Passages of Play in Urban India

In this book, Prasad Khanolkar offers a new way of thinking about "slums" and southern cities based on a grounded engagement with the relationship between media, objects, spaces, and people in the everyday life of slum localities in Mumbai, India.

Over the past few decades, Mumbai, like many cities in the global South, has experienced a series of overarching governmental missions to program it into an interoperable and profitable city. Its "slums," which house a majority of its population, don't fit within the dominant registers and continue to be deemed as excess. Urban residents inhabiting Mumbai's slum localities thus find themselves in the middle of missions, policies, and programs that are not of their making, just as often that they find themselves localized by lack of resources, caste system, communal conflicts, and territorial jurisdictions. Drawing on extensive fieldwork in slum localities of Mumbai, this book explores how its residents engage in different forms of play in order to extend and expand their field of possibilities, despite the limitations and fixities. The book attends to some of these playacts: imparting stories with different thicknesses, rehearsing roles on- and off-screen, engaging in deceptive performances, experimenting with repetitive everyday rhythms, and recycling matter and forms. Through these playacts, urban residents explore the virtual abilities of different mediums to put bodies, objects, and spaces into new forms of relationships and create passages to depart from programmed urban futures. By attending to these proliferating urban passages of different residents in slum localities, the book makes a case for rethinking southern cities as a labyrinth of passages in which urban lives converge and depart.

The book makes a significant contribution in the field of urban studies, urban anthropology, urban geography, and urban sociology. It will be of interest to scholars and students working on postcolonial cities, Southern urbanisms, infrastructure studies, and urban planning in the global South.

Prasad Khanolkar is Assistant Professor of Geography at the Department of Humanities and Social Sciences, Indian Institute of Technology, Guwahati, India. His research as an academic and urban planner has focused on urban issues in different cities, including Mumbai, Gurgaon, Portland, Nairobi, and Addis Ababa. His work has been published in journals and displayed through art and architectural exhibitions. He is also a coauthor of the book *Gurgaon Glossaries* (2012, coauthored with Rupali Gupte and Prasad Shetty).

Routledge Research on Urban Asia Series

Routledge Research on Urban Asia publishes high quality, original scholarship on cities and urban areas in Asia. The series welcomes research on the individual countries of Asia as well as comparative work from new and established scholars across the world. Themes include city cultures, urban policy and planning, megacities, urbanisation processes, sustainability, migrations and mobility, development patterns, civil society, politics and power, urban history, representations of the city, climate change, housing, gentrification and ghettoisation, social stratification and disaster risk.

Welcoming research from a wide range of disciplines, this series will be of interest to scholars of Asian Studies, Urban Studies, Sociology, Politics, Geography, Cultural Studies, History, Economics and Development Studies.

Jakarta
Claiming spaces and rights in the city
Edited by Jörgen Hellman, Marie Thynell and Roanne van Voorst

Time, Space and Capital in India
Longing and Belonging in an Urban-Industrial Hinterland
Atreyee Majumder

Community Arts and Culture Initiatives in Singapore
Understanding the Nodal Approach
Zdravko Trivic

Markets, Capitalism and Urban Space in India
The Right to Sell
Anirban Acharya

Passages of Play in Urban India
People, Media, Objects, and Spaces in Mumbai's Slum Localities
Prasad Khanolkar

For more information about this series, please visit: https://www.routledge.com/asianstudies/series/RRUA

Passages of Play in Urban India

People, Media, Objects, and Spaces in
Mumbai's Slum Localities

Prasad Khanolkar

Routledge
Taylor & Francis Group

LONDON AND NEW YORK

First published 2023
by Routledge
4 Park Square, Milton Park, Abingdon, Oxon OX14 4RN

and by Routledge
605 Third Avenue, New York, NY 10158

Routledge is an imprint of the Taylor & Francis Group, an informa business

British Library Cataloguing-in-Publication Data
A catalogue record for this book is available from the British Library

Library of Congress Cataloging-in-Publication Data
Names: Khanolkar, Prasad, author.
Title: Passages of play in urban India: people, media, objects and spaces in Mumbai's slum localities / Prasad Khanolkar.
Description: New York: Routledge, 2022. | Includes bibliographical references and index.
Identifiers: LCCN 2021061709 (print) | LCCN 2021061710 (ebook) | ISBN 9780367465674 (hardback) | ISBN 9780367509224 (paperback) | ISBN 9781003051848 (ebook)
Subjects: LCSH: Slums–Social aspects–India–Mumbai. | Urban poor–Social aspects–India–Mumbai. | Excess (Philosophy)–Social aspects.
Classification: LCC HV4140.M86 K43 2022 (print) |
LCC HV4140.M86 (ebook) | DDC 305.5690954/792–dc23/eng/20220131
LC record available at https://lccn.loc.gov/2021061709
LC ebook record available at https://lccn.loc.gov/2021061710

ISBN: 978-0-367-46567-4 (hbk)
ISBN: 978-0-367-50922-4 (pbk)
ISBN: 978-1-003-05184-8 (ebk)

DOI: 10.4324/9781003051848

Typeset in Times New Roman
by Deanta Global Publishing Services, Chennai, India

Contents

Figures

Acknowledgments

This book is about how urban residents inhabiting Mumbai's slum localities research and create an urban life despite all the delimitations. A lot of what they shared with me, particularly their stories and methodologies, forms the content of this book. Although based in Mumbai, the ideas, concepts, and questions in here are drawn from encounters with urban residents in lower-income and working-class neighborhoods of other cities, including Nairobi, Toronto, Portland, Addis Ababa, Gurugram, Guwahati, and New Delhi. To the residents of Toba Tek Nagar (TTN) in these cities, I owe a debt that I can never pay back. This book is an account of that debt, which includes the lesson: always look for what operates before, within, and beyond the scope of one's research and its target.

This book began as a doctoral project at the University of Toronto, Canada. I was fortunate to have worked with Kanishka Goonewardena, Katharine Rankin, Francis Cody, Kajri Jain, and Robert Lewis, who were more than generous with their time, words, and thoughts. Their questions, attention to details, and provocations taught me how to "read" texts and matter closely and to see my own writings from different angles. In Kanishka, Katharine, Frank, Kajri, and Robert, I found support and encouragement, which extends beyond this book, and without which this book wouldn't have been possible. Most importantly, I thank them, as well as all the other scholars in Toronto, for introducing me to a whole new world of literature, concepts, and ideas, which I wouldn't have otherwise.

This book features a few authors more prominently than others. But the citations don't do justice to their influence on the book. The textual and visual explorations of Walter Benjamin's ideas by Susan Buck Morss, Miriam Bratu Hansen, Samuel Weber, and Michael Taussig have been indispensable. And on a non-Benjaminian addendum, this book owes much to all those scholars—too many to name here, who have opened up a field for those of us in southern cities to play the game differently.

My interest in cities owes a huge debt to my friendships with Anand Ayare, Nilesh Rajadyaksha, Prajna Rao, Prasad Shetty, Rohit Mujumdar, Rupali Gupte, and Yogita Lokhande. They introduced cities to me in new ways and helped figure out ways of making my wasteful curiosities shareable with others. Their friendship is a part of everything that I write.

The "Reading Group" in Toronto, which took on different forms over years, with different incoming and outgoing members, has been foundational to the book. It provided a space to exchange thoughts and ideas, many of which have made into the book. Özlem Aslan, Prajna Rao, Katie Mazer, Meghana Rao, and Sawmya Ray read different parts of this book and helped me think through them, for which I am grateful. I am particularly thankful to Chitra Venkatramani, who read and commented on different versions of the monograph. Her suggestions on the text and visuals have been invaluable.

Over the course of this book, I have enjoyed friendships across different cities and institutions: Nishant Upadhyay, Katie Mazer, Jaby Matthew, Caitlin Henry, Makarand Salunke, Martin Danyluk, Sabin Ninglekhu, Patrick Vitale, Martine August, Melanie Richter-Montpetit, Preethy Sivakumar, Jacob Nerenberg, Özlem, Meghana, Asli Zengin, Ritika Shrimali, Mey, Begüm Uzun, Tania Tabar, Deepa Rajkumar, Saafi Warsame, Laura Pitkanen, Vivian Solano, Akshaya Tankha, Atreyee Majumder, Ponni Arasu, Hulya Arik, Katie, Martin Danyluk, Brett Story, Tarinigni Sriraman, Jyoti Neggi, Supriya Nayak, John Thomas, Kiran Keshavamurthy, Vasundhara Jairath, Daksha Parmar, Sawmya, Chitra, and many others. I name them here, in no particular order, knowing that I can't provide an account for their support in full.

This book wouldn't have been possible without grants and fellowships from different institutions. The Foundation for Urban and Regional Studies, UK (FURS) for their Studentship and the Writing-Up Grant funded my fieldwork and writing, respectively. The Center for South Asian Studies and the Department of Geography and Planning at the University of Toronto provided numerous grants for fieldwork and writing. The Center for Sciences and Humanities, New Delhi, generously provided a space to write the first iteration. Earlier versions of chapters 1 and 3 have appeared as a journal article in *Urbanization* and as a book chapter in *Bombay Brokers* (Duke University Press), respectively. I thank the editors and reviewers of these publications for their comments and suggestions.

The book also wouldn't have been possible without the behind-the-scenes logistical support of many staff members at different institutes: Jessica Finlayson, Marija Wright, Jenny Jung, Marika Maslej, Benjamin Potruff, and Mariange Beaudry at the Department of Geography and Planning, University of Toronto; Katherine Maclvor, Eileen Lam, and Rachel Ostep at the Center for South Asian Studies, University of Toronto; and Durga Sarma, Parag Kailta, Rubul Gogoi, and Khanthai Mala Basumatary at the Indian Institute of Technology, Guwahati. A special thanks to Kathy White for making my writing sensible.

This book is also an accretion of passages that extend beyond this work. And I want to thank those who were there alongside, while I struggled in these travels. Thanks to Prasad, Rupali, Jyoti, Katie, Meghana, Satyajit, Jo, Kabir, Avni, Anand, Chitra, Nilesh, Sawmya, Jaby, Yogita, Rohit, and Özlem, for their friendship, food, love, animals, playfulness, and patience. They made things joyful and light, while I struggled with writing.

Lastly, I would like to thank my family, who play a role that no one else can. My non-family family in Delhi, Mumbai, and Bangalore, who provide homes and love when needed. Amit and Vanadana, who step in the hardest of times and whose generosity has no bound. And most of all to my parents, for all their pain and toil over the years, and for assuring me, in their own ways, that they would be there no matter what.

Figure 0.0 Taking cities elsewhere

Introduction

This book forms part of a larger inquiry into cities and urban life that has been ongoing for the past 20 years or so and will not end with this book. It has taken on different forms along the way: architectural studies, design experiments, research apprenticeships, planning reports, purposeless wanderings, and organizational forms, to name a few. This book is its current iteration. To say it straightaway, this book is an experiment in thinking about the so-called "problem" of "slums" in cities from a different angle. And to that end, it posits and explores a specific proposition that goes as follows: The order of *the* city, be it a "just" city, an "efficient" city, a "smart" city, or a "world-class" city, is fundamentally based on nothing but myths, stories, and discourses that assign everything their "proper" place and everyone their "appointed" roles so as to create a "working community" (Rancière 2004). But any "working community" that desires to become coherent and complete also secretes an excess—an excess that is immanent to it but cannot be completely "put to work" by it, and is hence expended (Georges Bataille 1988[1949]). This excess, however, does not disappear or dissipate, but it seeps back in (Raqs Media Collective 2010). And this seepage entails creating passages through an interplay of bodies, things, and practices in different mediums, which make cities porous, incoherent, incomplete, and swollen (Benjamin and Lācis 1978[1925]). In what follows, I explore this proposition through an ethnographic study of how poorer residents in slum localities engage in different forms of play with others in different mediums to inhabit cities. But before doing so, I want to draw out the conceptual threads that interweave this book together, namely, excess, play, and abilities.

Excess Matters

By excess, following George Bataille, I refer to the residues of systems that are deemed as nonreproductive or inoperative and are hence expendable (George Bataille 1985 [1933], 1988[1949]). These residues include the laboring bodies that are in excess of labor needs, the capital that is in excess of what is minimally required for basic expenditures, and the energy resources that are in excess of what is required for the survival and growth of living organisms.[1] This is not to say that labor, capital, and energy are in infinite supply; they are finite. But they are in excess of that which is minimum necessary for the conservation and continuation

DOI: 10.4324/9781003051848-1

of life in a given society (Murphy 2017). The remaining share, or the excess, Bataille writes, can be wasted in nonproductive activities such as luxury, mourning, war, festival, play, spectacles, arts, and sex. These latter activities have no end or purpose beyond themselves but are a necessary part of human life. In a reproductive capitalist system, however, Bataille notes, this surplus isn't completely expended but put to work for further accumulation of capital and power. Thus, excess labor is either kept in reserve or made to perform unpaid labor; excess capital is either accumulated or reinvested to produce more capital; excessive energy is spent on extracting additional energy resources; and even expenditures on luxurious activities are made to reproduce societal hierarchies. In this utilitarian system, ends become means, and means serve ends. In other words, that which is rendered as surplus (lives, bodies, energies, and capital) is not spent unproductively but subjected to servility (Taussig 1995). This process of producing surplus and expending only to produce more surplus is an indispensable part of a utilitarian capitalist economy. Thus, excess matter, what Bataille terms as the "accursed share"—a share that is both sacred and cursed, is caught in this double bind of expendability and indispensability, of containment and secretions, and of being a surplus and a share, in the same moment. And this paradoxical nature of the matter makes it an unstable and vibrant matter that potentially threatens the coherency of the system. Class struggle for Bataille, then, is not the replacement of conspicuous consumption by total utility but the liberation of excess from servility.

Urban Excesses

Excess matters are also urban matters, historically. And they take on different forms and names in different urban contexts. For instance, in his seminal essay on the metropolitan psyche in 20th-century Europe, Georg Simmel noted that modern capitalism and the increased intensities in the circulation of money, people, and goods produced excessive sensory stimuli among residents of big cities (Simmel 1950[1903]). And these excessive sensations, he further writes, coerced individuals into becoming rational and blasé but simultaneously opened up possibilities for individuals to shed older identities and take on newer ones. For Max Weber, the 20th-century modern city-state in Europe, in contrast to older forms of spatial states, saw the emergence of political forms that exceeded or leaked beyond the confines of any controlling authority or state structures. And this excess and leakage, he suggested, were signs of emerging democratic forms in cities (Weber 1985[1921]). For Elizabeth Wilson, the 20th-century North American and European cities were chaotic and disorderly and presented a dangerous, squalid, and hard-working life for working-class women. But this urban chaos and disorder, she notes, also allowed them to loiter anonymously, to partake in urban pleasures, to explore sexual freedom, and to transgress social and spatial boundaries imposed by a patriarchal, racialized, and masculine order (Wilson 1992). It is no coincidence then that Alexis de Tocqueville perceived the chaos and disorder in cities (seen particularly in urban crowds) as a source of fear and danger to the order of the city republic and hence called for its containment and suppression through force and planning (ibid.: 6–7).

This containment and suppression of urban excesses, however, was not a blind restriction but an instrumental ordering of things to achieve specific ends (Osborne and Rose 1999). Thus, while nonreproductive excesses were contained and restricted, reproductive surpluses were encouraged—particularly, the circulation and accumulation of excess capital in cities. Over the years, Marxist urban literature has conceptualized the city as a space for investing, extracting, and accumulating surplus capital, and often through state planning mechanisms (Castells 1977[1972]; Smith 1990; Harvey 1978, 1989). Furthermore, while in earlier capitalist economies, this process involved a restructuring of urban space through the secondary circuits of capital (finance, real estate, and consumption), in advanced capitalist economies, the production of urban space itself became the primary instrument and source for accumulating surplus capital (Soja 1980; Lefebvre 2003[1970]). Today, this process of capitalist urbanization, backed by neoliberal state policies since the 1980s, has brought not just city regions across the globe (Sassen 2001) but the entire planet, including its atmosphere, within its fold (Brenner and Schmid 2015). Beyond the excesses of commodities, images, sensations, and capital, cities have also historically been a space for "surplus populations" (Davis 2006)—that is, people who are colonized and brought in as slaves to work on plantations and in industries (McKittrick 2006; Kawashima 2009); people who immigrate to and through cities to build new lives (McIntyre and Nast 2011); and also those lives are in surplus to the demands of industrial and postindustrial economies and are hence incarcerated or disposed of (Gilmore 2007; Wright 2006). These surplus populations are always above and beyond the "proper" count of the city and hence unaccounted for.

Such urban excesses are not specific to "Northern" cities but are common to cities everywhere. For instance, Vinay Gidwani and Rajyshree Reddy write of "waste" as a form of excess in Indian cities. By "waste" they refer to things, lands, ecologies, and lives that are cast outside the pale of capitalist value as superfluous, excess, detritus, and then erased and subsumed to create surplus value (Gidwani and Reddy 2015).[2] The declaration of commons (lands, resources, and waste too) as "waste" and their subsequent conversion into private property through enclosures and privatization points towards the reproductive consumption of excess by capitalist urban economies. Thus, waste, Reddy and Gidwani note, marks both the profitable and the expendable. These wasted lives and ecologies, however, do not vanish but linger as specters that haunt the city in different ways (Gidwani and Maringanti 2016). In the case of African cities such as Johannesburg, Achille Mbembe and Sarah Nuttall thus speak of a necropolis—an underground that lies beneath the surfaces of commodities, artifacts, and architectural forms in cities (Nuttall and Mbembe 2008: 1–36). This underground, they note, is made up of not just the infrastructures and subterranean spaces but also the laboring and racialized lower classes, the spaces of alienation and suffering, the detritus of the world above, and the subterranean utopias and forces of insurrection, which the apartheid rendered as unreadable (ibid.: 20–21).

Cities thus often "double up" into invisible second cities that emerge and operate in the shadows of carefully planned cities. In Kinshasa, as Filip De Boeck and

Figure 0.1 Urban excess

Marie-Françoise Plissart illustrate, this invisible city is a heterogeneous city made up of corporeal human bodies, of the occult and the imagined, and of immaterial words and signs, all of which form the infrastructures through which people make sense and operate in an urban context of economic scarcity and failing infrastructures (De Boeck and Plissart 2014). More than often, this urban excess is overnamed as "informal," "illegal," and "criminal" in order to bring it back into line—to formalize. But despite these efforts to enclose, cities remain "elusive" and "disappointing"—that is, they always exceed and disappoint the theoretical and analytical names assigned to them (Nuttall and Mbembe 2008: 25; Abbas 1997). Most urban economies, as Daniella Gandolfo argues, are always in excess of these names (Gandolfo 2013). They operate according to logics that exceed regulative systems, defy normative notions of value and productivity, transgress boundaries of what is "formal," "informal," and "criminal," at different moments, and contaminate the rational bureaucratic forms. And it is for this reason, she notes, that most urban economies are always under the threat of being formalized.[3]

In a broader sense, as Neferti X.M. Tadiar argues, cities everywhere have become sites of expendable lifetimes in today's neoliberal and postindustrial context (2012, 2013, 2016). They have exploded beyond what we knew as "the city" through a network of human-technological infrastructures, while subsuming the lives and rhythms inhabiting the peripheries and rural areas into a worldwide trans-territorial urban network (Tadiar 2016: 5). In this metropolitanist drive, Tadiar notes, land, people, and time have been rendered as surplus and disposable. Moreover, these disposable lifetimes of the surplus population are not completely dispensed but reabsorbed by the app-based human-technological infrastructures, thus making them into sites for securocratic control and accumulating surplus value in a postindustrial context of uber-urbanization (ibid.: 15). These residues and secretions, however, do not dissipate but seep back in through pores, underpassages, and leftover spaces using different material and immaterial infrastructures (Raqs Media Collective 2010). And in doing so, they contaminate cities, make them porous, elusive, swollen, and incoherent.

This book explores how this secreted excess—that is, how urban lives, entities, and rhythms that are rendered as unemployable and expendable in the making of the city seep back into the city in inhabiting it. And urban localities in Mumbai, which are inhabited primarily by poorer and lower-middle-class households and businesses and are identified as "slums," provide an apt avenue to take on such an inquiry. Slum localities mark the two sides of urban excess. As uninhabitable localities, they are in excess to the proper city and hence expendable. And as a source of excess capital, land, and labor, they are also indispensable to the making of "the city."

Slums as Urban Excess: A Short History

In the course of Bombay/Mumbai's[4] history of urbanization, the term "slum" has been used as a means of reducing urban localities[5] to utility-based concepts such as housing, built area, land tenure, and developmental value, and/or relegating them to the world of non-planning by representing them as chaotic, unhygienic, nuisance, and filthy. For instance, in her historical account, Sheetal Chhabria notes that the making of the "modern" city of colonial Bombay in the early 20th century, involved the concurrent discursive formation of "the slum" (Chhabria 2019: 17). The period saw three key formulations vis-à-vis the city. First, the conceptualization of "the city" as a bounded modern spatial entity and "the urban" as a calculable economic and demographic category. Second, the translation of shelter into "housing," which made dwelling practices governable and shelter a part of circuits of capital accumulation as a commodity. And third, the making of "the slum" by incorporating the former into the city, while simultaneously excluding it by drawing the discursive boundaries of what ought to be "the city." "The slum," as a result, became an agglomerative signpost for all that was constitutive of, but narrated out of, the story of "the city," namely, shelter, poverty, agrarian crises, disease, labor, migration, and hunger (ibid.: 18). Furthermore, this process involved mobilizing a whole institutional mechanism of reform, renewal, and finance, repeatedly, at different historical junctures and reorganizing the power of capital and the state at every turn. The city and the slum, Chhabria contends, were co-constituted, and yet, the "third world slum" came to be a marker of incomplete urbanization and modernization (ibid.: 19). These colonial conceptions of "the city" and "the slum," with the latter as the city's expendable other, continued to dominate the urban paradigm in postcolonial Bombay, despite the broader shifts in urban policies.

Postindependence, equitable distribution of housing was a major ideological force that characterized the planning agenda of the Indian state at different scales. At the state level, the Government of Maharashtra (GoM) established planning regulations and instituted planning agencies to meet the burgeoning housing demands in Bombay equitably. The city's housing delivery mechanisms were managed primarily by state agencies and a smaller share by landlords and cooperative housing societies.[6] Although private developers were active in Bombay's housing markets, their role was restricted to construction by limiting their access to finance (Searle 2016). Concurrently, past and present urban localities that were built outside the "official" purview were largely deemed as "slums"—that is, localities "detrimental to safety, health or morals" and were dealt with primarily through demolitions. These trends in housing and slum policies continued well into the 1970s, while Bombay simultaneously experienced growth in slum localities due to migration, urbanization, unaffordability, and a growing backlog in housing provision.

In the 1970s, the GoM began to slowly open up housing finance to private developers and simultaneously thought of other ways of addressing the growth of slums. With regard to the latter, the Maharashtra Slum Areas (Improvement, Clearance, and Redevelopment) Act was passed in 1971, new parastatal agencies were instituted, and a series of programs were launched. These programs included various "self-help" and "self-build" housing schemes, which provided land plots with basic infrastructure to lower-income groups to curb the growth in slum localities (e.g., sites-and-services schemes); the Slum Improvement Program (1970s) and the Slum Upgradation Program (1980s), which aimed to upgrade basic infra-structural facilities in existing slum localities;[7] and lastly, a state-led census of city's slum localities and its residents, whereby residents were provided with photo passes (1976). This census then became a basis for "regularizing" slum residents and "notifying" slum localities, that is, slum localities that were established prior to the "cut-off" year of 1976 and the urban residents who had arrived in the city before the same year, both were to be provided alternative accommodations in case of displacement. These new state initiatives, however, did not provide full protection to those living in slum localities; many were evicted between 1975 and 1977 (Weinstein 2014). This period marked the Emergency-era in India, during which the national government intervened heavy-handedly in city matters to restore discipline and carry out a modernization program. Given that multiple programs at work in slum localities, the latter, Liza Weinstein argues, have become sites of fragmented sovereignties (ibid.: 66).

While the 1971 Act and the subsequent programs set up new official avenues for accessing affordable housing, basic infrastructures, and quasi-legal protections against uncompensated displacements, they also introduced new qualifications for accessing the same, namely, "cutoff" dates, "regularized" and "unregularized" slum residents, and "notified" and "non-notified" slum localities. Furthermore, the 1971 Act also redefined slums as

> any area that is or may be a source of danger to health, safety or convenience of the public of that area or its neighborhood, by reason of the area having inadequate or no basic amenities, or being insanitary, squalid, overcrowded or otherwise.
>
> (State of Maharashtra 1971).

Such operational definitions have traveled across different kinds of organizations and have been instrumental in producing a commonsensical understanding of slum localities. For instance, in its seminal 2003 report, the UN Habitat defines a slum as "an area that combines, to varying extents, the following characteristics: inadequate access to safe water, inadequate access to sanitation and other infrastructures; poor structural quality of housing, over-crowding and insecure residential status." Similarly, the 2011 Census of India defines a slum as

> residential areas where dwellings are unfit for human habitation by reasons of dilapidation, overcrowding, faulty arrangements and design of such buildings, narrowness or faulty arrangement of street, lack of ventilation, light, or sanitation facilities.
>
> (Census of India 2011)

These operational definitions represent and identify "slums" through an absence of characteristics and thus enunciate that the only qualification of a "slum" is the absence of any qualification. This, in turn, has tied the rights of slum residents to qualify for housing, basic infrastructures, and protection against eviction to the disqualification of their localities as valid forms of habitation. Thus, residents of many urban localities continually work towards having their locality recognized as a "slum" by the state in order to access benefits from the different government programs (Burra 2005).[8] The term "slum" hence marks this struggle to have their localities recognized as a "slum" by the state, while simultaneously recognizing them beyond the disqualifications imposed by the state (see Chapter 3).

By the early 1990s, the Indian State had liberalized its national economic policies extensively and had altered its role from being a provider of public necessities to that of a market facilitator. This broader ideological shift was followed by the adoption of market-based housing policies in Bombay, which, in turn, made private developers the central agents of housing provision in the city. Today, Mumbai is one of the most expensive cities to own a house in. Just around 50 percent of the city's population can afford to access *pucca*[9] housing, while the rest access housing through slum localities.[10] This extreme unaffordability is a result of artificial price inflation produced by private developers and (national and international) investors coupled with a lack of adequate affordable public housing provision by the state. Thus, housing construction has not abated, neither have images of private luxury homes ceased to crowd the public realm in mass media, and yet, the commoditization and unaffordability has made housing a phantasy out of reach for the majority of the city's population (Appadurai 2000; Indorewala 2018b).

Post-1990, Mumbai's slum policies too followed this trend towards market-based policies (Bhide 2017). In 1991, the GoM introduced the Slum Redevelopment Program (SRD), whereby "regularized" residents in "notified" slum localities could partner with private developers to redevelop their localities. As per the program, the residents were to pay for 40 percent of the redevelopment costs, while the rest would be recovered by developers by building and selling additional housing units at market rates or by transferring those development rights to other parts of the city. The scheme, however, failed to attract both residents and developers and was replaced subsequently. In 1995, the GoM introduced the Slum Rehabilitation Scheme (also known as the SRA scheme) and established a parastatal agency called the Slum Rehabilitation Authority (SRA) to administer slum redevelopment projects. The SRA scheme, prevalent to date, is market-oriented, like its predecessor, but in a more extensive manner. It allows for the complete redevelopment of "notified" slums that were established in Mumbai prior to 2000. This process involves demolishing existing localities and rehousing its "regularized" (pre-2000) residents free of cost in high-density apartment blocks of 225 square-foot units, irrespective of household size, income, or occupation. In return, developers are guaranteed additional development rights, which can be used in situ, sold on the open market, or transferred to other areas with higher property values.[11] The scheme thus employs the property values of slum-occupied lands to cross subsidize and incentivize redevelopment of slum localities. SRA projects are highly profitable and sought after by developers, who make a profit of around 300 percent, since the scheme helps them avail land free of cost (Interviews 2013). Often, developers use fraudulent means to relocate slum dwellers to appropriate the entire land and/or provide housing for rehabilitation that is utterly dismal and under-provided in infrastructural terms. Furthermore, the SRA scheme requires consent from at least 70 percent of the slum dwellers as well as the registration of the slum as a cooperative society under the Maharashtra Regional Town Planning Act (MRTP Act). Nongovernmental organizations (NGOs) advocating for the rights and livelihoods of slum dwellers have been at the forefront in facilitating legal procedures, such as enumerating residents, organizing slum residents into communities, regularizing land titles, and producing city-wide governmental data on slum localities.[12] This active involvement of NGOs has fit well within the state rhetoric of "participatory governance," provided a conduit to convey the state and market ideologies down to the grassroots, while making the NGOs the proxy voices of slum residents in policy forums.[13]

In the early 2000s, governmental bodies, NGOs, private developers, corporate groups, and civil society organizations began mobilizing the "World Class City" vision to entice foreign capital and explore the economic potential of the city to its fullest (Bombay First and McKinsey 2003; State of Maharashtra 2004). In 2005, the central government launched the Jawaharlal Nehru National Urban Renewal Mission (JNNURM), which aimed at constructing massive infrastructural projects and building the governing capacities of governmental bodies in large and small Indian cities. Over the subsequent years, most Indian cities, including Mumbai, saw a proliferation of globalized infrastructures, including gated housing enclaves, office complexes and malls, and mega-infrastructure projects such as expressways, metro rails, and international airports; and promenades, boulevards, and private parks (Falzon 2004; Anand 2006; Roy 2011). This vision, as Asher Ghertner argues, was enacted not through disenchanted governmental tools such as cadastral maps or statistics but by producing a distinct re-enchanted aesthetic of a "World Class" city through planning, law, and mass media (Ghertener 2015). The "World Class" vision has instituted onto cities, including Mumbai, a new aesthetic economy of "value" and "order," wherein, a select few areas are preserved through discourses of heritage and environmentalism, while the rest of the city, characterized through aesthetics of fear and estrangement, gets reduced to "non-planned slums" (Rajagopal 2002; Benjamin 2010). Slums are thus brought to life by institutional process only to be expended. However, they are not expended completely, but reproductively—that is, they are made to perform the work of producing "the city."

Lines of Thought

This book is a response to and an intervention in this historical context. To be specific, it responds to three hegemonic phenomena (see below) that continue to affect the life and fate of slum localities in Mumbai. I use these phenomena as springboards to identify a set of questions and draw out lines of thought, which I pursue in the subsequent chapters.

First, historically, poorer and lower-middle-class urban residents have constructed and used different forms of urban localities as a platform to build urban lives in Mumbai (Chandavarkar 2009: 21). Even today, a majority of urban residents, that is, around 12 million people (a little more than 50 percent) live in localities that are identified as "slums." Despite their historical and social significance, over the years, colonial and postcolonial planning policies have continually invalidated these localities as uninhabitable, and have eradicated them through permutations of violent demolitions, urban renewal schemes, and market-based redevelopment policies (Nijman 2008). This judgment on the fate of slum localities has returned in the form of the state government's reiterative statement: "Mumbai is to be Slum Free" (1995, 2004, 2018). The statement enunciates that neither the urban majority nor their localities have anything to offer in terms of urban imaginaries and hence should be expended. In such a context, how do we describe these localities and the lives that reside in them while eluding the names and identities assigned to them and the partitions (planned/unplanned, formal/informal, and the city/the slum) imposed on them? This is the first line of thought.

Second: During an interview, a housing rights activist cum resident of a slum locality, who dreams of running a bakery someday, drew out a short narrative of how urban localities are put together out of nothing over years. Different migrants, she said, arrive in the city to fulfill needs as well as desires. After arriving, they acquire marsh by buying or occupying it, then convert the marsh into land by reclaiming it, assemble infrastructure (material and social) in myriad ways while simultaneously dealing with demolitions, and in doing so they build a locality through years of lifework. But once assembled, the state steps in and identifies the locality as a "slum" and converts it into mere "housing units" and "land" for urbanization or redevelopment. This process, she told me, entails separating people from their lifework, from experiences, and from social relationships. This separation is violent; it acts as a force, and they experience it, repeatedly (Tabassum et.al. 2010). Under the SRA scheme, this alienation results in the eradication of localities and the rehabilitation of their residents into pigeonholed high-rises. Here, as the slum residents often narrate in different forums, they are alienated from experiencing air, rain, heat, light, pleasure, as well as socialities. The forums where they speak of the estrangement through personal stories further alienate them based on the aesthetics of knowledge—what counts as knowledge for planning and what does not. I use the word "alienation" not to suggest a preexisting non-alienated human nature but to highlight a sensorial estrangement as well as a denial of the residents' abilities to see, hear, say, play, feel, and act. In short, to experience, to share and circulate these experiences, and to have them recognized as possible ways of affecting cities. In such a context, I ask, how do the majority of residents, those deemed as expendable, make sense of the city and act in it? What kinds of abilities are at play in the process of sensing, acting, and inhabiting cities? What kinds of relationships and forms are put together in the process? And how do they affect the city? This is the second line of thought.

In "Two Centuries of Planning Theory: An Overview," John Friedmann begins the history of planning with two figures: James Stuart Mill and Saint-Simon (1987:51–86). Both were influenced by the utilitarianism and social reformist agendas of Jeremy Bentham. For Saint-Simon specifically, the role of modern planning was to use the knowledge of society's "organic" laws to consciously set out its future course "according to a comprehensive plan." In this conception, the role of social physicians, such as scientists and engineers, was to use knowledge to predict future outcomes and to steer humanity's order towards a new industrious order. Different scholars have demonstrated how these reformist and progress-driven ideas were instrumental to colonization and imperialism (Stokes 1989; Mitchell 1991; McClintock 1995). They were seized upon by a nascent bourgeoisie as an ideological weapon for domination under the disguise of scientific planning geared towards humanity's liberation. This possibility of using knowledge as means for mastery can be ascribed to the instrumental reason within knowledge production (Horkheimer and Adorno 2002[1947]). The latter has provided planners and experts the will as well as the power to "improve" the world of "others" in the name of progress till date (Li 2007). Writing in reference to this instrumental relationship between knowledge production and imperialism in neocolonial times, Edward Said argues that it is important to pay attention to three key aspects (1989). First, how scholarly or monographic disciplinary work gets exfoliated from the relatively private domain of the researcher and their guild circle into the domain of policy making and policy enactment—something I experienced firsthand as an urban policy researcher and planner. Second, an awareness of how ethnography can shut out the points of view and expose tactical devices of those on the margins in favor of thick descriptions about the margins. And third, how ethnography acquires its power by reproducing the geography of a space through thick descriptions and, in doing so, produces the means of control over that space. Taking its clues from Said's provocations and Bataille's notion of expenditure, this book is an experiment in producing inoperative knowledge of the city. This is my third line of thought.

The City is Created *in* Play

To pursue these lines of thought, this book operationalizes the concept of play, which, similar to the notion of excess, is intimately tied to cities. For instance, in *Republic*, Plato puts together a treatise on what ought to be a "just" city-state but also suggests that despite this ideal image of the "just city" the construction of a city is a game. He then distinguishes between two kinds of play, "frivolous" and "motivated," and advocates for the latter as being more important since its instrumental to the development of individuals who can contribute towards the making of the "just city" (Krentz 1998; Livescu 2003). In *Rabelais and the World*, Mikhail Bakhtin attends to the ludic carnivalesque spectacles that flourished in Medieval Europe under feudalism (1984 [1965]). In contrast to the "serious official" days, the carnivalesque days were nonofficial, extra-political, and were filled with feasts and playful performances of folk humor. They offered the toiling ordinary masses time and space to engage as equals in playful mockery of authority and produced a sensuous awareness of their bodily self as a part of the whole. Despite the carnivalesque character, these days and activities had a structured nature. And yet, Sibaji Bandopadhyay notes, they invoked fear among the authority that the carnivalesque transgressions would bleed into the official days and raise the unofficial to the level of the official (2012). Thus, to maintain the order of the city-state, Bandopadhyay argues, artists and performers, including actors, storytellers, conjurers, clowns, and other entertainers, are either banned from the city or assigned specific roles to make them governable (ibid.: xx).[14]

For the Dutch historian Johan Huizinga, civilization has always been at play and a play in itself (2000[1938]). Society, culture, law, poetry, war, and music, he writes, all have emerged in play. Huizinga defined play as a free, nonpurpose-ful, disinterested, and joyous activity that occurs in a ritualistic space called the "magic circle." The latter is bound by spatiotemporal limits, governed by specific rules, and has an order that is distinct and separate from ordinary life. Building on Huizinga's ideas, Roger Caillois defined play as a free, indeterminate, and unproductive activity that is separate from life (2001[1961]). In free play, he notes, although rules and obligations of ordinary life are suspended, it is still governed by rules that are distinct to them and agreed upon by those involved. The free-natured play, however, they both argue, declined with the rise of fascism and World War II and took on new institutionalized forms in the postwar context, namely, leisurely and recreational activities, professionalized competitive games, and financial gambling in the stock market. Between the 1950s and 1970s, the Situationist International (SI), who identified themselves as a group of "explorers specializing in play and recreation," attempted to revive this lost element of free play through experiments in art, architecture, and urbanism in their own context. Their context was that of a technocratic and rationalist urbanism, where all aspects of everyday life were commodified by capitalism. Here, play too was commodified into pseudo-play, that is, recreational activities and shopping. The SI's experiments in different fields, such as the psycho-geographical drifting across cities (Debord 1996[1958]) and the labyrinthine futuristic city with mobile architectural and social forms (Nieuwenhuys 2005[1960]), were thus experiments to create a "unitary urbanism," wherein play would be freed from concerns of capital, and humans could live a "whole life."

Play and Its Abilities

While this book is influenced by these ideas of play and cities, particularly those of the SI, my sources of play lie elsewhere—where play is conceived of neither as an end in itself (free play) nor as means to an end (instrumental play). Instead, I am interested in the ability of play to suspend intent, judgments, and programs, that is, to render them inoperative and open up possibilities that aren't predetermined. In particular, I am drawn to Walter Benjamin's explorations of *spiel* (the German word for "play") and its multiple meanings.[15] The concept was central to his theoretical explorations of pedagogy, history, and revolution; his anthropological-materialistic elaborations on technological mediums such as language, photography, and film; as well as his search for passages in different cities, such as Paris, Naples, Moscow, and Berlin. Here, I briefly elaborate on the concept of *spiel* and its abilities, as it would help make better sense of how and why the book operationalizes the concepts ethnographically. To do this, I draw on the

Figure 0.2 The world is created in play

writings of Benjamin, and his interlocutors, specifically, Miriam Hansen (2011) and Samuel Weber (2008).[16]

The first meaning of the play is simply an activity in a medium (Hansen 2011: 184). For instance, when children play with toys or waste objects, the latter are the mediums in which they play. In this play, moreover, children practice an "inventive reception" of the world in their modes of collecting and organizing objects (ibid.: 150). For Benjamin, play is closely related to the mimetic faculty of humans. "Children's games," he writes,

> are everywhere interlaced with mimetic modes of behavior and their range is not limited at all to what one human being imitates from another. A child not only plays at being a grocer or a teacher, but also at being a windmill or a train.
>
> (1979 [1933]: 65)

In this latter case, the bodily gestures become the medium in which children play. This mimetic play, however, is not a representational practice but a relational practice—a form of exchange or correspondence between the self and the other, driven by the desire to become someone or something else. In other words, in playing with objects and bodily gestures, children do not merely imitate the world of adults but put objects and gestures that populate that world into new kinds of relationships. And in doing so, they rescue them from their instrumental destination and open them to new possible uses and configurations. Thus, what a child's play gestures towards is the ability of objects and gestures to be used in other ways (Weber 2008).

The play of adults is no different in this regard. They imitate the world in dance, singing, writing, film, and performance using the mediums of body, language, and modern technologies. For example, in performance or playacting—the second meaning of the term "play," an actor plays her subject matter on stage or in front of a camera by simulating and enacting the absent subject using bodily gestures (Hansen 2011: 184). Thus, receptivity and creativity, Benjamin writes, are present in equal parts in performance (1999[1928/29]: 201–206). Furthermore, performances, similar to children's play, involve repetitions—doing the same thing over and over. These repetitions, although similar, are not the same, but improvised iterations. For instance, in performance, back-stage rehearsals are improvised upon by actors in front of an audience or a camera. More importantly, in playacting, Benjamin writes in reference to epic-theater, actors make gestures citable (in Weber 2008: 97). The phrase "making gestures citable," as opposed to simply citing gestures, Weber argues, gestures towards the ability of playacting to mimic (cite) a gesture and interrupt (cite) it, in the same moment (see Chapter 2). Thus, an actor not only enacts an absent subject by imitating it with her bodily gestures but also gestures towards the possibility of interrupting the act by improvising it into something else.[17]

However, this mimetic play also has a darker side, which is driven by an impulse to identify the other and produce sameness. For instance, the state,

Michael Taussig argues, is a mimetic machine that exerts its power over its subjects by identifying them using mimetic technologies and copies such as fingerprinting and biometrics (1993: 61). Here, the medium (the mimetic technology) becomes an instrumental means to produce identities and exert power, and repetitions turn into eternally recurring sequences without breaks or escape. To break away from this self-similar cycle of history, one needs to play a hand or gamble—the third meaning of the term play. Here, the emphasis is on chance (Hansen 2011: 185). For example, as Gilles Deleuze notes in his elaboration on the relationship between chance and necessity in Nietzsche, there are two moments in a dice game: the dice are thrown, and the dice fall back (in May 2005). When dice are up in the air there is an affirmation of chance—the future opens up to multiple combinations, anything can happen. And when the dice falls back on the table, they crystallize into a combination, which might not be the winning combination. But despite losing, players gamble repeatedly to affirm chance and indeterminacy of the future (Marasco 2018). Furthermore, gamblers tend to wager at the very last instance (Benjamin 1999: 515; Hansen 2011: 186). This demands a heightened sense of awareness and fullness of bodily presence at the moment, rather than a reliance on accrued wisdom or waited contemplation. This form of playing, Benjamin notes, is driven not by the desire to win but by the desire to seize the chance and deceive the already fixed fate (Marasco 2018: 9–15). In other words, in playing her hand at the last moment, the gambler gestures towards the ability of gambling to interrupt the impositions and identities of the past and open up possibilities to move away from them.

Following its multiple meanings, this book operationalizes the concept of play in an expansive sense. By play, it refers to multiple acts: to mimic, rehearse, and improvise; to perform, pretend, deceive, and trick; to repeat, sense, and take a chance; as well as to receive, exchange, create, and waste. Moreover, I use play not as a framing device to study slum localities but as a conceptual device to draw attention to, first, how slum residents inhabit cities by engaging in different forms of play with others in different mediums and, second, the "abilities" in these playacts to open up other possible ways of inhabiting cities that haven't been calculated yet. I borrow this notion of *abilities* from Samuel Weber.

Abilities, he notes in *Benjamin's Abilities* (2008), is a mode of conceptualization that one finds in the writings of Benjamin (reproduce-ability, criticize-ability, translatability, cite-ability), as well as Jacques Derrida (iterability, repeatability), albeit differently. These abilities are not properties or attributes of particular subjects or objects but a way of reading and translating actions (actualities) into possibilities (virtualities) that are latent within different phenomena (events, texts, actions, gestures, and techno-infrastructural mediums). For example, Weber writes of Derrida's distinction between iteration of texts as something actual and iterability as a possibility that is a part of the text. So, a text might not have been repeated as of yet but has the implicit possibility of its iterability—yet to happen. Similarly, to impart a story is an act of sharing a story, which might have happened (actualized). But impart-ability (impartibility) of a story gestures towards the possibility of a story to be shared multiple times and in multiple ways, which might not have happened yet (see Chapter 1). Thus, a story might have been shared, but the process of sharing remains incomplete and unpredictable.

Furthermore, the term "impart-ability," wherein ability is a suffix, also includes a hyphen, which gestures towards the possibility of spatializing (spacing-out) the story as well as those involved in telling the story. In other words, it points towards the possibility in the act of storytelling to open up a space, wherein the elements of the story and the actors involved could depart towards an elsewhere. Thus, -abilities as a mode of conceptualization does not merely draw attention to what has happened (the actual) but also signals towards the possibility of that which is yet to come (the virtual). I emphasize this distinction between the actual and the possible (iteration and iterability) since the book does not aim to present stories of play as examples of actualized emancipatory possibilities, which can then be repeated as models elsewhere. Instead, it hopes to draw attention to how urban residents inhabit cities (the actual) and the unforeseen but possible ways of inhabiting cities that they gesture towards (the virtual).

Stories of Toba Tek Nagar

Toba Tek Nagar—the slum locality where this book is ethnographically grounded, is a generic locality. It can't be located on the map, but it does exist in actuality—since the book is based on an ethnographic study of different slum localities in Mumbai. Some of you might be able to identify the localities based on the details in the book, but those details can also be located elsewhere, in other localities, and in other cities, albeit in different iterations. The aim of using the name "Toba Tek" is not just to use a pseudonym and preserve the anonymity of the slum localities and their residents but also to suggest that the ethnographic details shared in this book are singular iterations of that which proliferates in the city.

The name "Toba Tek" has two sources. First, Sadat Hasan Manto's short story "Toba Tek Singh" (1970[1955]). The story is set on the Indian subcontinent in the post-partition context. The inmates of a lunatic asylum are being sent to their respective countries based on their religion: the Muslim inmates from Indian asylums are being sent to Pakistan, and Hindu and Sikh inmates from Pakistan are being sent to India. The story's main character is Bishen Singh, a Sikh inmate of an asylum in Pakistan, who is being sent to India. But he is disinterested in being in India or in Pakistan and wants to go back to his native village: Toba Tek Singh. Unable to return to his native village, Bishen Singh refuses to relocate and chooses to die in the uninhabitable no man's land between the two countries. He locates his Toba Tek Singh there. This is not to say that Toba Tek Singh doesn't exist in actuality. The actual place is situated in Pakistan, which is my second source for the name. The place, it is said, was a small town with a pond (*Toba* in Punjabi) that was located at the intersection of different travel routes. The history of the name can be traced to a Sikh saint, Tek Singh, who settled in this town and spent his life providing water and help to travelers who passed through it. Years later, the pond and the surrounding city were named Toba Tek Singh after the saint. The name Toba Tek thus gestures towards the desires

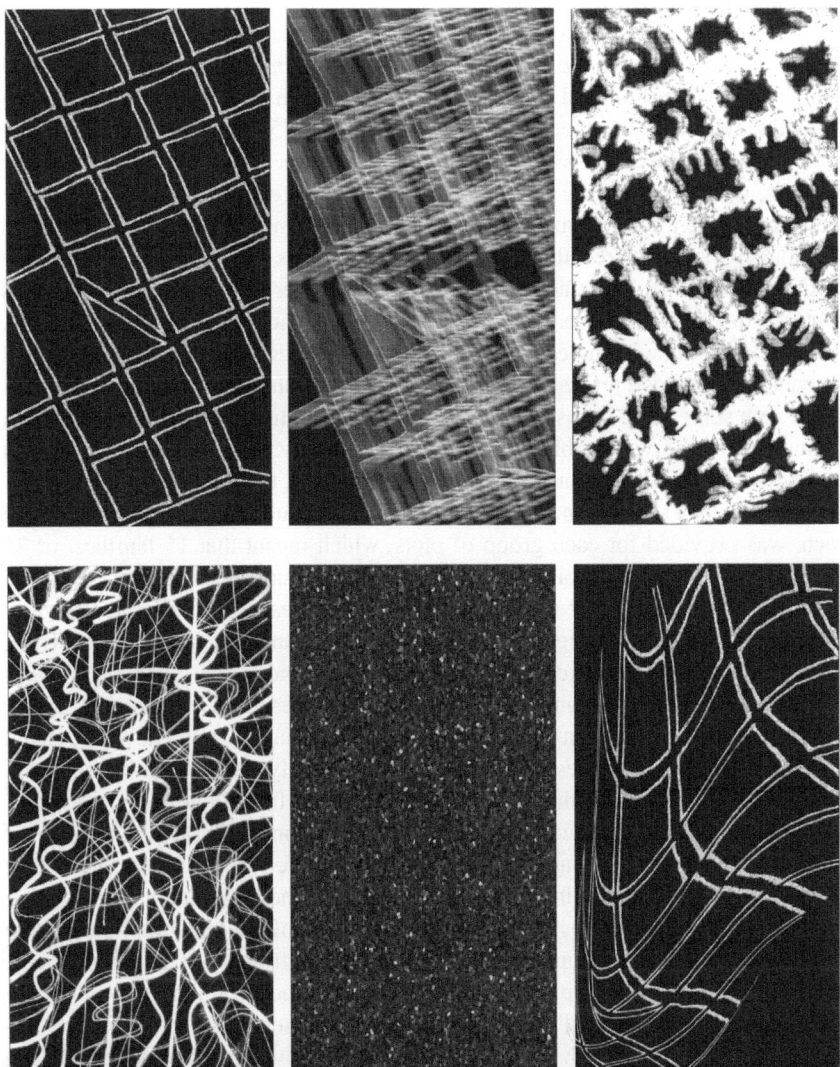

Figure 0.3 How do we draw a map?

How do we draw a map of a locality, which looks like any other locality but is also a singular iteration? A locality, which is always departing from itself? A locality that exceeds and secretes through its containments? A locality that slips through like dust when you try to grasp it? A locality where lines of thoughts and temporalities are going nowhere in particular? A locality with the abilities to become anything other than what it is?

as well as abilities of people and places to provide a space and resources for traveling elsewhere. This book hopes to share similar stories from a different city (Mumbai) under the name Toba Tek (Nagar).

Tob Tek Nagar, in this book, is a constellation[18] of different slum localities in Mumbai. It was set up in the early 1970s by the city municipality on the outskirts of Mumbai. It was established as a resettlement colony in order to rehabilitate urban residents evicted from other parts of the city. By 1975, in its first phase, around nine thousand households were rehabilitated. Of these, 60 percent were relocated from the central part of the city and the rest from different suburban areas. They were brought in trucks, en masse, and dumped on an empty piece of land. The land was marshy, as it was reclaimed from a creek, and was surrounded by the Deonar landfill on one side, a primary arterial road on the other. The colony was set up as a sites-and-services scheme. Each household was provided a plot of 10 by 15 feet, free of charge, but without legal security of land tenure. Residents had to pay a small amount that included a licensing fee and a land rent charge.[19] Each plot was provided with some basic infrastructures (water and sanitation), while the construction of houses was the responsibility of the residents. A few waterlines were set up and water was provided for four hours every morning and two hours in the afternoon (Interviews 2012). A common toilet block, with two cubicles for men and women each, was provided for each group of plots, which meant that 15 families, or 75 people, had to share one toilet block. Storm water drainage and garbage disposal were not provided, neither were postal services, recreational facilities, entertainment facilities, schools, religious institutions, public transportation, or parks. There were no electricity lines, except the one on the main road.

By the mid-1980s, around 15,000 families were resettled in Toba Tek Nagar and its "official" population rose to 74,000. Of these, only 70 percent were evicted and relocated, while the rest had moved to the locality and bought houses from the previous owners with the anticipation of eviction from their previous homes. Although the plots provided to the residents were nontransferable, a number of households had sold them and moved out by then. The secondary owners bought them at the risk of remaining unregularized. While the municipality was setting up the "official" colony, residents who were not part of the rehabilitation scheme were occupying land around it. They bought plots from touts and politicians. While the politicians sold plots to set up their constituencies, the touts sold them for money. The "unofficial" residents availed basic services such as water, toilets, and electricity through various means. This involved paying residents of the colonies who had access to some infrastructure, pressuring politicians and bureaucrats, traveling to other localities every day, and/or extending connections from existing infrastructural connections. This process of extending the colony into an expansive locality has continued till date, wherein new residents continue to buy plots and build houses. Furthermore, the non-regularized houses get evicted repeatedly, every two to three years, until the point at which they fall within the ever-extending "cut-off" date (1976, 1985, 1995, currently at 1 January 2000).

The locality, thus, has always consisted of heterogeneous residents, land tenures, infrastructures, and sovereign authorities. In terms of regional composition, a majority of the residents were from Maharashtra and the rest from Uttar Pradesh, Rajasthan, Kerala, Tamil Nadu, Karnataka, Gujarat, and Nepal. And in terms of religion, a majority consisted of Hindus and Muslims (in equal numbers), and the rest composed a minority of Christians and Buddhists. Today, the locality houses around a million residents, a majority of whom are Muslims (both Sunni and Shia). This change in the religious composition, and its transformation from a mixed neighborhood to a predominantly Muslim neighborhood, was a result of the 1992–1993 communal riots that followed the demolition of the Babri Masjid Mosque in Ayodhya, Uttar Pradesh, on 6 December 1992. The riots unfolded violently in a number of Mumbai's localities, including Toba Tek Nagar, and resulted in an out-migration of non-Muslims and an influx of Muslims from other neighborhoods (Contractor 2012). Some non-Muslim residents moved back to their villages, while others shifted to non-Muslim localities in other parts of the city. Recent writings on the growing marginalization of Muslims in Indian cities have shown that urban Muslims are being increasingly ghettoized in slum localities and victimized through state-led violence (Seabrook and Siddiqui 2011; Gayer and Jafferlot eds. 2012). This ghettoization involves denying these localities the physical infrastructures and exiling them from new urban as well as national imaginations (Anand 2012; Appadurai 2000). In the case of Mumbai, this exclusion is a result of the rise of Hindu regionalism in the city under Shiv Sena and the pervasion of Islamophobia into everyday urban life and state policies since the mid-1960s (Hansen 2001). Following the 1992–1993 riots, the official renaming of the city and city spaces (streets, parks, airports, and railway stations) became a way to establish the city as a Hindu regionalist place. Bombay was renamed Mumbai in 1995. It is also in response to this politics of naming that I chose to name the slum locality in this book Toba Tek Nagar. In doing this, I wanted to situate the locality within the history of partition, the appropriation of this history by regionalist and populist politics, and the impact of increasing xenophobia on poorer urban Muslims living in slum localities such as Toba Tek Nagar.

Despite recursive violence, Toba Tek Nagar has transformed a lot over the years. The locality has numerous toilet blocks, electricity transformers, cable television networks, markets, schools, spaces for religious worship, video theaters, *pucca* roads and houses, public transportation stops, parks, and so on. In terms of their legal status, the locality consists of a majority of notified slums that exist adjoining non-notified slums. Both consist a mix of regularized and non-regularized residents. During the fieldwork, my aim was to collect stories about how slum residents inhabit cities, despite the absence of resources and infrastructures? In what mediums? What forms of relationships are brought into play in this process? And lastly, what possibilities does this play open up?

Structure of the Book

In the subsequent chapters, I share some of the ethnographic stories that I collected while pursuing the questions and line of thoughts outlined above. And I use play, excess, and abilities as conceptual devices to narrate them and highlight the possibilities therein. To be clear, these concepts were not predetermined, nor are they meant to determine the stories to a specific conceptual framework. Instead, they are devices to retell the stories, which we might otherwise be familiar with, differently. Besides, this sharing, here, does not reduce their ability to be shared by others in their own ways. Stories, thus, are a significant part of the "semiotic commons" in cities, which can be used by many others, in multiple ways, without depleting their resourcefulness (Elyachar 2011). The first chapter attends to this aspect of stories and storytelling. Despite the lack of adequate infrastructures, security, and resources, stories circulate in Toba Tek Nagar excessively. They are shared, gifted, and exchanged every day by residents while waiting and idling in different spaces. Often, they are the medium for sharing personal experiences, events, news, encounters, travelogues, and what one knows about others and themselves. However, these stories aren't given their due in institutionalized "participatory forums," since they are personal and repetitive—"they don't work there." But in urban localities, where one doesn't need specific qualifications or addressee to tell stories, these shared stories become the mediums in which residents figure out other ways of inhabiting cities.

Each of the chapters in this book revolves around a medium: stories, films, toilets, and waste, respectively. But these mediums aren't at the center of things, they are located in connection with other mediums: bodies, spaces, performances, phones, memories, pipes, vehicles, bureaucratic documents, and money. By "mediums," I refer to the material and immaterial passages that move beings, ideas, experiences, and things in the process of transmitting them (Weber 2008). For instance, storytelling is not merely recounting experiences (repeating or imitating) from the past but also transforming them into a new singular iteration—that is, not just moving them from one time to another or one being to another but also reconfiguring the elements of experience in this process. This movement, thus, is not restricted to what is being transmitted but also involves the transmitter, who departs (to part with and to take leave) with and in the story. This book thus explores how slum residents engage in play with others (other residents, images, things, ideas, and experiences) in different mediums and the possibilities that this play opens up for them.

Following this line of thought, the second chapter attends to the interplay between residents and films in Toba Tek Nagar. The chapter is divided into two parts. The first part focuses on a YouTube crime series produced by members of a youth group, who aspire to become a part of the film industry while simultaneously struggling with stigmas and identities associated with living in a poorer Muslim slum locality. For them, filmmaking affords a space to rehearse, improvise, playact, try out new roles, as well as re-cognize spaces in the locality as sets for film scenes. This "recognizability" of the self and the locality in films, I show, allows the youth to depart from the hierarchies, identities, and roles assigned to them and their locality. The second part of this chapter focuses on film reception in the video theaters of Toba Tek Nagar. The latter are primarily spaces for local and immigrant men, who otherwise rarely interact with each other, to watch films from different parts of the country with each other. However, this audience isn't merely engrossed in watching films; they often sleep, spend their time between work and sleep, wait out time without work, talk on phones to their employers and families, and discuss films and everyday news. Furthermore, this film reception is every day and repetitive, whereby the audience watch the same films over and over again. These repetitions coupled with the movement across different times and spaces, I show here, extend and transform the space of the video theaters into avenues for journeying into other worlds.

The third chapter pursues the thread of playacting from the previous chapter further. It presents ethnographic studies of common toilets that were built under the Slum Sanitation Program (1997) in Toba Tek Nagar. The program was initiated by the Mumbai municipality in partnership with the World Bank to build financially sustainable sanitation systems in slum localities through community participation. There exists an abundance of literature that critically analyzes the discourses and practices of the program. This chapter moves away from this literature to explore deception as a way of inhabiting cities. It attends to how residents in Toba Tek Nagar engage in deceptive performances to get common toilet blocks built in their neighborhoods. To deceive is to pretend, to engage in charades and trickery, and to take on different appearances. It involves imitating someone or something but also deceiving that which is being imitated. These deceptive performances involve "citing" or imitating models and the roles that they assign, as well as "citing" or interrupting them by deceiving that which is being imitated. In doing so, I show here, residents make the developmental models and the roles they assign "citable." Thus, deceptive performances, I argue here, are a way of engaging with others, which involves deceiving not just the fellow residents and the developmental actors but also the analytical frameworks, the identities, and the roles that are imposed on them. They become a way of operating in an urban milieu that otherwise seems to be "fixed" and "programmed" (Simone 2012).

The fourth chapter travels between Toba Tek Nagar and the city by following the circuits of urban waste recycling. The slum locality, as mentioned earlier, is located on the edge of the city's oldest landfill. A number of its residents are involved in collecting, disposing, and recycling waste, in different capacities: municipal and private waste workers, waste pickers, scrap dealers, recyclers, and security guards. However, the occupational hierarchies and the access to waste resources in Mumbai are fixed by caste hierarchies. Thus, those belonging to the lowest castes, and more recently poorer Muslims, rely on waste picking for their livelihoods. Furthermore, although Indian cities produce an enormous amount of waste, the amount of recyclable waste that can go around for these multiple actors to earn a living is fairly limited. This chapter looks at how different actors, despite limitations of caste and waste, engage with others in order to expand their possibilities of partaking in the urban waste world. Specifically, it attends to the rhythms and exchanges that they devise to "swell" time, space, waste resources, and governance systems. In doing so, the chapter reviews the notion of "recyclability" from the perspective of these urban practices. However, since the 1990s, Mumbai has also seen an increase in partnerships between the municipality, private actors, civil society organizations, and nongovernmental organizations to achieve a "Zero-Garbage" city. The second part of this chapter attends to the practices through which these actors make urban waste manageable and governable and highlights how these practices affect the recyclability of the city.

How do we inhabit cities? The question is an invitation for thinking about how urban residents inhabit cities, as well as the possibilities that they open up for inhabiting cities otherwise. While the ethnographic stories in this book address the first part of this question, the concluding chapter extends these stories to make a few propositions for this otherwise. Urban residents use cities and engage with each other not according to any program or to reach a specific destination but in "whatever" ways possible so as to become someone or something other than who they are. Cities, in this sense, are a gathering of human and nonhuman lives that use each other as mediums to depart towards an elsewhere. These movements of converging and diverging swell cities beyond their limitations and their appearances into something that is unrecognizable and unclassifiable. In drawing attention to this swelling city, this chapter does not make a call to reclassify them or to program them to achieve a specific form. Rather, it makes a proposition for a "whatever city" that would render their programming and classification inoperative.

Notes

1 To cite an example, Allan Stoekl in his book *Bataille's Peak* explains that if a rural region can produce only so much food, its "carrying capacity" is limited. In which case, the surplus population present in the region has to be expended. Often, this leads to celibacy, use of contraception, warfare, and/or sacrifice (Stoekl 2007: 35).

2 Vinay Gidwani's broader scholarship has been seminal to drawing our attention to the waste-value dialectic underlying capitalism (1992; 2013; 2018). Also see Nicholas Blomley's narrative on the translation of indigenous lands into private property under settler-colonialism in Turtle Islands (2002).

3 An excellent example of the latter in the Peruvian urban context, but not particular to it, is the state's formalization of "informal" economies and habitats informed by ideas of the prominent Peruvian economist Hernan De Soto (2000). For a critique of policies influenced by De Soto's ideas see Mitchell 2008.

4 The name of the city was officially changed from Bombay to Mumbai in 1995. I use the two names accordingly.

5 Following Doreen Massey's elaboration on the concept of locality, I use the term locality in its extroverted and an interlinked sense (1991).

6 I have provided here a brief overview of Mumbai's postindependence slum and housing policies to ground this book. For more detailed accounts see: Mukhija 2017; Collective Research Initiatives Trust 2007; Weinstein 2014; and Indorewala 2018a.

7 Both these initiatives drew their ideological and financial sources from the World Bank. For a rich historical account of the multiple slum policies and programs in Bombay/ Mumbai, see Liza Weinstein's *Durable Slum* (2014).

8 Following the strategy of slum residents, I use the term "slum" in this book, despite all its problems, to mark this struggle as well as keep all avenues open.

9 *Pucca* housing (or pukka) refers to dwellings that are designed to be solid and permanent. The term is applied to housing built with substantial materials such as stone, brick, cement, concrete, or timber. It also refers to formal and legalized housing identified by the Indian Census as such.

10 A 2019 study by Reserve Bank of India (RBI) shows that on an average, households in Mumbai spend 43 percent of their monthly income on housing loan EMIs and the median house price to monthly income ratio is 74 (Economic Times, 2019).

11 In its first formulation, the policy capped profits from a slum redevelopment project at 25 percent, which deterred private developers from getting involved. The cap was later eliminated to further incentivize the scheme and attract private developers.

12 Nezar AlSayyad suggests that the shift towards market-based slum policies occurred concurrently with the rise in neoliberal rationalities in hegemonic international institutions such as the IMF and the World Bank, the decentralization and devolution of governance to local levels in India, and the increased participation of local and international NGOs in implementing developmental programs in postcolonial contexts (AlSayyad 2004: 13).

13 In some cases, particularly resettlement and rehabilitation schemes (RnR), NGOs have even taken up slum redevelopment projects themselves by partnering with developers, private investors, banks, and international funding agencies.

14 Bandopahdyay is referring here to Plato's Republic and Kautilya's 3rd BC state-craft treatise, the *Arthashastra,* respectively.

15 My other source of play is the concept of *līlā*. This Late-Sanskrit term for play is expansive and opens up the concept in many directions. In a general sense, it describes "any kind of playing," and more specifically, a spontaneous, carefree, and nonpurposive activity (Coomaraswamy 1941; Sax 1995). For instance, the art historian A.K. Coomaraswamy tells us that the term denotes a divine and indifferent activity through which gods created the world. He distinguishes *līlā* from *karma* or purposeful activities as well as from work that serves some sort of need, and suggests that the concept symbolizes a meeting point of extremes, such as action and inaction, work and play, and sleep and awakening (ibid.: 98). Furthermore, as other scholars have shown, *līlā* also signifies a continuous, flickering and playful movements through which one gains knowledge and enlightenment (Coomaraswamy, 1941); a performance involving swinging and oscillating that can induce trance (Gell 1980); and role-playing, trickeries, impersonations, and charades (Sax 1995). These conceptions of play share an affinity with Walter Benjamin's exploration of the German term *spiel* (play), which is what I elaborate on here.

16 The other interlocutors include Susan Buck-Morss (1977, 1989, 2000) and Michael Taussig (1992, 1995, 2006).

17 The concept of performativity in Judith Butler's work connotes a similar meaning (1990). Identities of gender and sexuality, she notes, are not given but performed or enacted by subjects through linguistic citing of dominant discourses. The subject thus does not precede given identities but is rather produced through performances of rehearsed scripts. She refers to these enactments and citational practices as performativity. However, these repetitive acts, she remarks, also entail going off the script and producing different scripts (such as in drag performances).

18 I use the term "constellation" as a gathering of disparate elements that are on their way to somewhere else.

19 The residents continue to pay the fee and charge till date. Today this payment amounts to INR 100 (USD 1.5).

References

Abbas, Ackbar. 1997. *Hong Kong: Culture and the Politics of Disappearance*. Minneapolis, MN: University of Minnesota Press.

AlSayyad, Nezar. 2004. "Urban Informality as a 'New' Way of Life." In *Urban Informality: Transnational Perspectives from the Middle East, Latin America, and South Asia*, edited by Nezar AlSayyad and Ananya Roy, 7–30. Lanham, MD: Lexington Books.

Anand, Nikhil. 2006. "Disconnecting Experience: Making World-Class Roads in Mumbai." *Economic & Political Weekly* 41 (31): 3422–29.

———. 2012. "Municipal Disconnect: On Abject Water and Its Urban Infrastructures." *Ethnography* 13 (4): 487–509.

Appadurai, Arjun. 2000. "Spectral Housing and Urban Cleansing: Notes on Millennial Mumbai." *Public Culture* 12 (3): 627–51.

Bakhtin, Mikhail. n.d. *Rabelais and His World*. Bloomington, IN: Indiana University Press.

Bandyopadhyay, Sibaji. 2012. "The Laughing Performer." In *Sibaji Bandyopadhyay Reader*, 1–37. Delhi: Worldview.

Bataille, George. 1985. "The Notion of Expenditure." In *Visions of Excess: Selected Writings, 1927–1939*, edited by Allan Stoekl, translated by Allan Stoekl, Carl R. Lovitt, and Donald M. Leslie Jr., 116–29. Minneapolis, MN: University of Minnesota Press.

Bataille, Georges. 1988. *The Accursed Share, Volume I*. Translated by Robert Hurley. New York, NY: Zone Books.

Benjamin, Solomon. 2010. "The Aesthetics of 'the Ground up' City: Some Insights from Bangalore." *Seminar* 612(August): 33–38.

Benjamin, Walter. 1979. "Doctrine of the Similar (1933)." Translated by Knut Tarnowski. *New German Critique* Spring 1979 (17): 65–69.

———. 1999. *The Arcades Project*. Edited by Rolf Tiedemann. Translated by Kevin McLaughlin and Howard Eiland. Cambridge, MA and London, UK: The Belknap Press of Harvard University Press.

Benjamin, Walter, and Asja Lācis. 1978[1925]. "Naples." In *Reflections: Essays, Aphorisms, Autobiographical Writing*, edited by Peter Demetz, translated by Edmund Jephcott, 163–75. New York, NY: Schocken Books.

Bhide, Amita. 2017. "Colonising the Slum: Changing Trajectories of State-Market Violence in Mumbai." *Economic & Political Weekly* 52 (7): 75–82.

Blomley, Nicholas K. 2002. "Mud for the Land." *Public Culture* 14 (3): 557–82.

Bombay First, and McKinsey. 2003. "Vision Mumbai: Transforming Mumbai into a World-Class City." Mumbai.

Brenner, Neil, and Christian Schmid. 2015. "Towards a New Epistemology of the Urban?" *City* 19 (2–3): 151–82.

Buck-Morss, Susan. 1977. *The Origin of Negative Dialectics: Theodor W. Adorno, Walter Benjamin and the Frankfurt Institute*. New York, NY: Free Press.

———. 1989. *The Dialectics of Seeing: Walter Benjamin and the Arcades Project*. Cambridge, MA: MIT Press.

———. 2000. *Dreamworld and Catastrophe: The Passing of Mass Utopia in East and West*. Cambridge, MA: MIT Press.

Burra, Sundar. 2005. "Towards a Pro-Poor Framework for Slum Upgrading in Mumbai, India." *Environment and Urbanization* 17 (1): 67–88.

Butler, Judith. 1990. *Gender Trouble: Feminism and the Subversion of Identity*. New York, NY: Routledge.

Caillois, Roger. 2001. *Man, Play, and Games*. Chicago, IL: University of Illinois Press.

Castells, Manuel. 1977. *The Urban Question: A Marxist Approach*. Cambridge, MA: MIT Press.

Census of India. 2011. "Primary census abstract for slum." Office of the Registrar General & Census Commissioner, India.

Chakrabarty, Dipesh. 2009. "*Adda*: A History of Sociality." In *Provincializing Europe*, edited by Dipesh Chakrabarty, 180–213. Princeton, NJ: Princeton University Press.

Chandavarkar, Rajnayaran. 2009. "Bombay's Perennial Modernities." In *History, Culture and the Indian City*, 12–30. Cambridge, UK: Cambridge University Press.

Chhabria, Sheetal. 2019. *Making the Modern Slum: The Power of Capital in Colonial Bombay*. Seattle, WA: University of Washington Press.

Collective Research Initiatives Trust. 2007. "Housing Typologies in Mumbai." Mumbai: CRIT and LSE.

Contractor, Qudsiya. 2012. "Unwanted in My City - The Making of a 'Muslim' Slum in Mumbai." In *Muslims in Indian Cities - Trajectories of Marginalisation*, edited by Laurent Gayer and Jaffrelot, 23–42. London, UK: Hurst Publishers.

Coomaraswamy, Ananda K. 1941. "Līlā." *Journal of the American Oriental Society* 61 (2): 98–101.

Davis, Mike. 2006. *Planet of Slums*. New York, NY: Verso.

De Boeck, Filip, and Marie-Françoise Plissart. 2014. *Kinshasa: Tales of the Invisible City*. Leuven: Leuven University Press.

Debord, Guy. 2006. "Theory of the Dérive." In *Situationist International Anthology*, edited and translated by Ken Knabb, 62–66. Berkeley, CA: Bureau of Public Secrets.

Economic Times. 2019. "Housing Affordability Worsened over Past 4 Years, Reveals RBI Survey - Mumbai Being the Least Affordable | The Economic Times," July 12, 2019. https://economictimes.indiatimes.com/industry/services/property-/-cstruction/housing-affordability-worsened-over-past-4-years-reveals-rbi-survey/mumbai-being-the-least-affordable/slideshow/70191730.cms.

Elyachar, Julia. 2011. "The Political Economy of Movement and Gesture in Cairo." *Journal of the Royal Anthropological Institute* 17 (1): 82–99.

Falzon, Mark-Anthony. 2004. "Paragons of Lifestyle: Gated Communities and the Politics of Space in Bombay." *City & Society* 16 (2): 145–67.

First, Bombay. 2003. "Vision Mumbai: Transforming Mumbai into a World Class City." McKinsey & Company, Inc.

Friedmann, John. 1987. *Planning in the Public Domain: From Knowledge to Action*. Princeton, NJ: Princeton University Press.

Gandolfo, Daniella. 2013. "Formless: A Day at Lima's Office of Formalization." *Cultural Anthropology* 28 (2): 278–98.

Gayer, Laurent, and Christopher Jaffrelot, eds. 2012. *Muslims in Indian Cities: Trajectories of Marginalisation*. London, UK: Hurst Publishers.

Gell, Alfred. 1980. "The Gods at Play: Vertigo and Possession in Muria Religion." *Man* 15 (2): 219–48.

Ghertner, D. Asher. 2015. *Rule by Aesthetics: World-Class City Making in Delhi*. New York, NY: Oxford University Press.

Gidwani, Vinay. 1992. "'Waste' and the Permanent Settlement in Bengal." *Economic & Political Weekly* 27 (4): 39–46.

Gidwani, Vinay. 2013. "Six Theses on Waste, Value, and Commons." *Social & Cultural Geography* 14 (7): 773–83.

———. 2018. "For a Marxist Theory of Waste: Seven Remarks." In *The Postcolonial Contemporary: Political Imaginaries for the Global Present*, edited by Jini Kim Watson and Gary Wilder, 187–207. New York, NY: Fordham University Press.

Gidwani, Vinay, and Anant Maringanti. 2016. "The Waste-Value Dialectic: Lumpen Urbanization in Contemporary India." *Comparative Studies of South Asia, Africa and the Middle East* 36 (1): 112–33.

Gidwani, Vinay, and Rajyashree N. Reddy. 2015. "The Work of Waste: Inside India's Infra-Economy." *Transactions of the Institute of British Geographers* 40 (4): 575–95.

Gilmore, Ruth Wilson. 2007. *Golden Gulag: Prisons, Surplus, Crisis, and Opposition in Globalizing California*. Berkeley, CA: University of California Press.

Hansen, Miriam Bratu. 2011. *Cinema and Experience: Siegfried Kracauer, Walter Benjamin, and Theodor W. Adorno*. Edited by Edward Dimendberg. Berkeley, CA: University of California Press.

Hansen, Thomas Blom. 2001. *Wages of Violence: Naming and Identity in Postcolonial Bombay*. Princeton, NJ: Princeton University Press.

Harvey, David. 1978. "The Urban Process under Capitalism: A Framework for Analysis." *International Journal of Urban and Regional Research* 2 (1–3): 101–31.

———. 1989. *The Urban Experience*. Baltimore, MD: Johns Hopkins University Press.

Horkheimer, Max, and Theodor W. Adorno. 2002. *Dialectic of Enlightenment*. Edited by Gunzelin Schimd Noerr. Translated by Edmund Jephcott. Stanford, CA: Stanford University Press.

Huizinga, Johan. 1998. *Homo Ludens: A Study of Play in the Element of Culture*. London, UK: Routledge.

Indorewala, Hussain. 2018a. "Housing and Dishousing in Mumbai - A Historical Outline of Slum Discourse and Policy." In *Urban Spaces in Modern India*, edited by Narayani Gupta and Partho Datta, 53–74. Shimla: Indian Institute of Advanced Study.

———. 2018b. "Mumbai's New Development Plan Is About More Real Estate for Developers." *The Wire*, 2018. https://thewire.in/urban/mumbais-development-plan-is -mostly-about-premier-real-estate.

Kafka, Franz. 1971. "Before the Law." In *The Complete Stories of Franz Kafka*, translated by Willa Muir and Edwin Muir 3:27–29. New York, NY: Schocken Books.

Kawashima, Ken C. 2009. *The Proletarian Gamble*. Durhman, NC: Duke University Press.

King, Tiffany Lethabo. 2019. The Black Shoals: *Offshore Formations of Black and Native Studies*. Duke University Press.

Krentz, Arthur A. 1998. "Play and Education in Plato's Republic." *The Paideia Archive*: Twentieth World Congress of Philosophy 29: 199–207.

Lefebvre, Henri. 2003. *The Urban Revolution*. Translated by Robert Bononno. Minneapolis, MN: University of Minnesota Press.

Li, Tania Murray. 2007. *The Will to Improve: Governmentality, Development, and the Practice of Politics*. Durhman, NC: Duke University Press.

Livescu, Simona. 2003. "From Plato to Derrida and Theories of Play." *CLCWeb: Comparative Literature and Culture* 5 (4).

Manto, Saadat Hasan. 1970. "Toba Tek Singh." Translated by Robert B. Haldane. *Mahfil* 6 (2/3): 19–23.

Marasco, Robyn. 2018. "It's All about the Benjamins Considerations on the Gambler as a Political Type." *New German Critique* 45 (1 (133)): 1–22.

Massey, Doreen. 1991. "The Political Place of Locality Studies." *Environment and Planning A* 23 (2): 267–81.

May, Todd. 2005. *Gilles Deleuze: An Introduction*. Cambridge, UK: Cambridge University Press.

McClintock, Anne. 1995. *Imperial Leather: Race, Gender and Sexuality in the Colonial Contest*. New York, NY: Routledge.

McIntyre, Michael, and Heidi J. Nast. 2011. "Bio (Necro) Polis: Marx, Surplus Populations, and the Spatial Dialectics of Reproduction and 'Race.'" *Antipode* 43 (5): 1465–88.

McKittrick, Katherine. 2006. *Demonic Grounds: Black Women and the Cartographies of Struggle*. Minneapolis, MN: University of Minnesota Press.

Mitchell, Timothy. 1991. *Colonising Egypt*. Berkeley, CA: University of California Press.

———. 2008. "The Properties of Markets." In *Do Economists Make Markets?: On the Performativity of Economics*, edited by Donald MacKenzie, Fabian Muniesa, and Lucia Siu, 244–75. Princeton, NJ: Princeton University Press.

Mukhija, Vinit. 2017. *Squatters as Developers?: Slum Redevelopment in Mumbai*. London, UK: Routledge.

Murphy, Michelle. 2017. *The Economization of Life*. Durhman, NC: Duke University Press.

Nieuwenhuys, Constant. 1998[1960]. "Unitary Urbanism." In *Constant's New Babylon: The Hyper-Architecture of Desire*, edited by Mark Wigley, translated by Robyn de Jong Dalziel, from an unpublished manuscript of a lecture at the Stedelijk Museum, Amsterdam on 20 December 1960, 131–35. Rotterdam, NL: 010 and Witte de With.

Nijman, Jan. 2008. "Against the Odds: Slum Rehabilitation in Neoliberal Mumbai." *Cities* 25 (2): 73–85.

Nuttall, Sarah, and Achille Mbembe. 2008. "Introduction: Afropolis." In Johannesburg: The Elusive Metropolis, 1–36. Durhman, NC: Duke University Press.

Osborne, Thomas, and Nikolas Rose. 1999. "Governing Cities: Notes on the Spatialisation of Virtue." *Environment and Planning D: Society and Space* 17 (6): 737–60.

Rajagopal, Arvind. 2002. "Violence of Commodity Aesthetics: Hawkers, Demolition Raids and a New Regime of Consumption." *Economic & Political Weekly* 37 (1): 65–76.

Rancière, Jacques. 2004. "The Order of the City." *Critical Inquiry* 30 (2): 267–91.

Raqs Media Collective. 2010. *Seepage*. Berlin: Sternberg Press.

Roy, Ananya. 2011. "The Blockade of the World-Class City: Dialectical Images of Indian Urbanism." In *Worlding Cities: Asian Experiments and the Art of Being Global*, edited by Ananya Roy and Aihwa Ong, 259–78. Malden: MA: Blackwell-Wiley.

Said, Edward W. 1989. "Representing the Colonized: Anthropology's Interlocutors." *Critical Inquiry* 15 (2): 205–25.

Sassen, Saskia. 2001. "Cities in the Global Economy." In *Handbook of Urban Studies*, edited by Ronan Paddison, 256–72. New York, NY: Sage Publications.

Sax, William Sturman. 1995. "Introduction." In *The Gods at Play: Līlā in South Asia*, edited by William Sturman Sax. New York, NY: Oxford University Press.

Seabrook, Jeremy, and Imran Ahmed Siddiqui. 2011. *People Without History: India's Muslim Ghettos*. New York, NY: Pluto Press.

Searle, Llerena Guiu. 2016. *Landscapes of Accumulation: Real Estate and the Neoliberal Imagination in Contemporary India*. Chicago, IL: University of Chicago Press.

Simmel, Georg. 1950. "The Metropolis and Mental Life." In *The Sociology of Georg Simmel*, edited by Kurt H. Wolff and Kurt H. Wolff, 47–60. New York, NY: The Free Press.

Simone, AbdouMaliq. 2012. "Ghostly Cracks and Urban Deceptions: Jakarta." In *In The Life of Cities: Parallel Narratives of the Urban*, edited by Mohsen Mostafavi, 121–33. Cambridge and Baden: Harvard Graduate School of Design and Lars Müller Publishers.

Smith, Neil. 1990. *Uneven Development: Nature, Capital, and the Production of Space*. Athens, GA: The University of Georgia Press.

Soja, Edward W. 1980. "The Socio-Spatial Dialectic." *Annals of the Association of American Geographers* 70 (2): 207–25.

Soto, Hernando De. 2000. *The Mystery of Capital: Why Capitalism Triumphs in the West and Fails Everywhere Else*. New York, NY: Basic Books.

State of Maharashtra. 1971. *Maharashtra Slum Areas (Improvement, Clearance And Redevelopment) Act, 1971*. Mumbai: Department of Urban Development.

———. 2004. "Transforming Mumbai into a World-Class City." Mumbai: Chief Minister's Taskforce.

Stoekl, Allan. 2007. *Bataille's Peak: Energy, Religion, and Postsustainability*. Minneapolis, MN: University of Minnesota Press.

Stokes, Eric. 1989. *The English Utilitarians and India*. London, UK: Oxford University Press.

Tabassum, Azra, et.al. 2010. *Trickster City: Writings from the Belly of the Metropolis*. Translated by Shveta Sarda. New Delhi: Penguin Books India.

Tadiar, Neferti X M. 2012. "Life-Times in Fate Playing." *South Atlantic Quarterly* 111 (4): 783–802.

———. 2013. "Life-Times of Disposability within Global Neoliberalism." *Social Text* 31 (2): 19–48.

———. 2016. "City Everywhere." *Theory, Culture & Society* 33 (7–8): 57–83.

Taussig, Michael. 1993. *Mimesis and Alterity: A Particular History of the Senses*. New York and London: Routledge.

———. 1995. "The Sun Gives without Receiving: An Old Story." *Comparative Studies in Society and History* 37 (2): 368–98.

———. 2006. *Walter Benjamin's Grave*. Chicago, IL: University of Chicago Press.

Taussig, Michael T. 1992. *The Nervous System*. New York and London: Routledge.

Weber, Max. 1958. "The Nature of the City." In *The City*, translated by Don Martindale and Gertrud Neuwirth, 65–90. Glencoe, IL: Free Press.

Weber, Samuel. 2008. *Benjamin's-Abilities*. Cambridge, MA: Harvard University Press.

Weinstein, Liza. 2014. *The Durable Slum: Dharavi and the Right to Stay Put in Globalizing Mumbai*. Minneapolis, MN: University of Minnesota Press.

Wilson, Elizabeth. 1992. *The Sphinx in the City: Urban Life, the Control of Disorder, and Women*. Berkeley, CA: University of California Press.

Wright, Melissa W. 2006. *Disposable Women and Other Myths of Global Capitalism*. New York and London: Routledge.

Correspondence

A Note on the Method of This Book

What follows below is an elaboration on the methodology that guided my fieldwork, writing process, as well as the final form of this book. It is not an elaboration on the methods used but an email correspondence between a friend just starting her field research and myself, while I was in the last phase of my fieldwork. We both shared a series of questions and reflections on methods and politics of research, on what kind of knowledge needs to be produced, and on how one locates oneself within a whole while immersing oneself in particularities. Writing these emails provided me (and hopefully her) a channel for sharing ideas, thoughts, experiences, reflections, and anxieties. A number of these ideas appear in this book explicitly, and others have made their way in implicitly. But before presenting the correspondence, I want to make two points regarding the choice of using correspondence as a way of writing about methods. First, it should be pointed out that the correspondence is between people working in two different contexts: one in the "Global South," the other in the "Global North"; one working on slum localities in Mumbai, India, and the other working on histories of economic transformations and the production of seasonal labor in Prince Edward Island, Canada. Despite the contextual differences, the correspondence allowed us to share experiences, similarities and differences, connections and disconnections, as well as how we were translating these into thinking about one's own world and its particularities without replicating them. I present this email exchange in the section on methods to preempt one possible way to reading cities and this book, as well as to think through what such correspondences could allow for in terms of devising methods, questions, and ways of thinking across different contexts. My second point is about the rawness or immediacy of the ideas and their articulations, when one is in the middle of things, inhabiting the field. The correspondence, in many ways, provided an avenue to share raw ideas, experiment and test out concepts, and have them heard and responded to, without judgment. It is hard, as my friend rightly points out, to find such "patient" spaces in formal setups today. I share this correspondence, and this book, with that spirit.

DOI: 10.4324/9781003051848-2

September 13, 2013
Toronto, Canada

Hi Prasad,
Thanks for these articles (on multi-sited ethnographies) (…)

I spent a lot of time this summer thinking about what it means to do research in a place that you know well, a place called "home," which is what I am trying to do. And it's complicated and really brought to light the degree to which (our) assumptions about research are rooted in ideas of apartness and outsider-ness; objectivity, even. And, obviously, in these places, there are layers of insider-ness and outsiders within them—geographic, classed, raced, colonial, etc. All of which make the questions that much more complicated. I was wondering if (a) this is something you are experiencing and struggling with in your own process, and (b) if you are, if you have found useful things to read that have helped you think through it. And this is the sort of sensitive and personal (though deeply political) stuff that I feel like we otherwise shrug off. It's hard to find patient enough spaces to talk about it all …. but it's really central to my research.

k.

September 15, 2013
New Delhi, India

Hi K,
I remember saying in one of the planner's PhD meetings at the department, what method do you use to write about a space that is your "home?" How do you study a place where you have lived most of your life? It didn't lead anywhere.

What helped me (as I reflect on it now) was reading (Walter) Benjamin on Proust.[1] There is no pure objectivity in knowledge; it's a dialectical relationship between living the thing and knowing the thing. You go back and forth, as you are suggesting a back forth between outsider-ness/insider-ness—a hybrid being of a stranger and a resident, always reflecting on what you knew or took for granted. But then a new experience or encounter transforms it.

In terms of reading: Benjamin's *Berlin Chronicle*.[2] Benjamin tries to recollect (or what he calls redeem—A Proustian redemption) memories of childhood to reflect on Berlin's fascist or capitalist becoming. His writings on encounters with telephone, his nanny, visits to places, are a conscious effort to write out what you know, and in writing them renew/re-know it in the present. Knowing, un-knowing and re-knowing—a process, which comes only from habit, which is what a home is (I think). Such writing also makes writing useless for its appropriation. (…)

It helped me with things that were habitually built into me. Like the matter-of-factness and being okay with walking through shit and dirt all the time. Now that I work on toilets, all those memories of watching children squat as I went to school, the smell, the visuals, the containers they use, men sitting in line at the railway tracks, or their disappearance during rains, provides new questions and makes me aware of what it means to be middle-class in the city. So I am trying to use those inbuilt memories to know more about what exists, what is taken for granted, but also unknow/reknow them through research and writing. A diary helps, when suddenly you see something and it flashes a memory—a déjà vu, and you write about it. A lot of these memories are of people around talking about the smell of shit, disgust with slums, rain and muck, about hatred for Muslims, living next to a slum.

I realized (while doing field work) that, as academics, we are very quick; we want to decipher signs and events in a Marxist or Foucauldian or Deleuzean way; move into analysis mode quickly. But I decided (during fieldwork) to rather enjoy or lose myself and then rethink those events in writing. It means a lot of everyday encounters from past and present, which are lived and need to be redeemed (in writing). I am trying to use the same method in talking to people about their lives. I decided to not ask residents of slums about their problems, but about memories and experiences. Problems demand solutions, which is what provides objective material for planners to provide violent solutions. But writing about experiences and memories of spaces, infrastructures, or events that made them happy or sad, objects they found and kept, encounters with government officials. In a way writing about experience helps me know the life and work that goes into making slum a livable place, but also avoids from seeing the place through the lens of problem/solution.

pk.

Sep 27, 2013
Toronto, Canada

Hi Prasad,
I owe you an email about the memory stuff (...) I remember you really struggling with it when you first came back. I have also been thinking about memory a lot—the way that history gets constructed and circulated and recirculated. The politics of memory in how they are so central to power and way the production of the present is imagined. And by whom. I am using some of this "method" to think about the construction of "locals" on the east coast (Canada)—people invoke very old histories of displacement and expulsion to assert their "roots," their being "from" the place (these are really the first European settlers here)—histories of the Scottish enclosures/clearances, and of the Acadian deportation by the British. It's weird. But I am trying to let what I know of these never-questioned histories from

being a kid, being educated there, circulating in daily life for 30 years provide the legitimacy for that being a thing that matters. But then, on the other side of my research is the state—producing very particular fantasies of what these settlers/ citizens/workers are supposed to be. And I have this feeling that, after British control was established over the region, the state didn't really know "what to do" with these characters. They were never good settlers—"irrational" with their farming techniques, blamed for being rural, unproductive, inbred, and over time, the "roots" that these people (settlers) had constructed/been "given" by the state, that they had learned to hold onto so tightly became a liability from the state's perspective. Now they are blamed for being "stuck in place" and a pariah on the nation (drain on the system for being seasonally employed and using employment insurance). They have been since WWII, when it became clear the region (and its people) was never going to become properly modern. The fantasy now seems to be to empty the region using the (state-manipulated) free market. So, I have these two sorts of logics (state and everyday life? Maybe the important thing is two governing logics of value?) and I don't know how to make them speak to each other. And in the middle, these sort of contradictory settler characters who have never really done anything right in the eyes of the nation, and who have been let in to the national project in a "major" (state, status, property) way, but maybe not in a "minor" way (ever the pariah)—and they assert their "ownership" over and "roots in" this region very strongly, even as it dies. Anyway, I'm not sure what any of this means and how to sum it up nicely in the form of questions and a proposal! Sorry to belt it all out, but I just started writing, and there you have it. thanks for the ear. If you see a way out of this mess, let me know!

What are you learning about on your journeys?

k.

Oct 9, 2013
Toronto, Canada

Hi Prasad,
It's too bad you are so far away, because I feel like we are thinking through similar things. We both have been meditating on a similar question about the governance (not the right word) of the very logic of life and the moments of possibility that contest or fracture the (dominant) logic (for a second or forever, which we would normally characterize as resistance), and introduce the possibility of other logics of time/space/sociality/ individuality. I always feel like you are articulating ideas that I am trying to articulate, often using different words and thinkers.

I have been thinking about time too. The places that I'm thinking about (in PEI) have really been commodified (through predictable rural tourism projects) as performances of the past. When I was 14 I had a job scooping ice cream. I had to wear a 19th century Acadian costume. It's a funny image: a 14-year-old Jew in 1997, charming the Ontario (British) tourists by presenting herself as a (English speaking) French settler whose people were deported by the British 250 years ago. There is tons of stuff going on in terms of how new times are being imposed through new work regimes of migration, and the question of time seems to be one of the biggest things that people are struggling against. When I talk to people in the east who are still in rural communities, still fishing, they talk a lot about time; their imagined time of the city. They feel like they can't move because they don't speak the language—the language of time. I'm trying to think how I can make my project really about understanding urbanization from the outside. Not through people who are moving there, but who have resisted for a long time (or tried at least), connecting to transportation, commodity, and capital circuits that they feel would speed up time. Now, that ability to separate (times) is being challenged and more of them feel like they are being entered into that system (not by going to the city, but by going to mines and the oil patch), which to them is basically an urban space. People out there actually understand that the urban is a process and they, seemingly inevitably, are part of it. Even in their rural communities, they are dependent on people from Toronto to come look at their Acadian costumes— which was a struggle in the 1970s and people felt like they were losing control and autonomy. And when that state-imposed regime fails, people move that much deeper into the system through new lived experiences of time and space with the migration regime. Its phenomenological element seems to bother people, gets under their skin. It's the product of state planning, the dismantlement of small-scale agriculture and fisheries, and driving people into (state-created) tourism industry.

There's this one story that I love. I was flying back to Toronto from home once and I sat beside a guy who was clearly an oil worker on his way to Alberta (this happens all the time). We started talking and I asked him about his life. He works two weeks in Alberta for every week off in Nova Scotia. He hates the whole thing and makes more money than he knows what to do with, but feels like he has no other option. Then he told me this, and I said (to myself) "that's what my dissertation is about!": even though the time change between "home" and "work" is three hours, he never changes his watch when he gets out west. It helps him stay rooted in the east; a little part of the logic of his life is reserved, is under his control. One tiny part! One tiny little thing that probably has no material impact on his life, at least not in any way anyone could possible argue and sound sane, but I feel like it's so significant. It was a moment of clarity for me—well, the sense of clarity. I can't really explain what it means. That's for the dissertation I guess.

Talk soon and thanks again for the thoughts and the ear.

k.

October 21 2013
New Delhi, India

Hi K,
I really like the way you articulated the meta-question: "we have both been meditating on a similar question about the governance (not the right word) of

the very logic of life and the question of the moments of possibility that contest or fracture this logic, even for a second (or, forever, but in an unremarkable way, more about persistence and being itself that anything we would normally characterize as resistance), that introduce the possibility of other logics of time/space/sociality/individuality."

It says a lot about my own thinking and I guess also yours. I say its a meta-question also because I have been thinking about postcolonial debates and cultural and contextual differences a lot. But my recent ventures into the work of Japanese critic Kojin Karatani, Jacques Rancière, and the Frankfurt school have been pointing towards a different way of thinking—about singularity-universality rather than particularity-generality. The idea that a singular phenomenon or singular break in time can make claims to universality rather than the notion of a particular phenomenon speaking of general state of things. It opens up singular events and their ability to claim universal emancipation vis-à-vis particular claims that are appropriated into generality (or normativity).

On time, a line keeps running in my head. In an essay on writing and time Rancière speaks of a French worker who writes, I no longer have faith in time because time is 'too twisted' (here twisted means encircling).[3] It cannot be attacked from front. One has to walk round it, to transform the space that it constructs, the gestures that it imposes. This transformation may involve a bodily disjuncture such as when in a workplace the worker's gaze falls on the landscape and his thoughts wander into space to make his arm stop work and transform time. I am interested in these moments of interruptions, disjuncture, bypassing time, short-circuiting time, and how those moments open up possibility without its eventuality. Isn't telos or the end already the tool of capitalism (M-C-M')? I feel your stories on time and dealing with time speak a lot about the displacing, confronting, interrupting time of capital and the state.

I think sending letters, writing emails and discussing is a great idea. All of us are doing such different works and reading different people, but there are still so many connections that can be built into each others' work. It's exciting to think through such connections.

pk

March 21, 2014
Toronto, Canada

Hi Prasad,
I would love to read your (field) update that you sent to KG. I'm so curious what you are making of all of this. It would be good for me to read some about your experience, as your reflections tend to resonate a lot. Overall, how have you found it? Have you sorted through some of the "going home to do research" issue?

Send me an update when you have the chance!

k.

June, 26 2014
Mumbai, India

Hi K,

I am actually not writing. Going through the material I collected to put an outline together.

The fieldwork turned out to be different than what I had intended. The project expanded beyond what I had started off with—which is looking at toilet projects. I ended up spending a lot time in the (slum) locality seeing movies, talking to people, drinking tea, walking, eating, renting out rooms in different localities, and doing some interviews by following links from one space to the other. The whole rise in surveys being done by NGOs, academics and activists about problems, have turned interviews into a problem solving exercise. I wanted to move away from that since the interviews I was conducting always ended up with talking about problems. It gave a glimpse into the development world of problems and solutions, which I want to move away from. I want to think of it in a more philosophical or political lens.

The question of what is it that I have to offer to them came up at two levels: one is what are the everyday things that one can work towards, and the other is a larger discursive shift in the way we "see"—where seeing is more about the experience (like in your article I read) than about abstractions through numbers and surveys, or abstraction of land into value.

How do we "write" about a place in a way that dies its own death without offering anything to the State or Capitalism to appropriate and reproduce? Reproduction is the theology of capitalism. Gramsci, Benjamin, Kafka, I feel, were attempting to work towards reproducing reality which self-closes, so that it offers no door for capitalism to enter. That's the struggle I am trying to explore in terms of writing. Somehow the idea of a fairytale—Grimm brothers, as well as the form of a movie helps a lot, because it's a tale and offers nothing in terms of a telos, and yet allows for tricks to be passed on.

Re: what is it one can offer to the locality? I think the fieldwork is that exercise, rather than the final writing. To offer what we know—sharing. To give whatever I collected in terms of policy documents, legal cases, distributing cards of NGOs and lawyers, archival material, passing information across divided groups, trying to apply for grants for their projects. I am planning to apply for a grant to do a film project with a local ad-hoc filmmaker youth group in the locality about "beauty." And second, a small community based slum redevelopment project came up in the process of the interviews. It is not a part of the PhD project but it comes up once you enter that world without having pre-ideas about what to do and offer—I think it's a process that gets defined during (fieldwork) interactions. Initially, I went with the eye of the researcher, trying to be critical, trying to figure out the discourse, the hidden system. But it is already known to them, the answer was not to be discovered.

So two tasks came up, one is how do we reproduce an idea, something capitalism does very well—reproduction, (but) how do we mimic it to reproduce its own death. And second, how do we move away from critical distance, again which capitalism does very well. It doesn't maintain a distance but enters into every part of our lives and hits you in an experiential way. How can our work do that? Hit you, put people on the edge …. Enter into the fairy tale world.

In terms of fieldwork, I think one needs to enter and move around like a rat in a labyrinth. And then move out at times of writing to see what we have gathered. It's also a process of our becoming through the fieldwork. That way you get to know the scene very differently and may be in terms of a fragment. But the fragment can have a lot to say about universality rather than totality. And it's good to leave totality as a set of fragments, where a door is left open for someone else to add other bits.

Sorry for rambling, just writing out thoughts.

pk

Sep 27 2014,
Prince Edward Island, Canada

Hi Prasad,
Sorry it's taken me so long to write back to this.

I laughed when I read this: "But in terms of fieldwork, I think one needs to enter and move around like rat in a labyrinth. And then move out at times of writing to see what we have in terms of food." Partly because only you would write something like that and mean it, and have me take it seriously and get it. And partly because I feel like that rat, but I'm running back and forth along the same passage looking for some turns. I'll find them eventually. I guess that is part of the labyrinthine experience.

There is a lot in your email. I really relate to a lot of this. I really hear you about the problem-solving thing. And it's an interesting thing to connect it to the history of people being studied. People here are very invested in the idea that there is a solution (and, for that matter, a problem). I spent most of the summer reading about the history of this big comprehensive social, spatial (land, industry), and economic planning project that was designed for PEI in the 1960s. I was trying to look at all the surveying and research that was undertaken in advance of the design of the plan, by planners and other professionals about peoples' poverty, (un)productivity, and conditions of living. You know, quantifying and mapping in a comprehensive way for the first time to show the fact that there was something wrong with the place and the people. And then the answer took the form of this neat and tidy (and fucked up) comprehensive development plan that promised to solve all of these new problems. They interviewed every land owner on the island with five acres or more—would have been a huge percentage of people at the time. I feel like this is what I hear today when I talk to people …. People have a strange way of relating to governance bodies. They are deeply suspicious but at the same time electoral politics is the only way people know how to talk about politics …. The idea that I might be studying something to better understand how it came to be and what it means about the world we live in is incomprehensible to a lot of people. To them, research is either about problems/solutions or it is about data, collecting numbers to prove something. So, how did you manage to run your interviews in a way that got away from problems/solutions?

I think that the obsession with problem solving is a problem in and of itself. I guess maybe this is one of the things I want to do with my work. Maybe this is part of what you are saying re: reproducing an idea? That there are layers of realities and logics and that when it comes to interacting with more molar structures like research, governance, imagining "improvement," people stick really closely to a hegemonic logic of history or something. But this is not the logic that guides daily life in so many ways—this is maybe the fairy tale moment. Finding other modes that allow the representation of these logics. I feel like people are stuck with a conversation that isn't theirs. Like they have been given a set of ideas that they are allowed to use in their own problem solving and are not to deviate beyond that. And I get the sense that people's adherence to these "rules" is guided by real fear. I don't know who they think is listening.

So, yes to work hitting people. This is why we need to learn to be good writers! We need to tell stories! We also, I am learning, need to be investigative, learn to navigate the law and the state—and this I find so hard. Research is funny because you never know where you are going. It's a different sense you have to follow—not a rational one, not one that thinks too much about the future. But yeah, I am trying to trace the everyday part and the state part and it's hard. But I like the fairy tale thing (if I get it) because I am increasingly down on the idea that I'm ever going to convince anyone of anything using logic or rational argument. Everything evil is way too naturalized. We have to appeal to other sensibilities maybe.

But I would like to hear more about how you managed your interviews. Good luck with the sorting, thinking and writing. I'll look forward to your next update!

k.

October 21 2014,
Bangalore, India

Hi K,
The work you are doing sounds really exciting. Hope we get a chance to speak at some point in person. Feels like we are struggling with same questions.

About interviews: I don't think I figured it out completely. I run from interviews because they are too formal for my liking. I conducted some interviews with two basic ideas: first, to ask them (residents) questions that I am asking myself. There is a nice essay called the "Eleventh Question" in a book called *The Hub*. The Eleventh Question, they say, is the question that comes after the first ten questions of survey, and it's a philosophical question—be it politics, about beauty, about love, about films, about strangers. So I tried as much as I could engage with residents at that level. It didn't turn out to be philosophical in some ontological way, but in a political sense: how they see things: fucked, melancholic .... and how does one then navigate it? I stuck to their idea of the world, rather than saying there is something hidden, which they don't see but I will show.

The second part of it was also to allow for characters to be mixed. I feel that urban poor is a completely stripped of person, like the proletariat who has nothing but labor to sell. Urban poor—who has nothing but poverty to show. I think that it hides the bastards of the world, those scoundrels who cheat and get cheated, who work and play. I felt everyone is like that, which meant they are not "only" ultimate surplus humanity of global imperialism. But people who participate in perpetuating it and fighting it too (at the same time)—people exist in doubles. We tend to strip them into pure forms. So most of the characters I focus on were these contradictory forms, somewhat anti-heroic tricksters who are active, not passive to be woken up out of ideological sleep. Will see how it goes and what it shows.

Sorry for rambling,

Pk.

Notes

1 Benjamin, Walter. 1968[1934]. "The Image of Proust." In *Illuminations*, edited by Hannah Arendt, translated by Harry Zohn, 201–16. New York, NY: Schocken Books.
2 Benjamin, Walter. 1978[1932]. "A Berlin Chronicle." In *One-Way Street and Other Writings*, translated by Edmund Jephcott and Kingsley Shorter, 293–346. New York, NY: NLB.
3 Rancière, Jacques. 2012. "I No Longer Have Faith in Time." In *Cybermohalla Hub*, edited by Nikolaus Hirsch and Shveta Sarda, 76–78. Berlin: Sternberg Press.

References

Benjamin, Walter. 1968[1934]. "The Image of Proust." In *Illuminations*, edited by Hannah Arendt, translated by Harry Zohn, 201–16. New York, NY: Schocken Books.
———. 1978[1932]. "A Berlin Chronicle." In *One-Way Street and Other Writings*, translated by Edmund Jephcott and Kingsley Shorter, 293–346. New York, NY: NLB.
Rancière, Jacques. 2012. "I No Longer Have Faith in Time." In *Cybermohalla Hub*, edited by Nikolaus Hirsch and Shveta Sarda, 76–78. Berlin: Sternberg Press.

Figure 1.1 Yahaan phaltu bethna sakht mana hai (Idling here is strictly prohibited)

1 On Idling, Storytelling, and Impartibility

Phaltu Bethna Sakht Mana Hai[1]

Toba Tek Nagar has around 35 mosques. During an interview, I asked the secretary of a local mosque about their significance in the locality. One part of its significance, he told me, is the act of praying in crowds: while praying, one kneels and touches one's head to the ground, and at that moment, one's head is at another's feet. This bodily gesture of praying together, he suggested, makes everyone equal in front of each other as well as before God. Another significant aspect of visiting a mosque, he further noted, is socializing with the *jamaat* (community). After the *namaz* (prayers) men and women[2] assemble in groups and inquire about each other's daily affairs and share what they know about those who haven't turned up.

On Fridays particularly, life in Toba Tek Nagar begins to fade around twelve-thirty in the afternoon. Shutting down their businesses early that day of the week, men begin to move slowly towards the mosques for the *jumma namaz* (the Friday afternoon prayer), while women start congregating in smaller groups in different houses. The streets approaching the mosques are partly shut and get occupied by men and children for praying. The police constables gather around the mosques with their walkie-talkies to avoid any incidence of communal violence. But before the *namaz*, while they wash themselves and prepare for prayers, the imams of different mosques give a sermon, the *khutbah*. They are narrated by the imams in a loud melodramatic way on mics and transmitted through loudspeakers installed on the roofs and minarets. Most often, the *khutbah*s narrated in the locality are about ethics of life vis-à-vis the difficulties faced by Muslims in today's world, and they are delivered in the form of stories of Nabi, the Prophet Mohammad. Each story ends with a lesson, reiterating how Islamic ethics can allow one to deal with everyday problems. But most times it is difficult to hear these stories in their entirety, as they collapse and merge into *khutbah*s from the nearby mosques.

On one such Friday, the story being narrated by an imam was like a Grimm's fairy tale. The devil had cast his spell of darkness on a village. The sun, the gift giver of energy, was nowhere to be seen. Its disappearance had stalled all life in the village: farming, the seasons, religion, and particularly praying. In despair, the followers decided to seek help from the prophet, Nabi. But none of them had ever seen him or knew where he lived. Everything they knew of him was through his

DOI: 10.4324/9781003051848-3

stories, *khutbahs*. One of the followers, a child who spent a lot of time grazing goats in the field, thought of a trick. He decided to kidnap one of Nabi's beloved goats from the common grounds and hide it. A while later, seeing that one of the goats hadn't returned, Nabi himself stepped out in search of the goat. On reaching the village, he found himself in front of the villagers with his goat tied to a rope held by the child. Unfortunately, the end, and the lesson of the story, drowned into another story from a nearby mosque, leaving the moral of the story open to interpretations.

What is intriguing here, to my mind, are three things. One, the trick the child plays on Nabi to bring him out into the world to cast off the spell of darkness. Second, equally intriguing is the imam's story of a child's trick and the curious play of hide-and-seek as a form of reverence and ethics, which makes religion, with its stories and its storytellers, an infrastructural resource of not just ethical values and ways of being but also tricks and passages to find light and to lighten life in times of darkness. And third, the multiple stories that circulate in the locality at any given time, which intersect each other, sometimes drown each other, other times supplement each other, and are open to be interpreted and used in different ways.

This chapter explores these different dimensions of everyday storytelling in the locality by paying attention to the ethnographic details of who is telling stories, to whom, about what, where, and when. It does this with a twofold aim: one, of exhibiting how and why stories that are shared, exchanged, gifted, and wasted are an important part of "semiotic commons" of urban life for slum residents; and second, of showing how storytelling becomes an important infrastructural medium for slum residents to transform their urban lives. By "semiotic commons," following Julia Elyachar (2011), I refer to the many linguistic and nonlinguistic signs that circulate across urban publics; which are available as a public resource for people to use in multiple ways; and which become the infrastructural mediums of urban life in a context of neoliberalism and marketization of common resources.[3] Given that stories are both resources and infrastructural mediums, they too, like most public resources and infrastructures, are embedded within the political economy of knowledge, time, and space in cities.

Eviscerating Urbanism: Making Everything Work

Indian cities are being increasingly restructured through dominant practices: deregulation of governance and planning systems; privatization of public resources and their provisioning mechanisms; displacement of obsolete industries and habitats; development of mega-infrastructure projects for the uninterrupted flow of goods, vehicles, and people; and expansion of cities across peripheries and rural areas (Anand 2006; Banerjee-Guha 2002; Coelho and Raman 2010; D'monte 2002; Roy and Ong eds. 2011). The broader goal of these dominant processes is to restructure and govern urban time-space in line with the rhythms of global capital (both real and speculative) and the returns on it (Banerjee-Guha 2009; Goldman 2011). Everything is to be "put to work" in this "eviscerating urbanism." Time, labor, land, and ecologies are colonized and converted into surplus value either by putting them to work or by expending them (Gidwani and Reddy 2015). The logic of work has become a pervasive and taken for granted social and political good not just in capitalist work societies but also in thought-systems that promise to set us free from it, albeit through work (Weeks 2011).[4] Work, Pierre Clastres suggests, is the imperative of modern state apparatus. And historically, it appeared with the constitution of surplus value, whereby work became overwork—alienated and commodified work (1987).[5] In this work model, everything is made calculable and measurable: money, miles, degrees, and minutes. And everything is made to perform the work of producing a surplus value: time, space, people, and things. It is in contrast to this work model that Paul Lafargue proclaimed "a right to laziness." This proclamation, Kristin Ross tells us, was not a demand for leisure, the constituted opposite of work, but a challenge to the division of time into work and leisure and a call to partake in the otherwise inaccessible time of pleasurable intellectual work (1988). But to look beyond work, as Tiffany Lethabo King proposes in her work on Blackness and colonial plantations, is to open up a space for other kinds of analytical concepts to view and perceive "something else," to open up a space for other forms of anti-work and postwork imaginations, which otherwise gets get crowded out by the analytic of labor (2019: 111–40).

In *Accursed Share*, Georges Bataille takes up a similar historical investigation of the logic of work within different systems, including knowledge, religion, economy, and energy, but with an interest in exploring the potentiality of the excess that these systems secrete (1988[1949]). What is of interest to me in this chapter is Bataille's take on the logic of work in G.W.F Hegel's knowledge system. For Hegel, Bataille notes, we can arrive at a higher form of knowledge by negating and conserving parts of our experiences. Experiences are not to be wasted completely but partly negated and partly preserved. And in doing so, both parts can be made to perform the work of producing a higher form of knowledge without allowing them to exceed or suspend the totality of the discourse being produced. Bataille calls this process "reproductive consumption," which he also sees at work in capitalism. In both, a speculative logic of accumulation is at work, whose aim is to reproduce values: value-as-money and value-as-knowledge (Gidwani and Maringanti 2016: 117). Furthermore, in this form of knowledge production, Jacques Derrida notes, although nothing is wasted, something is sacrificed to keep the totality of this discourse. And what is sacrificed is meaning—the meaning of nonabstract experiences such as unhappiness, anxiety, restlessness, forgetfulness, and laughter, which cannot be completely assimilated into the system (1978).[6] This sacrificed part is then relegated to the world of non-meaning or non-knowledge, and it is only in relation to this "other" that meaning and knowledge are produced in this world. For Bataille, this sacrifice or negation renders these parts of our experiences as inoperative or unemployable negativities—what he terms as excess. However, this excess doesn't dissipate in this process, rather it secretes and leaks out of its containment and takes on new unpredictable forms that haunt the system (Gidwani and Maringanti 2016: 117).

Putting Stories to Work

On an evening not so long ago, different apostles assembled for a consultation workshop in a municipal office in Mumbai. Platonist apostles, Habermasian apostles, Saint-Simonian apostles, Marxist apostles, had all arrived early and occupied seats around an oval-shaped table. The municipality was preparing a development plan for Mumbai. The city survey had been completed, and the process of assigning virtues and values to different pieces of land—the land-use plan—was ongoing. The workshop was organized to discuss the future of slums in that planned city.

The Habermasian apostles, the preachers of participatory planning and members of an NGO, sat at the head of the table. Next to them sat the Platonist priest. An ex-planner from the regional planning authority, the priest was a private consultant to both the municipality and the private consultants preparing the plan for the municipality. A Platonist par excellence, his aim was to establish an ideal city—a city of virtues, where justice was tied to the health of the city, and the health of the city to the right order of things. This order of things, like Plato's Republic, was to be established on a founding story—a "noble lie."[7] The sociological survey of land, the demographic census, the policy book, and the logic of the market were the basis and the tools of his story. The noble lie was that every piece of land is to have one use only, nothing more; one form of ownership only; no mixing; and no multiplicities. For this city to function efficiently, people, for their part, were to simply accept this noble lie and abide by it as the rule of law. It need not be justified, only told; it need not be believed, only accepted.

The meeting commenced.

The Saint-Simonian apostles were the first to speak. They projected onto the screen an array of cartographic maps, census data, pies, and graphs and evoked a dream world of affordable housing. In this enchanted world, they said, houses could fall from heaven onto the earth but *only* if the policy was right. And for the policy to be right, they needed more demographic numbers, more geographical maps, and above all a firm belief in progress and development. The Platonist priest intervened swiftly and cunningly sublated this image of heaven into a policy for the earth.

The next to speak were the Marxist apostles. They spoke of the squalor in slums and evoked the figure of the "urban poor"—that "surplus human of global capitalism dumped into the slums of the Third World." Things could change, they said, but only if the poor revolt. The problem of the policy, the revolt, and the noble lie, however, was the *only*; the *only*, which rendered the city life put together by slum residents as an illegible "mess" or "chaos" and stripped them of all their capacities to leave them standing as "bare lives" with poverty as their *only* ability.

The different apostles finished their presentations, and the dialogue was opened up for others to speak. The meeting invariably turned into a platform for slum residents to narrate personal stories, just like in an organized housing rights protest.[8] Stories about displacement, demolitions, bribes, all of which are intrinsic to the planning process, were narrated as experienced. Some residents cried, clapped, laughed, and hooted. Others debated with apostles about legalities and calculations pertaining to their localities. The Habermasian apostles intervened, "don't get personal or specific. We have heard that story." The rational discourse was getting too personal and repetitive. They demanded that comments be restricted to generalities so that they are useful to that third person, towards which every consultative dialogue is directed—the state, the judge, and the planner.[9] Despite the warnings, the residents continued to narrate stories.

During this whole time, the Platonist priest sat silently. He was unable to respond to these stories. The constraint seemed to be an impossibility of translating personal stories into reasonable policies. An impossibility that is built into the knowledge system to partition reason from experience, the participatory platform from the city, the noble lie from the cacophony of tales, and value from excess.

Stories in Urban Publics

In a non-synthesizing spirit, Walter Benjamin writes in his essay "The Storyteller" of differences between the values in information and story (1969[1936]: 83–109). Stories, he writes, do not aim to convey the pure essence of the thing, like information in a report. The value of information lives only at that moment; it has to surrender to it completely and explain itself without losing any time. A story, however, does not expend itself; it endures the passage of time. It preserves and concentrates its strength and is capable of releasing it even after a long time (ibid.: 90). And yet, stories are often made to perform the work of producing informational values in participatory forums, and if not, they are negated.

Participatory ladders, forums and platforms, like the one above, where the private self speaks and acts on public matters, have become a norm of neoliberal governance and planning in most cities (Guarneros-Meza and Geddes 2010). Within the planning discipline specifically, its roots lie in communicative planning theory and deliberative planning practice. They emerged in the United States and northwest Europe in the late 1980s as a response to modernist thinking and positivist technocratic planning. Both have gained much traction in planning pedagogy and practice across the globe over the last few decades (Watson 2002, 2011). Jürgen Habermas's writings on communicative rationality, and his conception of "the Public Sphere" as a realm of social life that mediates between society and the state, were foundational to these approaches (1991[1962]). Based on a historical narrative of increased circulation of newspapers, printed books, trading journals, and informal discussions in salons of 18th-century Europe, Habermas conceptualized the Public Sphere as an autonomous political space where critical public discussions could be held institutionally to produce public opinions on matters of common interests. However, for this sphere to function appropriately, he institutionalized two rules: first, access should be guaranteed to all citizens, and second, participants should bracket their individual interests and social status so as to engage in an impersonal and rational discourse on public issues.

Planning theorists drew inspiration from Habermas's conceptual model of the Public Sphere and argued that it is possible for rational and inherently democratic human beings to reach consensus and coordinate action through rational communication and deliberative action (Healey 1992; Forester 1999). In this schema, the role of a planner is to design these deliberative spaces, facilitate and encourage interested groups to tell their stories, provide an equal hearing to stories of all interest groups, and arrive at the best possible normative judgment. Here, stories are understood as expressions of value judgments and subjective norms, which are argued over through an intersubjective dialogue in institutionalized spaces in order to achieve a higher level of rational agreement.[10] However, producing consensus through rational communication, Jacques Rancière argues, is always based on introducing qualifications: rational speech, universal citizenship, discoursing over common interests rather than private needs, speaking in the public realm, and so on (2004b). Thus, words uttered with respect to private interests are always already illegitimate with regard to domestic matters and find no place in the public realm. Such qualifications, he notes, predetermine what is proper to politics, who is qualified to participate, and which is the proper space where politics can be performed (ibid.: 43–60).

Cities, however, are not *a* public sphere but constituted of multiple intersecting publics that are mediated by different technological mediums (Fraser 1990; Hirschkind 2009; Cody 2011).[11] Cities are also the loci where different urban actors, who have "no part in anything," arrive in cities to become something other than what they are (Simmell 1950[1903]; Rancière 2004b). These urban actors navigate and negotiate urban precarity through practices whose logics and rationales are often incongruous and in conflict with the planning rationalities (Roy 2007). In such a context, participatory platforms and forums, with their rules and qualifications, often work as institutionalized spaces that are carved into cities to enact modern forms of power and produce good neoliberal citizens (Warner 2002; Muehlbach 2012). And in these spheres, stories that do not perform the work of producing a consensual community are often disqualified. Departing from such qualifications, Abdoumaliq Simone imagines urban publics as forms of being connected that go beyond what a person does and where they come from (2010: 117–21). To be part of a public, he notes, is to be part of a larger set of addressees, which is not predetermined by a specific character or identity, but comes into being simply by sharing an experience or an event. And what is shared affects ways of thinking and living in a wide range of contexts, and can be potentially opened up by others to a wider set of uses than originally intended (ibid.: 119). In other words, gestures of speaking or acting in public, what Elyachar refers to as the semiotic commons, are always open to translations and citations.

But why tell stories in urban publics?

Poverty of Experience and Experience of Poverty

I had accompanied my colleagues for their meeting with a few residents of Toba Tek Nagar. These residents, five men, were building contractors. They were trying to acquire a contract for repairing dilapidated infrastructures in a Rehabilitation and

Resettlement scheme (RnR) from the city development authority. The RnR scheme, located at the southern edge of Toba Tek Nagar, was a cluster of six high-rise buildings, where slum residents displaced under Mumbai's Urban Transportation Project in 1997 were rehabilitated. The norm under the RnR scheme, which was formulated by the state government, and approved and funded by the World Bank, was to relocate displaced slum residents into high-rises in low-value real-estate areas in the peripheral suburbs. And the high-rises near Toba Tek Nagar, like most RnR schemes, were built with minimal safety regulations, poor construction standards, and insufficient amenities, as a result of which they had been dilapidating over the years. The resident-contractors, with whom we were meeting, were trying to not only acquire work but also address some of these infrastructural problems.

Halfway through the meeting, my colleague asked the resident-contractors, "Why is it that the collaborative practices that we see in slum localities have disappeared in the RnR schemes? How did they dilapidate in the first place?" After thinking for a bit, one of the contractors answered, the "social relations developed in a habitat over years disappear when habitats get demolished and rehabilitated on terms that aren't one's own; what is built over years gets taken away." The violence of displacement and alienation from habitat brings to mind the anthology of writings, entitled *Trickster City* (Tabassum et.al. 2010). Its section "Eviction" is a collection of blog posts, field diary entries, and reflections on urban eviction in New Delhi (ibid.: 137–227).

On 1 April 2005, Rakesh Khairalia writes in "Like a slow fire spreading through a dense forest":

> Wind, space, objects, time—everything turns to oblivion when the terror that fills the heart appears before the eyes. That sight which makes one tremble, when it finally manifests, makes the body feel as if it's being stung by a thousand needles. Right now, the tearing down of houses in the settlement is in progress.
>
> (ibid.: 151–52)

On 30 March 2006, Suraj Rai writes in "Remains":

> It takes many kinds of people, from different kinds of environments, to come together and make a settlement. But at this time, when the settlement is being demolished, everyone looks alike. The same kind of household things, the same kinds of wishes—gathering which all of them prepare to leave for a new place … . Many people have emptied their houses. But they have left their shadows behind on the walls. Each wall tells of those who lived by it. It's as if people leave, but the stubbornness and desires they lived with remains, printed on the walls.
>
> (ibid.: 163)

In "Spreading in the air," 31 March 2007, Rai writes again:

> It takes many years for a place to become a settlement, but a settlement is turned barren in merely two days. All around things are being broken, felled.

Some people are watching houses being pulled down. Each time dust rises when a house falls, they don't turn their faces away. They seem to be trying to take it all in. They had plastered the walls and roofs of their houses with memories. Today those memories have turned into dust and are spreading out in the air.

(ibid.: 155)

In "Objects of desire," 20 April 2006, Neelofar writes:

I think there are two kinds of objects in a home—those that fulfill our needs and those that express our desires. When we leave our homes, we leave behind our desires, and take along with us those things which fulfill some necessity.

(ibid.: 168)

Filled with observations, notes, questions, and thoughts, the words of these writers recount the disappearance of their homes while creating a new language to express violent urban experiences (ibid.: 298–311). Memories, experiences, and desires, which reside in other individuals as much as in things and spaces, built through years, get demolished, leaving people with nothing but necessities. Experience has indeed fallen in value.

In his 1936 essay, Benjamin comments that experience has fallen in value with modern capitalism—we are impoverished (1969[1936]). The shocks and rhythms of modern industrial capitalism, the fast-paced urban life, modern technology, modern warfare, economic inflation, and the rise of information culture, had diminished the capacity to experience and tell a story about that experience. Exploitation for Benjamin was a cognitive category, not an economic one—"it injures every one of the human senses, paralyzing the imagination of the subject, alienating the subject from itself" (Buck-Morss 1989: 17). During the same period, as scholars of colonial histories and discourses show, modern capitalism under colonialism was accompanied by modern forms of information, bureaucracy, and disciplinary practices, and was transported to the colonies and tested in different areas of life, including economy, governance, planning, bureaucracy, architecture, education, and religion (Birla 2009; Legg 2007). It was this rationalization, or the disenchantment of life through the cunning use of reason, and its simultaneous re-enchantment under capitalism and fascism that Benjamin associates with the poverty of experience and death of storytelling. Both reason and myth, he wrote, have cast their spell on humankind (Buck-Morss 1977). But if sensory alienation was the source of the aestheticization of politics under fascism and capitalism, Benjamin's response to it was to politicize art—that is, to undo the alienation of the corporeal sensorium and to restore the instinctual power of the human bodily senses through different technological mediums, such as films, photography, and writing.

However, I find it rather strange for someone like Benjamin, whose entire oeuvre was dedicated to evoking life in dead and petrified objects through what he referred to as child's play, to announce a death—a death of experience and the art of storytelling. I want to take up here the task of giving experience and the art of storytelling a new life. And what better way to do this than through fairy tales. With the words "once upon a time," as Benjamin puts it, children get transported in fairy tales into an enchanted world where they learn cunning tricks to outwit the hellish spell cast on humankind with courage.[12] In the figure of the fool, (the tale) it shows us how mankind can act dumb before the myth (...) (...) (I)n the shape of the animals which come to the aid of the child in the fairytale, it shows that nature not only is subservient to myth, but prefers to be aligned with man. The wisest thing (...) it teaches is to meet the forces of the mythical world with courage, high spirits, and cunning. (1969[1936]: 102) In contrast to Hegel's cunning of reason, Benjamin saw in fairy tales a different kind of cunning—a cunning of trickery by which children could shake off the nightmare of reason and capitalism.[13] The similarities between Benjamin's cunning in tales and the imam's *khutbah* at the beginning of the chapter are not merely coincidental.

Mimetic Play and Impartibility of Stories

Before delving into the ethnography, I want to highlight here two interrelated aspects of storytelling: first, the mimetic play in storytelling, and second, the impartibility of stories. Both are closely related to Elyachar's concept of semiotic commons and Benjamin's concept of cunning.

When someone makes a journey to a faraway place or listens to those who have stayed at home, Benjamin writes in his essay on Nikolai Leskov, they have a story to tell (1969[1936]). Lived experiences that are carried from far and near are the source of all stories, which are then passed on repeatedly. Storytelling is the art of repeating stories (ibid.: 91). In his account, folk tales emerged as the passing on of experiences by artisans, tillers, and traders, as pieces of wisdom about everyday practicalities (ibid.: 84). For this reason, the storyteller is always someone who knows what has to be done. But to receive counsel, you have to share something too—a story or the gift of "listening" to others (Chandola 2020). However, the wisdom held in stories is not the same as explanations that one finds in informational news. Stories might narrate experiences or events with great accuracy, but the psychological connections among its elements are not forced on the reader or listener, and they are open to interpretation (Benjamin 1969[1936]: 89). Thus, each storyteller leaves their own trace or imprint on the story in the process of repetition. So, on the one hand, storytelling is this mimetic play of carrying, repeating, sharing, interpreting, exchanging, gifting, and listening to experiences between self and the other, which give stories an amplitude, rather than depleting their resourcefulness or energy. And, on the other hand, storytelling as a technological medium, like most medial forms, is cunning in its impartibility (impart-ability and im-partability) of experience. Let me elaborate.

In his astute reading of Benjamin's theory of language and media, Samuel Weber (2008) draws attention to the different abilities that Benjamin saw in both: translatability, criticizability, and citability, among others. The one that concerns us here is "impartibility." Rather than "communicability" in language, which one finds in Habermas, Benjamin uses the term "impartibility" in language. The word *impart*, Weber writes, gestures towards two acts (ibid.: 38–44). One, to share—that is, *partitioning* and *sharing*. To think of it in terms of stories, the storyteller parts with or shares a part of their experience with the other in storytelling, and receives a part in listening. Second, in imparting, Weber further notes, what is imparted also takes its leave or it splits off from what it was—that is, it is transmitted and transposed into something else. In this process, what is shared and the sharers are transposed both towards somewhere else and into something else. But there is a caveat here, which refers to the im-partability or the impossibility of sharing experience completely. In other words, stories do not fully mediate the experiences that are being shared, but partly. And that part which is im-partable is open to translations. Thus, the process of storytelling is never complete, and its ability to impart is inexhaustible. It is these virtual abilities in storytelling that, to my mind, make stories a form of semiotic commons and an infrastructural medium for slum residents to transform themselves and their localities. In what follows, I explore these dimensions of storytelling using ethnographic stories from Toba Tek Nagar.

Finding Passages in Stories

The urban space of *adda*,[14] Dipesh Chakrabarty shows, was instrumental to transgressing boundaries of gendered and undemocratic participation in urban Bengal (2009). The *adda*, unlike civil society, was an anti-teleological space—a space for idle talk, literary circulation, and conversational pleasures. The culture of *addabazi*, he further notes, was important to establish a sense of home and belonging among the urban middle classes in the face of effacing modern capitalism. In the present context, however, and in a slum locality more so, establishing a sense of being and belonging is tied to acquiring bureaucratic objects (Sriraman 2018). Slum residents spend a lot of their time waiting and idling, repeatedly, over many days, in and around bureaucratic offices to acquire these objects. Permanent Account Number card, *Aadhar* card,[15] driving license, voter ID, ration card, Below Poverty Line cards, and Waste Pickers Organization card, among others, are instrumental to access benefits of governmental programs and policies. The aura of these objects lies in their authenticity and the distinct identity that they assign to each individual. And for a policy to address everyone, it is essential that everyone be identified using these objects, as well as for everyone to identify themselves with these objects. The state, in that sense, is a mimetic machine that produces mimetic copies through bodily contact (photographs, fingerprints, signatures, biometrics) and uses these mimetic copies to organize and order cities into their ideal image—a plan, a program (Taussig 1993). However, the bureaucratic object is also a material object that circulates, gets duplicated, and forged, which, in turn, allows urban residents to both contest state practices and reproduce them in illegible ways (Hull 2008; Das 2004). This imbues the bureaucratic objects with mimetic powers to reproduce power relations but also interrupt and alter them. My interest here, however, is to explore how this mimetic play between the copy (the bureaucratic object) and the contact (the lived experience) churns out other forms of mimetic copies, particularly stories, and how slum residents use stories as passages to travel the rational and magical bureaucratic structures of the state and alter their lives. This play is most visible outside the ration card office in the locality.

The ration card office in Toba Tek Nagar is located on the southern side of the settlement. It is a small cream-colored building with an extended asbestos roof. The open space in front of the building is always crowded. While the clerk calls out names of particular residents, others remain seated outside on concrete seats under the roof. Legs folded, bodies rested against the wall, avoiding cracks, spit stains, and the burning sun: these bodily gestures speak of their repeated visits to the place and their corporeal familiarity with the space. If waiting, as Kafka hints in his short anecdote "Before the Law" (1971[1915]), is an essential part of the enchantment of modern bureaucracy, stories too begin to pass along with the time of waiting: Which officer arrives at what time and at which window; which clerk or peon is more helpful; why is someone there, why someone's work got done, why someone else's didn't, which officer to go to or which officer to avoid, which documents work better, and which don't. The tricks of navigating the bureaucratic world, and locating the "ins and outs" of urban bureaucracy based on one's repeated experiences at the office, all get shared outside the ration office. These mundane tricks then circulate into other publics through stories. An instance of this circulation was the identity-card-issuing process at a *balwadi*[16] in Toba Tek Nagar.

I was waiting that day at the *balwadi* to interview Nargis, the head of a Waste Pickers' Organization (WPO) in Toba Tek Nagar. She lived in a non-regularized part of the settlement, which meant that her house got demolished by the city municipality every three to four years. Given the precarity, she had worked with *Medhatai*[17] on housing rights early on and was currently involved in the city-level housing rights organization as an active member. In her capacity as the head of the WPO and as a housing rights activist, she had visited different cities, met new people, learned about their experiences, and attended various meetings and protests. At the *balwadi* that day, Nargis was filling out forms, collecting identity proofs, and issuing new ID cards to new and old waste pickers of Toba Tek Nagar. Residents were crowding around her, waiting for their chance, while observing others, making a list of the required documents, and simultaneously informing other residents' details of the process on their mobile phones. Two women, recent migrants to the settlement, were sitting at the table, waiting to register themselves with the WPO. "Which dumping ground do you work at?" Nargis asked them. Unaware of the formal name, they simply pointed in the direction of the land-fill. "Toba Tek Nagar Dumping!" Nargis rejoined sternly. "What do you collect? Which WPO are you a part of? Where do you live?" Without waiting for an answer, she filled out the forms herself, while verbalizing the answers out loud. At that moment, it struck me that Nargis had translated the procedure of issuing ID cards into a theatrical performance, which involved mimicking municipal officers that she had encountered herself in her past, adding her own improvisations, and simultaneously training other residents to mimic her at the landfill entrance. This was important, Nargis told me later, since a wrong answer to the security guards at the landfill could cost them their access to livelihoods. When Nargis asked the women for their ID proofs, they had none. Instead, the women began narrating how and why they had come to Toba Tek Nagar. Meanwhile, the others who were waiting aside for their turn began exchanging their own stories of arrival to Mumbai, what documents they have been collecting, and who they contacted to get them. In how urban waste was central to their current livelihoods, they discussed the purpose of the waste pickers' ID card and the arbitrariness of their efficacy in some instances. The stories then gradually moved outside the *balwadi*, and onto the concrete benches where others were waiting and idling. Residents compared documents, signatures, photographs, and stories of how they had come to acquire those documents, including the tricks they had used to expedite the process. Some just listened in on them. Such storytelling about bureaucracy and bureaucratic documents is an everyday activity in Toba Tek Nagar. And these repetitive retellings become a way of understanding the architecture of modern bureaucracy as well as finding passages to seep into them.

Kafka's Assistant

On another occasion, I was reading a book while waiting for my interviewee at a teahouse in the locality. The teahouse was a preferred location for most male residents for an interview. That day, Abdulbhai was sitting at the next table with the secretary of the local ward councilor and a young man. He introduced me to the secretary and asked me to interview him for my research. I thanked him and continued to read my book. Over the next few minutes, Abdulbhai made arrangements with the councilor for reclaiming a piece of land at one end of the locality. Sand trucks were to arrive that night. The young man and a few of his friends were to accompany the truck across the nearby octroi tollbooth. The secretary made a few phone calls and shared his number before leaving to make sure that the sand arrived without hassle. The conversation lasted about ten minutes. On my next visit a few weeks later, I saw new houses erected with shining asbestos roofs and blue tarpaulin.

I first met Abdulbhai during my research on the Human Rights Commission offices in Toba Tek Nagar. I have renamed him Abdulbhai because of his resemblance to the character Abdul from the movie *Shaan* (1980). The character in the film sings "*Naam Abdul hai mera sabpe nazar rakhta hoon*" ("My name is Abdul and I keep an eye on everyone") and is the go-to guy for counsel on local matters. Located in the back alley of the Nagori teashop, Abdulbhai's Human Rights Commission office has a peculiar character. Bright blue in color, the office has a small table with a computer, where he checks his Facebook page in the English language, which he cannot read but deciphers from images. A sheet of glass covers the table. In-between the table and the glass is a photocopy of the only map of the locality that was prepared by the municipality in the 1970s. The table is usually covered with books on planning regulations for slums and a few folders

Figure 1.2 Passages

with grievances filed by local residents. Human Rights Commissions offices are established by the Maharashtra State Human Rights Commission in slum localities for making people aware of their rights and providing them institutional support for the same. But the Human Rights Commission offices in Toba Tek Nagar are multifunctional. Most often, they are run by ex-touts or aspiring politicians. They deal with all kinds of issues ranging from domestic violence, divorce procedures, family conflicts, labor disputes to running election campaigns, acquiring ID cards, and storing make-shift furniture for festive events. They also function as gathering spaces for old and young men in the evenings. Each complaint made by a local resident is archived in files. Matters are resolved one way or another, since these heads of offices are involved in the community affairs in more than an official capacity. Deals with politicians and contractors for reclaiming land and building houses; negotiations with municipal officers and contractors to carry out civil work; and deals with politicians and local leaders in return for political support during elections, are all conducted in this space over conversations and mobile phones. Here, tensions between personal and impersonal, rights and politics, and planning and non-planning get played out through everyday occurrences.

Idleness: time slows down, mild boredom takes over, pushing one into a state of mental relaxation. Boredom, the character essential for experiencing and storytelling, as Benjamin tells us (1969[1936]), is the main reason for Abdulbhai and his friends to gather at the Human Rights Commission office during the twilight hours of the evening. Storytelling has become somewhat of an evening ritual for them during these gatherings. The ritual begins with the different objects on the table each day: an electricity bill, an Aadhar card, a PAN card, a driving license, a pocket photo of Mecca, a bureaucratic file, a ration card, the development plan of the locality, or slum policy books. The men then take turns discussing these different objects and narrating stories of their encounters related to these objects. As they go around, their recollections are interspersed with short stories by Abdulbhai. For example, on the allusion of a high electricity meter reading by someone one such evening, Abdulbhai narrated stories of the first transformer in the locality, his meetings with the politician who brought electricity to the area, the illegal electricity connections, and the use of a legal connection to accumulate bills as proof of residence.

Abdulbhai was a tout in his past life. He was involved in stealing electricity and water, occupying and selling land, striking deals with local party members to reclaim the land. He gave it all up, he told me, because of the increasing violence in the dealings and took charge of the Human Rights Commission office. He was well traveled in the world of bureaucracy and development. He often narrated stories of dusty files in the filthy small municipal offices; of the enormous wooden tables behind which sat small-sized powerful officials; of the enormous framed photographs and paintings in these offices; of his encounters with clerks in white safari suits who transported files from one table to the other through the lobbies and corridors of government offices; of visits from the district collector's officials who sought his help with the data that had burned in a mysterious fire incident at the Mantralaya; and of the fights and attacks at night that he had had with other touts over land occupations and sale. Often, he would request me to share with him the official documents and reports that I had collected, particularly municipal plans. He would then sit with me and narrate stories of old mosques, infrastructural objects, and demolished slums, and of how they have disappeared from municipal surveys. The arbitrariness of the state and the sheer excess of capital in land deals were the other themes of his stories. A story he often narrated was of the maze of corridors in a real-estate developer's office. At the end of the maze, he said, was a hidden room, dark with just one tube-light, where huge piles of cash were stored to strike deals. To my mind, Abdulbhai was like Kafka's assistant. He had traveled the world of bureaucracy and development but was neither a member of nor a stranger to any of the groups, just a messenger of stories from one place to the other. In the two years that I met him regularly, never did he tell me what he did for a living.

Idle Space, Idle Time, and Idle Stories

Noorani Teahouse is located in the municipally rehabilitated section of Toba Tek Nagar. The teahouse is a 10 feet by 15 feet unit with pistachio green walls. The walls have swollen up in some places due to moist air flowing in from the nearby creek; in other places, the paint has peeled off revealing a different color beneath. There are four wooden tables in the teahouse. Each table is covered with a white laminate that is kept in place by nails along the edges. The laminate makes it easier to wipe off tea stains left by the numerous cups of tea consumed by people every day. And yet, the tea glasses leave their imprints on the tables in the form of stubborn stains. Each table has an old plastic glass holder with six steel glasses. The glass holders on different tables are alternated by colors: blue and red. A colorful board on the back wall lists the items available at the teahouse using photos: "Hot Milk, Nagori Tea, Lassi, Cold Drinks, Desi Ghee, Yogurt, and *Maska Pav* (buttered bun)." Religion is integral to the teahouse in terms of conversations as well as interior decorations: A clock with an image of mosque domes is hung on the back-most wall, the celebratory Eid poster from the previous year is stuck on the left wall, and the Sunni Razvi Calendar, also from the previous year, with its page turned to November, since it has a printed advertisement of Noorani Teahouse, is next to it. The owner of the teahouse, Husain, nicknamed "Nagori," is a young, shy, and quiet man. Dressed in worn-out white jeans, a polyester gray shirt, and a white *taqiyah* (cap), he sits on a stool behind the cash counter most days, while his younger brother, also nicknamed "Nagori," prepares tea on the gas stove located right at the entrance. Next to the tea counter is a small old wooden cupboard, like the old showcase units disappearing from middle-class houses, where the daily supplies of sweet buns, butter, biscuits, tea, sugar, and ginger are stored. The first tea gets made at seven every morning, and then at regular intervals till ten in the night. The Nagori tea, specific to the Nagori caste of Muslims from Gujarat, is prepared with a two to one ratio of milk to water, a ratio inversed by Mangal, a Marwari from Rajwadi, Rajasthan, who runs the Ganesh Tea Stall at the other end of Toba Tek Nagar.[18]

At the entrance to the Ganesh Tea Stall, a *nimbu-mirchi* (lemon and green chilies strung together) is hung off the rolling shutter to ward off evil spirits. Its swollen yellow ochre walls are crowded with photo-frames of Hindu gods. On the left wall, a laminated poster lists four ways to earn *punnya*[19]: feeding ants, feeding dogs, feeding cows, and praying to the *kalpavriksh* (a wish-fulfilling tree).[20] Amidst these gods is a framed photocopy of the municipal license to run the commercial establishment, and to keep out the evil spirits of illegality and demolition. At the right-most corner of the entrance, an L-shaped table covered with thin aluminum sheets serves as the kitchen. Three male teenagers work in the teashop. They are recent migrants from the same village as the owner, Mangal. They work as servers, as well as cleaners, and sleep in the teashop itself at night. The unit is subleased by tenants who live in the unit above. The owners of both these units live in a rental unit away from the main road.[21] The left-most corner space at the entrance is further subleased by Mangal to a pan and cigarette shop. The *panwalla*, Sahil, is a young Muslim man from Muzzaffarnagar, Uttar Pradesh. Often dressed in a checkered *lungi* (a wraparound), a white *baniyan* (vest), and a polyester half-sleeve shirt, he sits on a marble slab, which serves as a countertop. A plastic bucket is placed next to this base for the water from the countertop to drip into through a small metal gargoyle. Below this counter is a cupboard, which forms the base of the shop. The entire structure of the pan shop is built from scrap-iron angles. A second cupboard fixed on the countertop houses and displays cigarettes and other ingredients. The top of this cupboard is decorated with gothic forms made from scrap iron. The shop is mobile in form and yet fixed to the entrance of the tea stall.

Teashops in Toba Tek Nagar are open to everyone. And no stories are taboo either: gods, kings, family, sex, love, money, drugs, deals, cars, domestic issues, community issues, mosques, contracts, and happenings of the day all meander in and out of this space. Everyone enters and exits on their own terms. But to say that everyone can use the shop would be an overstatement. It is a male space, like most enclosed public spaces in Toba Tek Nagar. However, one does see women in these teahouses every now and then. They do not interact much with others; they sit on an empty table or on the outer edge of the seat if it's already occupied. Most often, they are accompanied by men and are part of a conversation that involves paperwork and files regarding family matters. Both tea stall owners keep a small diary to maintain an account of tea consumption and individual credit on a daily basis. A diary, to me, was a good device to keep an account of events and conversations.[22]

Offerings, 4 July 2013: A middle-aged woman, dressed in a nightgown and a nice *dupatta* was sitting at the last table. She was crying with two broken phones in front of her. Another man, sitting at the table across from hers, struck a conversation. They never looked at each other; instead, they stared straight ahead at the street while speaking to each other. He inquired about her work. She was a real-estate agent in the slum locality and a broker for cloth trade in Bhivandi in the eastern suburbs of Mumbai. The business was doing OK, she said. Having led her attention towards other things, the man asked her the reason for her crying.

She explained that her husband, who had suffered a paralysis attack a few years back, had beaten her that morning and thrown the phones at her in anger. Further, he wasn't taking his medicines and was instead drinking alcohol. The man in the teashop offered to visit their house with a few other residents and speak to her husband after the *jumma namaz*. The woman agreed, finished her tea, and then walked away without thanking him.

Investments, 13 August 2013: It was a Sunday morning. Two friends, young men in their late 20s, were sitting at the table next to me discussing their new jobs. They shared their experiences on starting work, their travel times, their travel routes, and their office work culture. A few minutes later the discussion turned to questions about the future. The first friend suggested working at their new jobs for a year or two and then branching off to start their own business. The friend agreed, but their savings, he suggested, wouldn't be enough to start a new business. They needed a third person to invest money in their future company. They indexed a list of different possible partners, shared stories about them, and finally agreed to ask a school friend, a car mechanic who had returned with some savings after a year of work in Muscat. They finished their tea, which was a treat from one of them on receiving his first paycheck, and then walked out to meet their possible third partner.

Cuttings, 28 August 2013: They split two cups of teas into four cuttings.[23] The garage owner put forth his problem: an official from the Regional Traffic Office (RTO) was harassing him for buying and selling cars without registering the sales with the RTO. The officer was insisting on getting a commission on each sale that was made without registration to avoid being reported. The second person, a mechanic in a renowned car-servicing center that subcontracted their repair work to the garage owner, shared how his company deals with such deals. He then suggested meeting his acquaintance, another RTO official in a higher position, who could help him for a lesser amount. The discussion then turned towards traffic rules and ways to trick the traffic officials in order to avoid fines. The other two on the table listened closely to the conversation. They all finished their tea and walked away their separate ways. A week before, five others were discussing problems with municipal water tankers … A week before that, proof of residence … fights within families over land … unemployment of their kin … and so on.

Prospects, 1 September 2013: Four young men were staring and comparing their cell phones over tea. One of them began sharing about his family's financial troubles and how they were looking to rent out the ground floor unit of their house. Mangal, the teashop owner, overheard and interjected. He inquired about the rental rate, the required deposit amount, if it was being leased or subleased, and possible commission. The young man answered. Mangal sifted through his mobile phone while simultaneously stirring tea on the stove. He then made a call. In a few minutes, a middle-aged man appeared at the teahouse buttoning up his shirt. He had moved to Mumbai recently from Uttar Pradesh and was looking for a place to start a waste recycling unit. Two of them moved to a different table and Mangal joined them with three glasses of tea. They spoke for about two minutes, and the young man then guided his prospective tenant towards his unit. A number of such deals and negotiations get made and broken here.

What causes something? September 5, 2013: Rahimmiya, a frequent visitor to the Nagori teahouse arrived at 11 in the morning. As usual, he was dressed in his crisp white *kurta* and a *taqiyah*. He had just returned from his trip to Shirdi.[24] He struck up a conversation about his trip with Sajidbhai, another frequent visitor to the teahouse. He began with an observation that the Hindus have taken over Shirdi, as if Saibaba is a Hindu god. The Muslim *jamaat*, he commented, is not organized enough to reclaim their right to the place. The conversation then turned towards the closure of a mosque in their neighborhood in Toba Tek Nagar. Rahimmiya argued that the infrequency of its users, and the shift of residents to the mosque in the next neighborhood, was the prime reason for its closure. Sajidbhai suggested that the reason was the improper management of the mosque by its new secretary that had resulted in diminished donations from Bollywood actors and technicians to the mosque. The issue and its causality remained open ended. A few months later, a member of Rashtriya Swayamsevak Sangh (RSS), the militant Hindu organization, had made a call in popular media that Hindus shouldn't pray to Saibaba as he was a Muslim.

Love, November 9, 2013: Rahimmiya, a regular at the teahouse, and Husain, the owner, were arguing about who is the greatest of Mughal kings: Aurangzeb or Akbar? Rahimmiya suggested Akbar and narrated a story. One day the king disguised himself as a *fakir* (a beggar) and sat in the center of a market square where no one would recognize him. The point of this disguise was to spend his time as an ordinary subject and understand the true state of his subjects. That story for Rahimmiya was greater than any conquest of any king. Nagori argued that the story wasn't about understanding his subjects. Akbar had actually disguised himself as a *fakir* to go listen to Mirabai's songs, which he found mesmerizing. Sajidbhai, who had joined in by then, argued it was actually to go meet Jodha, his love interest. Regardless of a resolution, the conversation moved from Akbar to the present politicians. Would any of them ever do anything like that to experience people's problems? "No! They are not imposters in love."

Divorce, 15 October 2013: Parents of a married couple were sitting with a lawyer on the table across from mine at Ganesh Tea Stall. They were discussing the ongoing divorce between their daughter and son. They were meeting that day to find a solution that could help avoid a divorce. The lawyer arrived and called for tea for everyone. They each put forth their perspectives on the issue. The father of the husband suggested to the wife's parents that they convince her to return, and resolve issues with the husband in person and within the house. The wife's father agreed. Their wives were having a parallel conversation with each other about the same issue. The lawyer paid for the tea and they all walked out after saying their goodbyes. A few days later, the men (fathers and the lawyer) returned and exchanged the divorce papers.

Heat, 21 June 2013: It was scorching hot and the teashop was crowded today. BEST[25] bus drivers, salesmen with ties, construction workers as well as their contractor, and some local residents all had packed themselves in the teahouse.

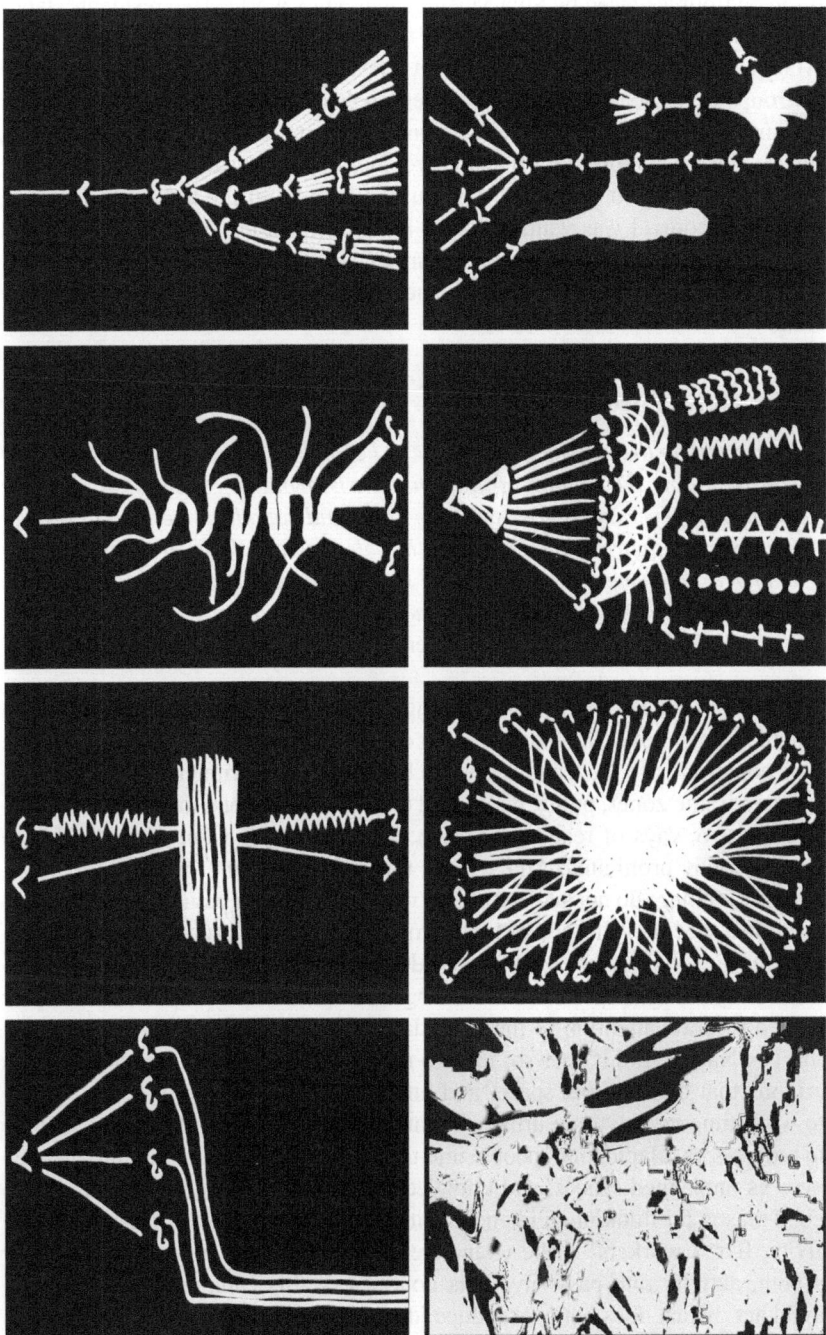

Figure 1.3 Storylines

Outside on the street in a makeshift tent, the local Shia imam was delivering a sermon on troubles faced by Shia Muslims in today's world. Two residents standing at the counter explained the details of the difference between Shias and Sunnis to Mangal. He, in return, told them about a heated fight between members of the two groups in the locality. The bus drivers looked harrowed and discussed their problems with the new bus routes assigned to them. These routes were longer, congested, and had more stops than the previous ones. The salesmen finished their paperwork over tea. It was a hot day, but the hotness of the tea seemed to cool down their bodies. I was waiting for an interview, writing down questions, and reading Benjamin and Lācis's piece on urban porosity in Naples. The similarities between their observations in Naples and mine in Mumbai evoked an uncanny feeling.

Making Cities Porous

> *In everything they preserve the scope to become a theater of new, unforeseen constellations. The stamp of the definitive is avoided. No situation appears intended forever, no figure asserts its "thus and not otherwise." (...) Porosity results not only from indolence [...] but also, above all, from the passion for improvisation, which demands that space and opportunity be at any price preserved(...) Porosity is the inexhaustible law of this city.*
>
> (Benjamin and Lācis 1978[1925]: 166–68).

"*Phaltu Bethna Sakht Mana hai!*" "Idling here is strictly prohibited!" is written in bright red paint over the fading yellow ochre walls of the Nagori teahouse. The sign is not specific to the teahouse; it can be found in government buildings, public spaces, traffic zones, public parks, and tourist spots, among many other spaces. There are two ways of reading this sign: first, time is of value (money); hence idling is strictly prohibited. And second, this space is meant for a specific use— buying and selling; do not sit here idling, without buying or paying. Both readings determine a specific value and order of time and space. In a broader sense, the sign highlights the ideology of "work" that orders time, space, and knowledge production in a city being shaped by eviscerating urbanism. In this context, this chapter has tried to draw attention to the everyday playact of idling and storytelling in Toba Tek Nagar. And it does so, for two reasons. First, comes from anxiety with partitions that divide time, space, and knowledge in cities: partitioning of time into work time vs playtime; urban habitats into habitable vs inhabitable; change into progress vs dilapidation; people into useful vs expendable; cities into planned spaces vs unplanned spaces; and knowledge into meaning vs non-meaning. The second reason for thinking in idleness is its paradoxical nature. Idling is a passive activity, like a workers' strike (Rancière 2012). It is neither one nor the other but both, activity *and* passivity. This doubleness, this cunningness, makes it a playful act, which does not ever reduce idling to one *or* the other. Thus, idling is not the passive time of inactivity but a paradoxical union of activity and passivity, a heteronomy—"and" not "or." Furthermore, idling also marks a refusal or a dis-identification with the time-space model based on the logic of work—a logic that partitions time, space, and knowledge into oppositions. This refusal is articulated through the creation of another, altered time-space in storytelling.

In a locality where resources are scarce, stories circulate in excess at any given point in time. These stories are about the numerous events, experiences, encounters, happenings, rumors, futures, travels, and plans, both past and present, that are exchanged and gifted while waiting and idling in different spaces, including bureaucratic offices, teahouses, WPO offices, NGO offices, streets, cigarette shops, streets, and so on. In these stories, everyday encounters with people, objects, spaces, and the experiences these encounters produce are woven together to present a story to the other. By weaving together different temporal and spatial elements, the story also weaves together a new space. In this space of the story, the exchanges and gifts between the self and the other play an important role. The story draws the other out and into the space conjured by the story. At the same time, the storyteller splits the self by imparting or sharing their experience with another. Thus, in this time of idling and storytelling, both the self and the other are drawn out of their selves into this conjured space of the story. In this space, the tensions between activity and passivity, between the useful and the useless parts, between the self and the other (embodied in the act of storytelling) are not sublated to create a higher meaning (à la Hegel and Habermas) but kept in play so that other translations and citations of stories are possible.

In addition to idling and storytelling, this chapter also focused on stories as repetitive imparting of experiences that circulate in excess in different publics but are negated in institutionalized participatory platforms. In other words, these stories are sacrificed and relegated to a world of non-meaning within the schema of knowledge production that is driven by the logic of work and producing consensus. For Bataille, these excessive experiences are significant since they hold the possibility of interrogating and transgressing what is commonly understood as meaningful. And for Derrida, such experiences are unique; they exist as singularities that cannot be translated into a universality but are universally transmittable and repeatable (1978). This non-translatability into a singular universality does not prohibit the possibility of imparting and transmitting these experiences infinitely so that others can use and/or repeat them in multiple ways. This impartability of stories, however, does not square with the communicative planning model that is based on Jürgen Habermas' idea of communicative reason. In the latter case—as is evident in the participatory platforms—stories are bound by rules (impersonal and non-repetitive), are to be addressed to a third party (a planner or judge), and are told with the specific aim of arriving at a consensus (a higher level of knowledge). Contradistinctively, stories do not dissipate but accumulate over the years in documents, built forms, and in people, and get told and retold in multiple ways. For slum residents in localities like Toba Tek Nagar, they become infrastructural mediums, in which those expended figure out tricks and ways to navigate the system and locate passages to travel towards becoming something other than who they are. In doing so, the structures become porous. Other times, these stories are of no use to anyone in particular when shared. They are simply

Figure 1.4 Yahaan phaltu bethna sakht mana hai 2 (Idling here is strictly prohibited)

shared and they lay idle, like the ones shared in the teahouse. And yet, they don't disappear but gather around as an excess that can be used by others at a time, which is not here yet. It is this ability of stories to store excess energy that makes them a semiotic commons and infrastructural mediums for urban inhabitants to move and make moves, despite limited means.

Notes

1 Translation: Idling Here is Strictly Prohibited.
2 Women aren't permitted to pray in the mosques. They gather in each other's houses to pray in groups. However, they do stop by outside the mosques on their way home to. When I asked the secretary about this exclusion, he suggested that there are parts of Islamic beliefs that need a rereading, particularly the inclusion of women in affairs of the mosque.
3 In saying that stories are a resource and a medium, I am referring to Friedrich Kittler's notion that the content of mediums are other mediums (1996).
4 At a broader level, Weeks, informed by a range of thinkers and social movements, including the anti-work Italian autonomists and the 1970s feminist movement for waged housework in the Anglo-American world, among others, is interested in imagining a utopian "postwork" life and society.
5 I draw this set of arguments from Kristin Ross's book *The Emergence of Social Space: Rimbaud and the Paris Commune* (1988: 47–71).
6 There are forms of dialectical thinking that depart from sublation—for example, see Gidwani 2008.
7 Jacques Rancière argues that the ideal order of the city and the order of the discourse are based on nothing more than a noble lie put forth by the king-philosopher. The use of the term "noble lie" here is not to suggest that stories tell truths (2004a: 267–91).
8 At a protest organized by the *Ghar Bachao Banao Andolan* (Save Houses, Build Houses) against slum demolitions the scene was similar to the meeting. The protest began with a march to the municipal ward office. After reaching it, the protesters, primarily slum residents, seated themselves on the road and blocked off the entrance of the ward office. After a short speech by prominent activists, different slum residents came up to the front and began narrating stories through a handheld speaker. These stories were about demolitions, corruption, bribery, and they pointed particularly towards the arbitrariness of state planning. The stories I heard there were similar to the ones narrated at the consultation workshop.
9 For an elaboration on how rational intersubjective public spheres and dialogues are always oriented towards the third person—a judge or the state, see Michael Warner, "Publics and Counterpublics" (2002); and Jacques Rancière, "The Rationality of Disagreement," in *Disagreement: Politics and Philosophy* (2004b: 43–60).
10 A second way of thinking argues for planning itself as a persuasive form of storytelling about a future (Throgmorton 2003). Planners, it is argued, produce texts: maps, plans, policies, and articles. These texts employ characters, settings, points of views, and languages to express conflicts and propose resolutions that persuade people and shape their view in a particular way. In this schema, planning stories are future-oriented stories that shape meaning and tell readers what is important and what is not, what counts and what does not, and what matters and what does not, in order to guide the sense of what is possible and desirable. The third way of thinking draws on the previous two as well as extends them (Sandercock 2003). Stories, it is argued, are to have specific qualifications: temporal or sequential framework to provide tension, explanation or coherence, potential for generalizability—seeing universal in the particular, a plot structure and protagonists, and moral tension. These characteristics are drawn from Aristotle's conception of mimesis as a representational act of producing a concordance

between community and its image, whereby the latter become a tool for improving the former. In this model, stories are used in a multicultural and settler-colonial context to find common threads and priorities, to resolve conflicts, and represent diversity.

11 In his essay "The Public Realm," Richard Sennett (2000) traces another trajectory for how the realm of the public as a proper domain for free speech got formed. In Georg Simmel's conception of the metropolis, he argues that individuals in the city withdrew their emotional beings and became rational to protect themselves from the over stimulation of the city. It was a necessary withdrawal of the emotional and at the same time a construction of the rational. Thus, strangers in the city developed a new way of relating; without giving out too much information they developed a new code of being with each other in the same space—bodily gestures, lack of staring, peeking and glimpsing, handshakes, raised eyebrows. It was a way of being within the same space, understanding each other without *voice* but still developing a stranger relationality where everyone could coexist and understand each other. The shift to speech occurs, with Arendt, who took Simmel's rational individual as repressive and opened onto him a public domain, wherein he could exercise the right to free speech, not as someone attached to a class or race but as a mere being. Arendt's formulation, Sennett suggests, shifts the role of bodily politics and body politic from movement and gestures to speech and writing.

12 For Michael Taussig, storytelling is similar to the practices of shamans, who use storytelling as a form of healing. Using certain objects, shamans conjure a story, a mental image of the form of power from which one was to be healed (2012).

13 For Hegel, cunning of reason is the process by which reason itself finds its absolute meaning, its freedom. In this process, reason uses the passion of powerful rulers and nation-states to achieve its freedom. For Hegel, the realization of this reason was itself the goal of history. For Benjamin, Hegel's cunning of reason is a process by which reason finds its emancipation while humans remained colonized by the myth of progress that is hidden in the idea of linear historical progress. For a detailed discussion on the different takes on cunning in Hegel and Benjamin see, Buck-Morss, *The Dialectics of Seeing* (1989: 272).

14 It is difficult to define an *adda*. The essay in Chakrabarty's book uses literary as well as other historical sources to complicate the definitions as well as to point out spe-cificities of what makes up an *adda*. But to put it simply using his own words: The word *adda* (pronounced "uddah") is translated by the Bengali linguist Suniti Kumar Chattopadhyay as "a place" for "careless talk with boon companions" or "the chats of intimate friends (2009: 180). It was "(a) site where several of the classic and endless debates of modernity played out—discipline versus laziness, women's confinement in the domestic sphere versus their participation in the public sphere, separation of male and female domains versus a shared public life for both groups, leisure classes versus the laboring classes, an openness to the world versus the responsibilities of domestic life, and other related issues (ibid.: 219)."

15 *Aadhar* card is issued by the Unique Identification Authority of India, which assigns every individual a unique identification number, which is required to access many of the social security benefits.

16 The *balwadis* provide preschool education to children in the age group of 3–5 years. These are run in urban areas where children from low-income families do not have access to an *Anganwadi* center run by the government or any other preschool facility run by the private sector including other NGOs. The Waste Pickers Organization does not have an office of its own and uses different spaces to hold their monthly meetings. This specific *balwadi* was housed in an extension to a community toilet block in the neighborhood. *Subhash Mitra Mandal,* the neighborhood organization, had built the *balwadi* using contributions from residents. The space was then rented out to different NGOs to run day-care centers for infants or organize monthly events in the neighbor-hood.

17 Medha Patkar is a prominent social activist. She was involved in founding the *Narmada Bachao Andolan*, the National Alliance of People's Movement (NAPM), and in recent years, the *Ghar Bachao Ghar Banao Andolan*, a housing rights movement in Mumbai.

18 The tea at the Nagori teahouse is milky and smooth while at the Ganesh Tea Stall it is made by boiling water with black tea powder, green tea leaves, beaten ginger and cardamom, and milk, which smells and tastes spicier.

19 Merits or virtues earned through good deeds.

20 These posters and calendars also serve other uses. For instance, the calendar in *Noorani* teahouse is printed every year by the Islamic educational institute Raza Academy, Mumbai and sold at local roadside stalls. Every year, the institute seeks donations from different big and small entrepreneurs to advertise their businesses and the calendar is produced from these donations. The calendar serves as a directory of institutional and commercial establishments. Each page lists names and information of schools, medical institutes, hospitals, madrasas, and businesses.

21 It is profitable to rent out units closer to the main streets and live in rental units located in the interior lanes. A number of residents rent out their units along the main streets to shops, NGO offices, doctors, theaters, recycling units, and so on to secure an extra monthly income. Besides, one cannot buy or sell units here; they can only transfer property by transferring power of attorney to the other.

22 Business owners and migrant workers, in particular, consume tea on credit, and the accounts are cleared at the end of the month. The credit system is also used in the local food messes called *bisi*, which are used mostly by migrant workers who get salaries at the end of the month or bimonthly.

23 *Cutting* is a colloquial word for half a glass of *chai*.

24 A holy place in Ahmednagar, Maharashtra, where the secular demigod Saibaba resided till the early 1900s.

25 BEST stands for Brihanmumbai Electric Supply and Transport, the public bus transit system providers in Mumbai.

References

Anand, Nikhil. 2006. "Disconnecting Experience: Making World-Class Roads in Mumbai." *Economic & Political Weekly* 41 (31): 3422–29.

Banerjee-Guha, Swapna. 2002. "Shifting Cities: Urban Restructuring in Mumbai." *Economic & Political Weekly* 37 (2): 121–28.

———. 2009. "Neoliberalising the'urban': New Geographies of Power and Injustice in Indian Cities." *Economic & Political Weekly* 44 (22): 95–107.

Bataille, Georges. 1988. *The Accursed Share, Volume 1*. Translated by Robert Hurley. New York, NY: Zone Books.

Benjamin, Walter. 1969. "The Storyteller: Reflections on the Works of Nikolai Leskov." In *Illuminations*, edited by Hannah Arendt, translated by Harry Zohn, 83–109. New York, NY: Schocken Books.

Benjamin, Walter, and Asja Lācis. 1978[1925]. "Naples." In *Reflections: Essays, Aphorisms, Autobiographical Writing*, edited by Peter Demetz, translated by Edmund Jephcott, 163–75. New York, NY: Schocken Books.

Birla, Ritu. 2009. *Stages of Capital*. Durhman, NC: Duke University Press.

Buck-Morss, Susan. 1977. *The Origin of Negative Dialectics: Theodor W. Adorno, Walter Benjamin and the Frankfurt Institute*. New York, NY: Free Press.

———. 1989. *The Dialectics of Seeing: Walter Benjamin and the Arcades Project*. Cambridge, MA: MIT Press.

Chakrabarty, Dipesh. 2009. "*Adda*: A History of Sociality." In *Provincializing Europe*, edited by Dipesh Chakrabarty, 180–213. Princeton, NJ: Princeton University Press.

Chandola, Tripta. 2020. *Listening into Others: An Ethnographic Exploration in Govindpuri*. Theory on Demand 36. Amsterdam, NL: Institute of Network Cultures.

Clastres, Pierre. 1987. *Society Against the State: Essays in Political Anthropology*. Translated by Robert Hurley and Abe Stein. New York, NY: Zone Books.

Cody, Francis. 2011. "Publics and Politics." *Annual Review of Anthropology* 40: 37–52.

Coelho, Karen, and Nithya V. Raman. 2010. "Salvaging and Scapegoating: Slum Evictions on Chennai's Waterways." *Economic & Political Weekly* 45 (21): 19–23.

Das, Veena. 2004. "The Signature of the State: The Paradox of Illegibility." In *Anthropology in the Margins of the State*, edited by Veena Das and Deborah Poole, 225–52. Santa Fe, Ca: School of American Research Press.

Derrida, Jacques. 1978. "From Restricted to General Economy: A Hegelianism without Reserve." In *Writing and Difference*, translated by Alan Bass, 251–77. Chicago, IL: University of Chicago Press.

D'monte, Darryl. 2002. *Ripping the Fabric: The Decline of Mumbai and Its Mills*. Oxford, UK and New York, NY: Oxford University Press.

Elyachar, Julia. 2011. "The Political Economy of Movement and Gesture in Cairo." *Journal of the Royal Anthropological Institute* 17 (1): 82–99.

Forester, John. 1999. *The Deliberative Practitioner: Encouraging Participatory Planning Processes*. Cambridge, MA: MIT Press.

Fraser, Nancy. 1990. "Rethinking the Public Sphere: A Contribution to the Critique of Actually Existing Democracy." *Social Text* 25/26: 56–80.

Gidwani, Vinay. 2008. "Capitalism's Anxious Whole: Fear, Capture and Escape in the Grundrisse." *Antipode* 40 (5): 857–78.

Gidwani, Vinay, and Anant Maringanti. 2016. "The Waste-Value Dialectic: Lumpen Urbanization in Contemporary India." *Comparative Studies of South Asia, Africa and the Middle East* 36 (1): 112–33.

Gidwani, Vinay, and Rajyashree N. Reddy. 2015. "The Work of Waste: Inside India's Infra-Economy." *Transactions of the Institute of British Geographers* 40 (4): 575–95.

Goldman, Michael. 2011. "Speculative Urbanism and the Making of the next World City." *International Journal of Urban and Regional Research* 35 (3): 555–81.

Guarneros-Meza, Valeria, and Mike Geddes. 2010. "Local Governance and Participation under Neoliberalism: Comparative Perspectives." *International Journal of Urban and Regional Research* 34 (1): 115–29.

Habermas, Jürgen. 1991. *The Structural Transformation of the Public Sphere: An Inquiry into a Category of Bourgeois Society*, translated by Thomas Burger. Cambridge, MA: MIT Press.

Healey, Patsy. 1992. "Planning through Debate: The Communicative Turn in Planning Theory." *The Town Planning Review* 63 (2): 143–62.

Hirschkind, Charles. 2009. *The Ethical Soundscape: Cassette Sermons and Islamic Counterpublics*. New York, NY: Columbia University Press.

Hull, Matthew S. 2008. "Ruled by Records: The Expropriation of Land and the Misappropriation of Lists in Islamabad." *American Ethnologist* 35 (4): 501–18.

Kafka, Franz. 1971. "Before the Law." In *The Complete Stories of Franz Kafka*, translated by Willa Muir and Edwin Muir 3:27–29. New York, NY: Schocken Books.

King, Tiffany Lethabo. 2019. The Black Shoals: *Offshore Formations of Black and Native Studies*. Durhman, NC: Duke University Press.

Kittler, Friedrich A. 1996. "The City is a Medium." Translated by Matthew Griffin. *New Literary History* 27 (4): 717–29.

Legg, Stephen. 2007. *Spaces of Colonialism: Delhi's Urban Governmentalities*. Malden: MA: Blackwell-Wiley.

Muehlebach, Andrea. 2012. *The Moral Neoliberal*. Chicago, IL: University of Chicago Press.

Rancière, Jacques. 2004a. "The Order of the City." *Critical Inquiry* 30 (2): 267–91.

———. 2004b. "The Rationality of Disagreement." In *Disagreement: Politics and Philosophy*, translated by Julie Rose, 43–60. Minneapolis, MN: University of Minnesota Press.

Ross, Kristin. 1988. *The Emergence of Social Space: Rimbaud and the Paris Commune*. Minneapolis, MN: University of Minnesota Press.

Roy, Ananya. 2007. "The Location of Practice: A Response to John Forester's 'Exploring Urban Practice in a Democratising Society: Opportunities, Techniques and Challenges.'" *Development Southern Africa* 24 (4): 623–28.

Roy, Ananya, and Aihwa Ong, eds. 2011. *Worlding Cities: Asian Experiments and the Art of Being Global*. Malden: MA: Blackwell-Wiley.

Sandercock, Leonie. 2003. "Out of the Closet: The Importance of Stories and Storytelling in Planning Practice." *Planning Theory & Practice* 4 (1): 11–28.

Sennett, Richard. 2000. "Reflections on the Public Realm." In *A Companion to the City*, edited by Sophie Watson and Gary Bridge, 380–87. Berlin: Blackwell.

Simmel, Georg. 1950. "The Metropolis and Mental Life." In *The Sociology of Georg Simmel*, edited by Kurt H. Wolff and Kurt H. Wolff, 47–60. New York, NY: The Free Press.

Simone, AbdouMaliq. 2010. *City Life from Jakarta to Dakar: Movements at the Crossroads*. London, UK: Routledge.

Sriraman, Tarangini. 2018. *In Pursuit of Proof: A History of Identification Documents in India*. New Delhi: Oxford University Press.

Tabassum, Azra, et.al. 2010. *Trickster City: Writings from the Belly of the Metropolis*. Translated by Shveta Sarda. New Delhi: Penguin Books India.

Taussig, Michael. 1993. *Mimesis and Alterity: A Particular History of the Senses*. New York and London: Routledge.

———. 2012. "The Stories Things Tell And Why They Tell Them." *E-Flux*, 2012. https://www.e-flux.com/journal/36/61256/the-stories-things-tell-and-why-they-tell-them/.

Throgmorton, James A. 2003. "Planning as Persuasive Storytelling in a Global-Scale Web of Relationships." *Planning Theory* 2 (2): 125–51.

Warner, Michael. 2002. "Publics and Counterpublics." *Public Culture* 14 (1): 49–90.

Watson, Vanessa. 2002. "The Usefulness of Normative Planning Theories in the Context of Sub-Saharan Africa." *Planning Theory* 1 (1): 27–52.

———. 2011. "Communicative Planning: Experiences, Prospects and Predicaments." In *International Handbook of Urban Policy*, edited by H.S. Geyer, 133–45. Northampton, MA: Edward Elgar Publishing.

Weber, Samuel. 2008. *Benjamin's-Abilities*. Cambridge, MA: Harvard University Press.

Weeks, Kathi. 2011. *The Problem with Work: Feminism, Marxism, Antiwork Politics, and Postwork Imaginaries*. Durhman, NC: Duke University Press.

Figure 2.1 Sirens

2 On Films, Recognizability, and Spacing Out

Double Dekho[1]

Quicksand and the Sirens

The Hindi film *Dharavi* (1991), written and directed by Sudhir Mishra, opens with a film scene (a film within a film): A don and his henchmen are standing atop a water tank overlooking a slum. The don instructs his men, *"Jala dalo is basti ko!" "Burn down this settlement!"* At that instance, the hero of the film, a benevolent don, walks into the screen space.[2] This film scene, we are shown, is being screened in a small video theater in Dharavi, one of the largest clusters of slum localities in Mumbai. The camera pans onto the slum residents in the theater. They are completely engrossed in watching the film and their faces are filled with anticipation. The onscreen hero screams, *"Yeh basti meri hai!" "This settlement is my home!,"* and then goes on to kill the don and his henchmen. The slum residents whistle and clap as a heavy-throated voice booms across the video theater: *"Yeh koi na samjha, yeh koi na jaana, garibo ki thokar main hai yeh jamana"*; *"No one understood, no one realized, that the world is at the blows of the poor."* Then, the title of the film (in the film) flashes on the screen: *"Shahar Ka Shahenshah"* (The Supreme King of the City). At that very moment, the video theater's screen gets set on fire. The offscreen don's henchmen are shown beating up one of Dharavi's residents. The violence escalates and the video theater eventually burns down. A second title flashes on the screen: *"Dharavi,"* translated as *"Quicksand."* A bullet hits the title text, which then bleeds onto the screen. The reality, we are told, is more violent than the fantasies on-screen.

At an overall level, Mishra's film narrates the story of four slum residents who aspire and struggle to get themselves out of quicksand—a metaphor used to describe the poverty, squalor, and violence in Mumbai's slum localities. The four residents, four male friends, devise a business scheme to buy and run an old cloth-dyeing factory in Dharavi. The film's main protagonist, a taxi driver named Raj Yadav, invests all his resources and networks into starting this factory. However, as the film's narrative advances, their plan fails for various reasons. And by the end of the film, the four residents find themselves at the same point from where they started, but worse off. In the last scene, Raj is shown sitting in a taxi next to one of his friends-cum-partner narrating a new business scheme. Despite this new beginning at its end, the film's narrative represents a

DOI: 10.4324/9781003051848-4

cyclical movement of time, which is indicative of the eternal recurrence of the same, without an escape, in a hellish modern world. This hellish interpretation of life in slum localities is symbolized by another metaphorical figure in the film: a beautiful and popular female actor in a red *saree*.[3] She is a fictional imagination of Raj's mind. She draws him in, gives him hope, enchants him, and seduces him, but commits neither her love for him nor the hope that his dreams will indeed come true. In the film, Raj chooses to follow her advice and decides to buy the factory to fulfill his dreams. But when his plan fails, his dreams and the female actor both die. This figure of an imagined actress, to my mind, resonates with the sirens in Ulysses' story. However, the Ulysses of the film, the one with reason, is neither the taxi driver who follows the song of the siren-actress nor the alienated slum residents that are deaf and blind to this fantasy. Instead, it is the film director, the one demystifying the fantasy to show that the reality in slum localities is not as wishful as onscreen fantasies.

If the film *Dharavi* oscillates around the Siren—a figure central to Theodor Adorno and Max Hokheimer's critique of Enlightenment and their call for the autonomy of art from the relations of production (2002 [1947]), the figure that fascinated Walter Benjamin was the "Angel of History" (1969 [1942]). The latter saw in it a figural depiction of a dialectical historian: An angel is standing amidst the temporal storm called progress, with its face turned towards the past, while the storm is violently propelling it into the future. It wants to stay, collect pieces from the past ruins, and create a dialectical image out of these pieces so as to awaken the past in the present and gesture towards the possibility of a different future. And while Paul Klee's painting, "Angel Novus" was a figural depiction of this dialectical historian anachronistically playing with historical elements, Benjamin found the same principles at play in the technological medium of films.

Cinema as Play Space

With the mechanical reproducibility of artworks, Benjamin notes in his essay "'The Work of Art in the Age of Its Technological Reproducibility," the aura of the artwork—that is, the distance (both spatial and historical) separating the artwork and its recipient, which also imbues the former with a uniqueness, has declined (2010[1935]). But this decline in the aura, he points out, is matched by an equal gain in the scope of play. Since, as reproductions, artworks are freed from their established site and made accessible to human experience in situations particular to them. This scope of play, Benjamin further notes, is widest in film. And he ascribes this increased scope of play to the abilities in the film as a technological medium. For instance, cinematic techniques such as camera movement, slow motions, scene-cuts, and close-ups helped humans surpass the anthropological limits of the human body and offered a sensory-perceptual device to comprehend and reconceive ordinary life in the mode of play (in Hansen 2011: 192). Similarly, for an actor, the film offers a wider set of technological tools to play their roles, as compared to in the theater, where the actor relies primarily on the medium of her body. Furthermore, as Miriam Hansen emphasizes, Benjamin conceptualizes film in the essay as "a technological medium of repetition par excellence," refer-ring specifically to its technological structure, that is, the "infinite reiterability and improvability at the level of production (numerous takes)," as well as its ability to be distributed and exhibited in unlimited and variable formats (in Hansen 2011: 195). Given this repeatability, films, Benjamin argues, make the world accessible to human experience in an experimental mode of play and hence are assigned the task of awakening the masses. This awakening is both therapeutic and trans-formative and is closely related to film's ability to articulate different forms of interplay between the body and technology (ibid.: 183). With regard to the latter, he suggests that human experiences in a particular milieu are presented back to it on-screen through mechanically regulated repetitions of different rhythms, which allows the body to domesticate them, enjoy them, be shocked by them, as well as transform them into something else. Hansen thus writes, following Benjamin, that films offer a "play space" to experiment in (2011).

Borrowing Benjamin and Hansen's theoretical construction of cinema as a "playspace," this chapter undertakes an ethnographic study of the interplay between films and slum residents in Toba Tek Nagar. The reasons for this are threefold. First, cinematic representations of slum localities have received much attention in scholarly literature. Their portrayal in films such as *Slumdog Millionaire* and Rem Koohlas's *Lagos* has been influential to unpack the Euro-American discourses on Southern cities as well as to rethink urban theory from the Global South (see Roy 2011: 225; Rao 2006: 227). However, the life of cin-ema in slum localities itself has not received much scholarly attention, with a few exceptions.[4] Second, in the scholarship that does pay attention to the latter, the relationship between slum localities and films has been understood as either one of reflection—films represent the point of view of the slum dwellers (Nandy 1998)—or one of incongruity—films are spectacles that provide slum residents with an aspirational fantasy and temporary relief (Dickey 1993). Lastly, most scholarship on infrastructures in slum localities, albeit with a few exceptions, tends to focus on utility-related infrastructures such as water, toilets, roads, and houses, among others, while infrastructures and technologies of pleasure get rel-egated to the realm of excess—or in Bataille's words, they are sacrificed.[5] In his essay on media piracy, Lawrence Liang draws out a similar parallel (2010). The figure of the pirate and the practice of piracy, he argues, have remained an anom-aly in conceptions of urban commons and intellectual property rights due to their association with the world of pleasure and desire, rather than with "pure needs." The links between pleasure, desire, aspiration, and trespass, he notes, have always been complicated, and the closer a transgressive act is to the domain of pleasure, the more difficult it seems for it to be redeemed socially. The (information) needs of the poor have to be something other than wanting to watch films or become a filmmaker to be taken seriously. Thus, while projects and practices that deal with questions of livelihood and survival are easily justified, projects that deal with new subjectivities and pleasurable transgressions, he argues, are excluded. This chapter aims neither to discern if films are spectacular constructions of reality nor to show that they are ideological tools for phantasmagoric reality. Instead, it draws attention to how films afford slum residents a spatial medium to play—that is, to participate in a world of globally circulating images, to experience them sensorially, to connect them to one's own life, to mimic and produce them, and in doing so, to conjure altered worlds.

The chapter is divided into two parts. The first part focuses on Shivaji Nagar Boyzz (SVJ Boyzz), a youth group, and their YouTube crime series, titled "*Govandi ka CID*" (Govandi's Crime Investigative Department). The series is produced, directed, scripted, and performed by the members of the youth group. Its stories revolve around local issues, particularly high drug use among youth and water shortage. In this part, I focus specifically on the youth group, how and why they produced the series, the different cinematic elements in their films, and the life of the series postproduction. In doing so, I show how films provide a medium for the youth group not just to fulfill their desires of becoming filmmakers but also to play with the roles, hierarchies, and identities assigned to them and their locality. This specific story, I should note, is based in Shivaji Nagar, a slum cluster adjoining Toba Tek Nagar. The second part of the chapter attends to film reception through an ethnographic study of video theaters in Toba Tek Nagar. These video theaters are small neighborhood-scale cinema halls that screen movies from different genres throughout the day, seven days a week.[6] Its audiences are primarily men, both old and new migrants. Here, I attend to cinema as a "total event." This includes paying attention to the spectacular affective image, the arresting sounds, the narrative devices internal to the films, the urban space of the video theaters, the financial and technical workings of the video theater, the encounters among the audience, how the audience use the space, as well as how the sensory field relayed by the cinema relate to the sensory experience of urban life in cities (Larkin 2008: 161; Vasudevan 2003). My broader aim in this second part is to highlight how the rhythms of these disparate elements that are brought together in the space of theater interact and break away. For residents, this breaking away, I show, involves "spacing out" into other worlds.

Part 1: Production

Religion, Drugs, and Films

During my fieldwork, I was invited by Sagirbhai, a secretary of a neighborhood mosque, to attend an event at a local youth center in Toba Tek Nagar. He wanted me to listen in and learn more about the difficulties faced by the local community. The event, however, was organized to discuss a very specific issue: How to deal with the high usage of drugs among the local youth? It was one of the many events that were being organized by different local organizations to deal with the same issue. I arrived early and sat at the back, while others started to trickle in. The attendees were primarily men, who included *maulvis* (religious scholars), *imams*, community elders, mosque secretaries, and a few residents. As the event proceeded, the *maulvis*, the *imams*, and the local elders were invited on stage to share their views on the issue. In their mediations, they framed the question exclusively:

How do we as a Muslim community deal with the high usage of drugs among our youth? The different speakers then turned to religious texts, religious learnings, and their past experiences with similar issues to put forth their views on the issue and devise a way forward. Their proposals included strengthening everyday religious practices such as going to mosques and *madrasas*, regular reading of the *Quran* under the guidance of *maulvis*, everyday surveillance of youth activities, disciplining the youth by partnering with local police and politicians, checking the growth of alcohol stores in the locality, and restricting the access of youth to the "corruptive" technologies such as mobile phones and the Internet. Such self-reflective mediations, Sagirbhai told me after the event, are a way to look inwards and discipline oneself rather than channeling vexation outwards towards others or seeking intoxications.[7] They are also a part of their broader strategy to reconstruct their image as "good Muslims" and discard the territorial stigmatization attached to Muslim-dominated slum localities such as Toba Tek Nagar. This re-imag(in) ing of a community, although a necessity in the contemporary context of Muslim minoratization in Mumbai, was based on excluding others, particularly women, the youth themselves, and technological mediums such as mobile phones, computers, Internet, and films that were deemed as corrupt.

Around the same time that I attended the event, I also met the SVJ (Shivaji Nagar) Boyzz—a youth group in the adjoining slum locality of Shivaji Nagar. They weren't connected with the event in any specific way, except that they were part of the same milieu and had decided to speak about one form of intoxication: drugs, through another: films. Moreover, religion, drugs, and filmmaking share affinities with each other; they are all mediums that mediate the relationship between experience and illumination in different ways—divine, hallucinogenic, and profane, respectively.[8]

SVJ Boyzz

I first became aware of the SVJ Boyzz through an outdated poster next to a garbage bin in Toba Tek Nagar. The poster was put up to advertise the premiere of the second episode of their crime series, *Govandi ka CID* (*Govandi's Criminal Investigation Department*). After inquiring around for a few days, I finally got to meet the members of SVJ Boyzz at a teashop in Shivaji Nagar. The teashop, where the group meets every other day, was also where the group conceived of the crime series in 2011. Back then, they were a small group of seven young men: three college students interested in acting, a street-side food-stall owner who wrote scripts in his free time, two men in their early 30s with regular office jobs, and a polytechnic—an actor, singer, and director, who worked as a technician in small-budget B-circuit Hindi films.[9] Regardless of their background, or their line of occupation, all of them wanted to be a part of the Hindi film industry. Unfortunately, none of them, except the polytechnic, had any experience or the technical know-how of filmmaking.[10] The group thus decided to make a film in order to learn the technicalities of filmmaking and produced an audition tape to seek work in the Hindi film industry. Specifically, they wanted to learn how to face the camera, the commands of "cut" and "action," how to rehearse and act out dialogues, how to write out a script, how to put up sets, as well as post-filming technicalities such as voice over and editing (Interviews 2012). The idea of a crime show came from the group's storywriter, the food-stall owner, who thought of it while watching the popular series *C.I.D* on prime-time television at home. But rather than choosing a random crime as the subject of the show, they decided that the show should revolve around an issue in their own locality. Thus, the first episode *Khoon Pani-Case No. 1* (Blood Water) revolves around a murder committed due to extreme water shortage in the locality; and the second episode *Lapata Baccha Govandi Ka-Case No. 2* (Govandi's Absconding Child) revolves around a child kidnapped by someone with a drug use problem.

Talent

For a while now, the city media as well as city residents have perceived Govandi, the eastern suburb of Mumbai where Shivaji Nagar and Toba Tek Nagar are located, as a place of crime, drugs, and violence. This stigmatization can be ascribed to their location next to the city's landfill, the high concentration of slum localities in the suburb, the high levels of poverty in the area, and the suburb's locational centrality to the two Hindu-Muslim communal riots (1986 and 1992–1993). The SVJ Boyzz, who are born and brought up in Shivaji Nagar, have also experienced this stigmatization on their own. During a conversation, one of the group members stated: "If a resident goes for a job interview with Govandi as the address on their resume, no matter what their qualifications are, they don't get a job." Another member noted: "Even lovers suffer due to the blacklisting of Govandi. One can't express their love to someone from a different area, just because they live here." A third member added, "The name represses our *talent* ... *Talent*," he elaborated,

> is closely related to money in this world. We go for auditions, but never get in. You need money, a lakh (USD 1800) at least, to get even a small role. We don't have money, but we have *talent*. We have grown up in Shivaji Nagar. We have seen the struggles of our residents, their experiences, their sufferings ... and we wanted to show it to others through our films. We want to prove that Govandi has *talent*.
>
> (Interviews 2012, my emphasis)

Etymologically, the word "talent," as the member of the SVJ Boyzz explained to me, is related to two sets of meanings: one, weight, scale, and sums of money; and second, will, desire, and ability. The former is implied in how the world measures "talent" and assigns it value, while the SVJ Boyzz referred to their and Govandi's talent in the former sense: will, desire, and ability. But a will, desire, and ability for what? Their crime series references "talent" in this latter sense: a desire to represent the everyday struggles in their locality as well as their own ability to become filmmakers. The former is overtly conveyed in the first episode of the crime series through explicit monologues that are dramatized with sound effects and camera work. And the latter is presented in the second episode through a text that runs across the screen at equal intervals: "This is a student project show, not commercial. Made by Shivaji Nagar Boyzz (SVJ) for their acting improvement, only that." However, I want to thicken this notion of "talent" here and explore the different abilities that emerge in the interplay between the youth and the technological medium of the film. To do this, I focus on the crime series itself.

Recognizability in Films

At an overall level, the crime series has a standard format. Each episode, of which there are just two,[11] revolves around a specific local issue: shortage of water and high drug use among youth, respectively. This everyday issue is then scripted into a crime mystery that unfolds in the locality: a murder in the first episode and kidnapping in the second.[12] The members of the youth group, who play the roles of crime investigators (as well as perpetrators), then go on to solve the case. So, in one sense, the representation of the locality through a crime case doesn't necessarily depart from the usual perceptions of Govandi circulating in the popular media. But within this standard format, I want to focus here on a few key cinematic elements: the aesthetics of the film, their performances, the films' opening and end credits, the shooting locations, and the instruments used to solve the crime.

In the first episode, *Khoon Pani—Case No. 1* (*Blood and Water*), the film has an amateurish quality. There are abrupt zoom-ins and zoom-outs; the film is edited like a PowerPoint presentation; the dialogues aren't well scripted; there is no art direction; and the actors are neither aptly dressed for their parts nor does their body language convey the roles they play. Furthermore, in certain scenes, one can see the director shouting at the actors for screwing up, which are then muted to show just the visuals.[13] The hardest parts of producing the first episode, the members of SVJ Boyzz told me, was financing the film and finding time to rehearse for the film. They rehearsed for their parts during late evenings and nights after their daily routines and on weekends. Furthermore, to keep production costs at a minimum, the film was shot in a short timeframe with a borrowed handheld digital camera and then quickly edited by one of the members on his laptop. While this first episode was produced to simply acquire some technical experience in filmmaking and prepare an audition tape, by the second episode the endeavor had become a project on its own.

The second episode, *Laapata Bacchaa Shivaji Nagar Ka—Case No. 2* (*The Absconding Child of Shivaji Nagar*), has a slightly advanced aesthetic quality. A part of this change can be ascribed to the use of a rental high-definition camera, planned art direction, use of rented costumes, and editing by a hired professional, all of which cost around INR 80,000 (USD 1,300). This money was put together using the pocket money of the nonearning members and a more substantial contribution from the earning members of the group. Another part of this change in aesthetics can be ascribed to the expansion in the number of group members. By the time they shot the second episode, the youth group had expanded via YouTube

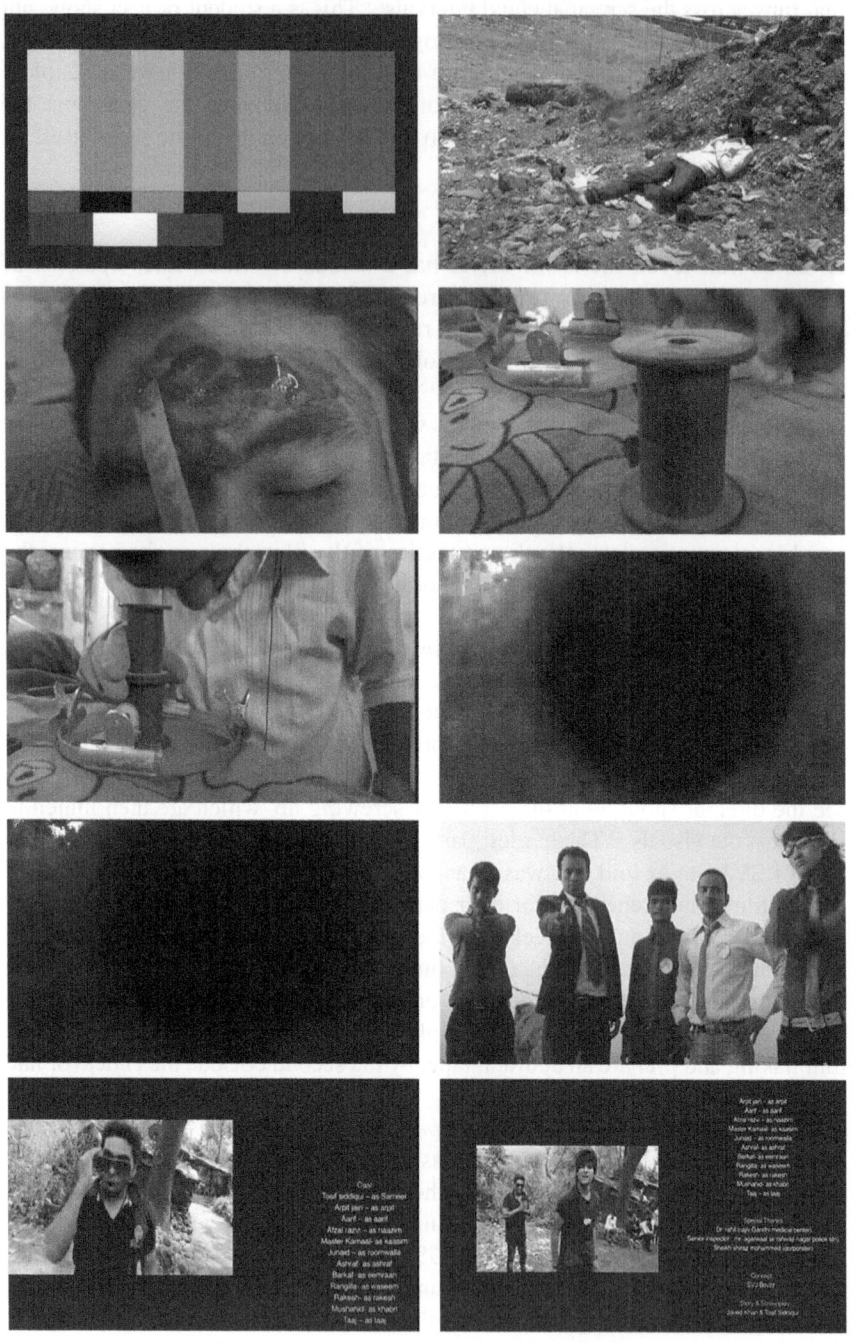

Figure 2.2 CID

and Facebook to include many more local and nonlocal members, who volunteered during the shoots. A third part can be ascribed to the acting skills of the members, who play their part aptly by mimicking the body gestures of their characters and through voice modulations. An instance of this skill is the "making of film" section at the end of the second episode, where group members impersonate different popular Hindi film actors on camera in a comic style using voice and body gestures.

My aim here is not to point out their growing acting prowess but to highlight how films provided a space for the group to recognize their ability to become someone else. This is most evident in the opening and end credits of the second episode. Here, they recognize themselves—which is also a play of re-cognizing while making something recognizable in the film—as film technicians: creative team, actors, art director, writer, videographer, editor, storywriter, and so on. This re(-)cognizability in films is also extended to the everyday spaces and things in the locality. For instance, the scenes are shot in different local spaces, such as *Farooq's Chinese Stall, Dr. Ali's Clinic, 90 Feet Road, Shivaji Nagar Bus Depot, Shivaji Nagar Primary School*, and *Teesri Khadi* (Third Creek). These spaces are acknowledged in the end credits of both the episodes, alongside names of the crew members. Thus "CID Forensic Lab" is credited as *Shivaji Nagar Primary School*. In another instance, two wooden spindles, a plastic lid, and metal paper clips are used to assemble a microscope in a makeshift lab (in a local school classroom) without any prop-work to examine blood samples from the crime scene. This use of bodies, spaces, and things in films as if they are something else, but nothing specific, gestures towards how films provide a space to make the self and the locality re(-)cognizable. And what is made recognizable is not a specific identity of the self or the locality, rather their ability to interrupt the specific identities assigned to them so that they can become whatever, infinitely. It is in this sense that I take Benjamin and Hansen's construction of the film as a space for transformative play and awakening.

But if films provided the youth group a space to play, what possibilities do they offer the community? What kind of collectives does it make recognizable? I ask this question with a particular reference to the opening vignette in this part of the chapter, where local organizations in Toba Tek Nagar chose to address community issues by drawing stronger boundaries.

After the second episode was finalized, a trailer was cut and shown to the local councilor. The councilor, in turn, offered to finance a premiere screening of their film in Shivaji Nagar. The screening was held at the local community hall.[14] More than three thousand residents, both men and women, attended the premiere. It was the first time that men and women from the locality were present in a non-private enclosed space for a movie screening. The screening received an unexpectedly great response from the local residents and family members of the youth group. One of the peculiarities of the second episode is the presence of a young female actor, although not from the locality, who plays the part of a female crime investigator. The presence of a female character on-screen encouraged Muslim young women from the locality to participate in filmmaking. Post-screening, a few of them approached the group and expressed their interest in becoming part of the group's next film project, which wasn't expected by the youth group. Furthermore, many others saw the series via YouTube and decided to start similar endeavors in their own localities. Thus, the crime series had unintended effects. My intention here, however, is not to idealize the SVJ Boyzz or their crime series, since the youth group too is based on a model of community that excludes youth with criminal records, those with a history of drug use, and young temporary migrant workers.[15] Instead, my aim here, and in this chapter at large, is to highlight how films in slum localities provide a space to bring bodies, spaces, and things into an interplay, in which unanticipated configurations become recognizable. And what these unanticipated configurations make recognizable is the possibility of interrupting judgments and closures imposed on communities. In other words, they make communities impossible.

Part 2: Reception

Anand Video Theater

Located right opposite the Toba Tek Nagar bus depot is a small cinema hall called Anand Video Theater.[16] At its entrance is a small verandah whose walls are covered with film posters. These posters form the backdrop for Hasan, the manager of the video theater. A short, middle-aged man with gray hair, he usually sits behind a waist-height cupboard selling tickets while smoking cigarettes. The tickets for the next two film shows are placed on the top of the cupboard alongside the VCD or DVD covers of the movies being screened. The ticket collections are kept in the top drawer of the cupboard, and the VCDs and DVDs are stored in its main compartment. An unpolished wooden box, which houses the two DVD and VCD players, is located at the top corner of the right wall in the verandah. The sound amplifier for the theater's audio system is located on a black granite seat, below which all the film posters are neatly shelved and stored. At the entrance to the screening hall is a red sign that says, "In case of power failure money won't be refunded. In case the video player stops working, money won't be refunded."

The screening space of the video theater is a 25-foot-wide and 40-foot-long rectangular hall. The entrance to it is through a bright-green wooden door, draped with an overused, heavy, red, velvet curtain. The curtain prevents the sunlight from traveling in and the sound inside from traveling out. A 50-inch LCD television is fixed at the center of the wall at the opposite end of the entrance. It's dark inside, and the constantly moving images on the screen gleam over the entire space. The sloping roof above is built with L-shaped iron sections and covered with asbestos sheets. These sheets fail to meet at the center, allowing faint rays of sunlight to enter. But these light rays don't distract the viewers engrossed in the film, or even those sleeping. The off-white walls of the screening space are covered up to waist height with white ceramic tiles. There are about 25 benches in the theater for seating. These benches are about a foot deep and made of cast iron.[17] They vary in height from the back of the hall to the front, creating a stepped seating arrangement for better viewing. The benches are narrow and hard to sit on. And yet, about a hundred men sit on them cramped up with their bodies touching each other, while smoking, sleeping, flipping through their mobile phones, and watching the films. The floor is laid with green *kota* stone that Hasan cleans meticulously every morning before the first show. The showtimes are painted in red on the right wall of the hall: "9 a.m., 12 p.m., 3 p.m., 6 p.m., (and last show) 9 p.m." Next to them is a sign that reads: "No Spitting or Smoking … Fine INR. 200." Despite the sign, the walls of the theater are covered with spit—dark red, layer upon layer, hardened over time, as fossils of the times passed by different men in the video theater. "Time-pass," which is what Hasan says the residents visit the theater for every day.

Everyday Time in a Video Theater

There are five shows daily at the video theater. The choice of the film to be screened depends on the audience for that particular show as well as the films being screened in the neighboring theaters. The early morning 9 a.m. show is a randomly chosen Bollywood film from the 1990s; it's the least-watched show. Its audiences include a few *hammals* (porters), who work late nights and early mornings at the manufacturing units or at the nearby city octroi booth, and a few young boys from the locality who wander into the theaters on their way to college. The 12 p.m. shows are Bollywood films from the late 1980s and 1990s or Bhojpuri films.[18] Hindi-dubbed Telugu and Tamil films, which feature male megastars such as Rajnikant, Nagarjuna, and Chiranjeevi are screened on rare occasions.[19] The Bhojpuri films, too, usually feature popular male actors such as Sujit Kumar, Manoj Tiwari, Ravi Kishan, or Dinesh Lal Yadav. The noon shows attract the manufacturing-unit workers in Toba Tek Nagar. They are seasonal migrants from the region around the borders of Uttar Pradesh, Bihar, and Jharkhand, where the Bhojpuri language is spoken. They work overnight in the manufacturing units, watch films until the afternoon, and then go on to sleep till late evening so as to work again through the night.[20] Often, tired from working through the night, these workers and porters end up sleeping during the film screenings, while others are half-awake trying to watch the film. The other audience of the morning and noon shows is the daily wage laborers from Toba Tek Nagar. They congregate outside the video theater early in the morning (around 6:30 a.m.) and wait to be picked up by contractors for daily wage work. Those who do not get hired that day enter the video theaters to pass time. But they are never completely engrossed in the films. They move in and out of the theater responding to calls on their mobile phones. They watch films in the intervals while waiting for a call from their contractor or friends for work. After a while, they give up and end up watching the film, while continuously flipping through their phones to arrange for work for the next day or to see photographs of families, homes, and fields that they have left back to come to the city. This audience thus moves across different times and spaces in the video theater: the films, their life in the locality, their work-life in the city, sleep, and their native homes.

The 12 p.m. show starts off half-empty most days, but by the end of the show, the theater is overcrowded with viewers. These new viewers are the older residents of Toba Tek Nagar—the shop owners, the landlords, the manufacturing-unit owners, who do not work through the day and who come to watch half of the film after their *namaz* and lunch. They enter the screening hall and crowd its corridor, making it impossible for others to enter. At that moment, the show is stopped midway and the tube lights are switched on. Hasan then rushes in and begins to walk back and forth frenetically, swearing to awaken those sleeping or lounging on the seats. Once everyone is up, he pushes and squeezes the audience to accommodate those standing. A few viewers get tired of the crowded space inside the theater and walk out to converse with Hasan on the verandah. Others, who are bored with the movie, walk out to wait on the verandah for the next show to start. The new migrants sit by quietly overhearing the conversations between the older residents and Hasan. These conversations cover a range of topics (see Chapter 1). The video theaters are one of the few places in Toba Tek Nagar where older residents encounter and share space with seasonal migrants. The more typical lack of interaction owes to the routines of the migrant workers—they sleep during the day, eat at a *bisi* (a food mess), and work through the night, as well as to the common perception of seasonal migrants as temporary residents with no attachments to the locality and with no moral boundaries (Interviews 2013).[21]

The 12 p.m. show is about to end. The movie gets stopped just when the end titles begin to roll on the screen. The lights are switched on. Hasan walks in and shouts for everyone to show their tickets. Those sleeping wake up and sit up, while others begin to walk out. Those who hold tickets for the next show are allowed to stay, and those without one are rudely pushed out of the theater. They all exit and stand outside on the verandah smoking, flipping through their mobile phones, discussing different aspects of the film, and staring at the posters, all at the same time. The evening shows, similar to the early morning shows, are randomly chosen Bollywood films from the 1990s and don't attract many viewers. On Sundays, however, the video theaters screen the latest Hindi film releases throughout the day and on a loop. They are usually downloaded through torrents at a nearby cybercafe or bought from vendors at railway stations. The everydayness gets suspended on Sundays as male residents, old and new, young and aged, seasonal and permanent, all watch films at the video theater without any routine. But as the day passes and night approaches, the theater begins to empty and the audience start moving towards their homes to prepare for the routine that is to follow the next day.

The Climax

There is an everydayness to the life in the video theaters, but one that is filled with encounters, both on-screen and off-screen. The films screened at noon usually tell stories about male migrants in the city or about male protagonists in rural north India. Their narratives revolve around urban encounters, revenge, and redemption. For example, a common film narrative is of two male friends who migrate

Figure 2.3 Video Theater

to Mumbai to make new urban lives. But as they move through the city, they encounter crime, corruption, love, death, and money.[22] The films show how these encounters transform their lives and their personhood. Many a times, the narratives involve cruel landlords in a rural setting, who grab land from farmers by forcing them into debt. Here the story is one of seeking revenge in the name of family, land, and love.[23] Other times, the narratives entail conflicts between the male migrants and an urban gangster. In these narratives, the male migrant takes on the nexus of the slimy urban politicians, the corrupt police, the capitalist businessmen, and their crime world in the city.[24] The cruel world in the film, governed by money and greed, becomes a space for encounters, accidents, transformations, and realizations for the film's male protagonist.

Most days, as the movie is about to end, one of the spectators hurriedly walks out to alert the others that the climax of the film is about to start. Everyone on the verandah leaves their conversation abruptly and hurries back into the screening hall to watch the film's climax. The climax is usually a fight scene. The hero, beaten up by the villain's goons, is lying half dead on the ground. But at that very moment, just when it seems as if there is no hope, the hero gathers the strength to get up and destroys the villain. This redemptive power is usually associated with an utterance or a flash of a past moment that involves the death of the hero's beloved one: a mother, father, sister, or friend.[25] The viewers are well aware of this turn, not because of the usual climax-scene structure in Hindi films but because they have watched this climax scene many times before. And yet, they repeatedly enjoy this moment when things turn around. During my interviews at the video theaters, or while I hang out on the verandah making notes, the managers and interviewees would often interrupt me and urge me to go watch the climax. They would narrate the climax and its details and tell me what details to pay attention to while watching it.[26] At that point, I would wonder what drives this pleasure in cinematic repetition? And what does it do?

On Cinema and Repetition

For children, Benjamin writes, repetition is the soul of play; nothing makes them happier than doing the same thing over and over again (in Hansen 2011: 194). Repetition, he notes, plays two roles: one, a therapeutic role of domesticating trauma by transforming a shattering experience into habit through repetition. And second, repetition as difference entails reliving the past moment repeatedly with the aim of redeeming its elements for a different future; the same is reproduced over and over to the point of it becoming unrecognizable—different. Repetition in Benjamin's writings, Hansen suggests, oscillates between these two notions: first, an eternal return of the same, which we saw earlier in the narrative structure of the film *Dharavi*, and second, repetition as difference, wherein the past is reproduced in order to produce a difference. For Benjamin, Hansen notes, film as a technological medium of repetitions tilts towards the latter (ibid.). And given this repeatability, which is therapeutic and redemptive, he invested in cinema in the hope that it could heal the wounds inflicted on human bodies by technologies predicated on the mastery of nature. The hope was that as a sensory-reflexive medium of technology, films offered a second chance of reversing sensory aliena-tion and the numbing of human sensorium in the modern world. It is in this sense, or these senses, that I see the repetitive act of the audiences in the video theater: watching the same climax scene, where the actor on-screen redeems the strength to take over the evil forces at the flash of a past, over and over again, with the same intensity every time. However, while a few of them enjoy the scene, there are others who use films as a therapeutic moment to sleep in the video theaters; those that remain half-awake and move between the psychic unconscious and the optical unconscious on-screen; and then there are those that move in between the world of the theater, their attempts to find work for the next day, and their mobile phones. So, what does this redemptive moment look like when one watches films, the same films, over and over again to enjoy specific moments while moving between different worlds? What sort of moments does the video theater offer to them? And lastly, what is it about the exhibition practices in video theaters that provide an impulse for the emergence of these moments in the everyday life of Toba Tek Nagar?

The Last Show

Unlike the empty theaters on Sunday nights, the night shows (9 p.m.) are packed with audiences the rest of the week. The last show at Anand Video Theater is an old Bollywood film from the 1970s or 1980s. Its primary audience is made up of the older male residents of Toba Tek Nagar. They return home from work in the evenings, have dinner, and then come to watch films at the video theater. The show goes on till midnight, and the discussions then continue over smokes, pan, tobacco, and spit for another hour or so, outside the theater.

On one such night, two friends, Khalid and Jackie, were standing outside Anand Video Theater having a conversation about films. They, like me, had just walked out of the 9 p.m. showing of the 1975 film *Khel Khel Mein* (*All in the Play*). Khalid, a man in his late sixties wearing a white shirt and a checkered lungi, was an older resident of Toba Tek Nagar and a cinephile who loved old Hindi films. He had been a frequent visitor to the night show at the video theater for the past 15 years. One of the reasons for showing older films in the evenings, Hasan stated, was the demand from viewers like Khalid. The latter's love for films goes back to his days in the city as a young teenage migrant. Jackie, a man in his early seventies, wearing a pink shirt and gray pants, was not from the locality, or even the city, but was visiting Khalid. He was new to the video theaters but had dabbled in questions of film theory, art, and aesthetics in his writings. They lit their cigarettes, as I stood by my motorbike waiting to overhear their conversation. As they exhaled the smoke, Khalid initiated a conversation:[27]

Khalid: When I came in the 1970s to Mumbai, I was working as a daily wage *hamal* near Kamathipura,[28] just like some of the new migrants in this locality. The area was filled with single-screen cinema theaters where I could watch films at an affordable price. They screened all kinds of films, English as well as Hindi. Most of the businesses in the area were owned by Muslim business-men. Work used to be slow on Fridays, since the day of the businessmen revolved around the *Jumma namaz* (the Friday afternoon prayer). I would take the day off to watch films in the theaters. I would watch three shows on the same day in the same or in different theaters. I relive that feeling today while watching those films in this video theater. I live in that world today through films.

Jackie: Do you mean through memories?

Khalid: It's the experience of those moments—of youth and the city then, which for me are attached to those films. Those films, now considered old films, had and have *mohabbat* (love). They (the films) remind me of the city's *mahol* (milieu) then, and my life in it as a young migrant. I relocated with my family to Toba Tek Nagar in 1980. We had to because of the demolition of our older house in Byculla. After we moved, the first religious riot between Hindus and Muslims broke out in Toba Tek Nagar soon after (1984). Things have changed since then. They are more violent now.

Jackie: Which means although your individual time is governed by the time of the city, your individual time, the time you live in, that is, through films, is not the same as the time of the city.

Khalid: We have to live in this time of violence. But I also want to live in that world, a different world; in the world of those older films, and the world in which those films were screened. Today, films in theaters are violent, but that is because *duniya ka mahol hi vaisa hai* (it's the milieu we live in). This is not the violence of the *bhais* (gangsters); their time has waned. But the violence of religion and money; everyone is after land and money. Even the dead are not safe here; their bodies get excavated and burned to accommodate new ones. The younger generations, my children, they can relate to it; they have grown up with it. They find their way in and out of it. I can't, I am too old. I live, or want to live, in that old world. I do it through the old films in this video theater.

Jackie (interrupts): "*Duniya ka mahol!*" Foucault uses a similar concept of "milieu." He collapses the boundary between the social and the natural but shows how they are all entrapped within forms of power. Is that what you mean by your idea of violence? And are there intervals in this milieu? For me, intervals are created when individuals and collectives renegotiate the ways in which they adjust their own time to the divisions and rhythms of domination dictated by the system.

Khalid: The films in this video theater, you must have seen, don't have intervals. But the film itself is an interval for some, not for all. Today, things do come and go very fast; nothing lasts. That is how time is made to work. So, we watch films to relive time.

Jackie: I also feel that it doesn't take long to think. Intervals allow for that time to appropriate the breaks in work to become breaks for leisure, par-ticularly for workers, whose time is governed by rhythms of work, like the migrant workers here who work overnight and then come watch films in the mornings.

Khalid: Ours is a time governed by elections, religious conflicts, work, development, demolitions, evictions, and violence, among other things. At this time, watching a film is an overwhelming experience. You relive the lost moment and enjoy it. And at the same time, you long for it since it's not here. The overwhelming feeling has its sadness and pleasure ... In the old films, there was always a song, a *shayari* (poetry), a dialogue, or a scene that would stick with us. We would repeat it to each other, over and over again, find moments to use it in ordinary moments. It made the film and that time a memory, which we relive today when we see that dialogue or scene or song in the same film again.[29] Watching it today, in this theater, reminds us and lets us enjoy that time. Just that song, that dialogue, and you get transported into a different world.

Jackie: And that world is also in this world; that time is also in this time.

(As they turned to exhale their cigarette smoke away from each other's face, Khalid saw me overhearing the conversation and turned back towards Jackie.)

Khalid: But don't get so serious. Look at this guy listening with such seriousness. The film is about entertainment: the pleasure of feeling the sorrow as well as the sorrow of not having pleasure today.

On Cinephilia and Spacing Out

In his essay-cum-interview, the film theorist Paul Willemen makes a case for writing critical film-theory from the point of view of cinephilia (1994: 223). At a basic level, cinephilia, he suggests, is a loving relationship with films and an act of viewing with attention to the moments of revelation that are experienced in the coded cinematic reproductions. What distinguishes cinephilia from critical analysis, he notes, is the attention to excess—that which is seen beyond what is coded in the film. This excess in films, that which is seen but not there, is the ghostly matter; something that is dead but alive in memory. Cinephilia, he thus suggests, has a close affinity to necrophilia. This attention to excess in the moments of their revelation, he further comments, allows the viewer to fantasize a "beyond" of cinema, a world beyond representation. And what is revealed in the moments of revelation, I argue, is not a structure of reality or the phantasmagoria in films, but the ability of the video theaters to provide a space to "space out". This spacing out is a disarticulation between the film and the human experience, the present and the past, the body and the self, wherein the self—a bodily self that is involved in habitual repetitions— gets dislocated from its location (the theater and the body) and drawn out into other worlds (Weber 2008: 173). This dislocation is an effect of sensations in the body—a song, a visual image, or a dialogue experienced in the film. And in this movement away, one is going nowhere and yet not standing still; one is located in the theater on the cast iron seat and yet moving away. In that sense, the video theaters in Toba Tek Nagar are not spatial containers to watch films but a medium in which images, sounds, phone calls, and bodies are brought together, in which they encounter each other, and in which they space out. In this extended space, as Khalid points out, one becomes aware of that which is not present: memories, expectations, and fantasies (ibid.: 174).

Such spacing out, however, cannot be experienced by everyone in the video theaters. Since video theaters are a space primarily used by men. Even the narratives of the films screened there revolve around male protagonists. Thus, women are never able to participate in this pleasure,[30] neither are children, who watch films in their homes or at the nearby single-screen theaters and multiplexes. They are discouraged from visiting the theaters. While the extensive use of theaters by seasonal male migrants is a significant reason for residents' contempt towards the theaters, another reason for this contempt has also to do with the history of video theaters in Toba Tek Nagar.

Workings of Video Theaters

Up until a few years back, there were around 15 video theaters in Toba Tek Nagar. They were located along the main street that connects the locality to the city highway. These older theaters screened Hindi movies, just like the newer ones, but their primary source of income was screening porn films. They screened porn openly, in a literal sense. Curtains used to be half-open, Hasan told me, so that the moaning and orgasmic sounds would creep their way out to attract more audience. This audience was primarily young men, both local and migrants. The theater managers earned a lot those days. "We earned so much," Hasan claimed, "that I even took a trip with my family to Dubai and a Haj to Mecca." But the days of porn waned a few years back. Often, after watching the films, the audience would come out and tease women from the locality. That aggravated members of the *jamaat* (community) and got them together against the video theaters. They filed a complaint at the police station, and the video theaters were forced to shut down. Today, there are just about seven video theaters in Toba Tek Nagar. Its managers try to maintain a cordial relationship with the community and try projecting the image of the video theater as a respectable business, like any other. The video theaters that share a wall with the plot of a temple or a mosque refuse to screen Hindi-dubbed English films. Film posters with women on them are chosen carefully. And managers purposefully drive away children who are hanging around the theater or staring at it.

As the days of porn and its substantial income have waned, running video theaters in Toba Tek Nagar isn't profitable anymore. It has become a risky business that is slowly declining. The unit next to Anand Video Theater used to be an old video theater too. It was shut down a year back due to lack of income and converted into a warehouse for construction material. At another video theater that was located next to the city landfill, part of the screening hall was being used as a storage space for waste recycling, while the verandah was used to sort waste. Its manager, who had leased out the theater from its owner for five years, was unable to sustain the theater without this parallel business. And yet, he could

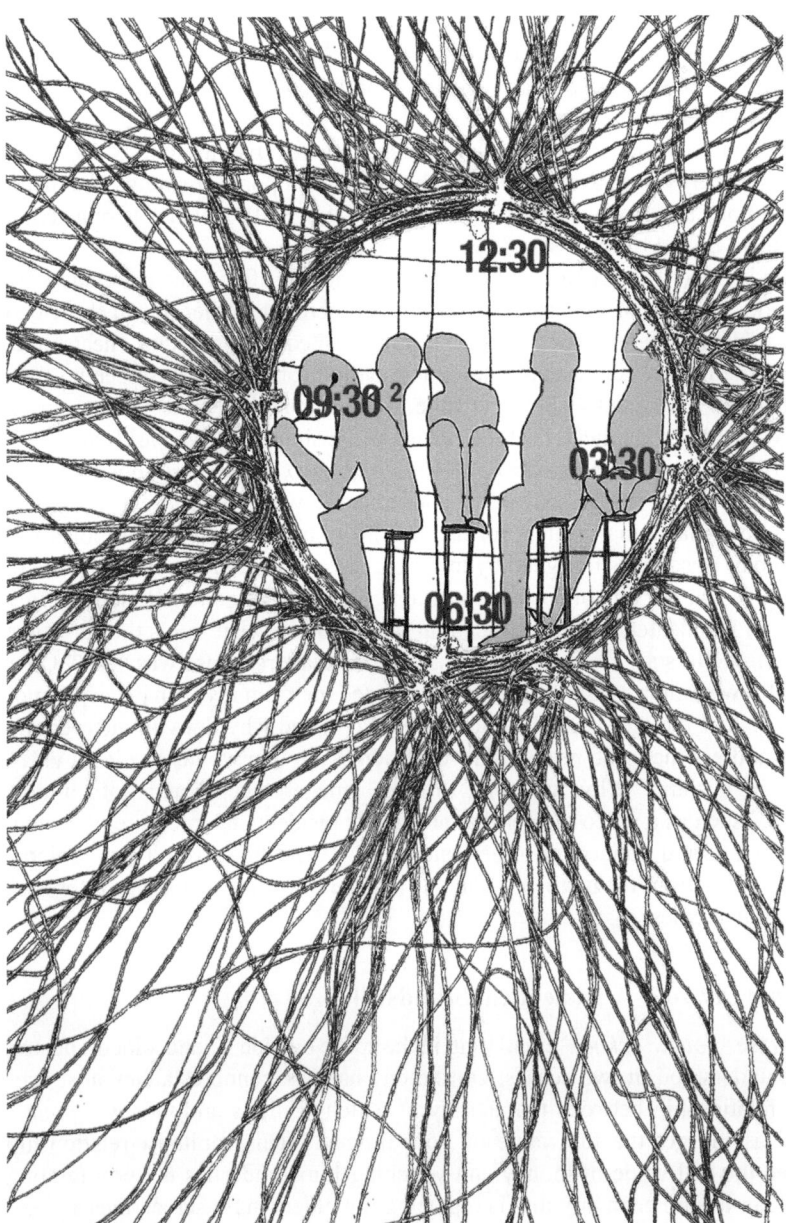

Figure 2.4 Timelines

survive just for another year. The units in which video theaters are housed are rented for INR15,000 (USD 240) per month. Most owners, which include police inspectors, municipal bureaucrats, or other government officials, live in other parts of the city and lease out their theaters on a five-year basis to managers. The latter have to deposit an amount of INR 500,000 (USD 8,000) and share parts of their weekly collections, which is agreed upon beforehand. The owners pay for the entertainment tax and arrange for the license from distribution companies to screen movies. Besides these costs, the managers also pay a monthly *hafta* (an informal weekly bribe) to the police. In the old days of porn screenings, the theaters would pay a monthly *hafta* of INR 18,000 (USD 300), which was reduced to INR 7,000 (USD 110) post-shutdown.

Anand Video Theater too shut down a few months after I had concluded my fieldwork. A group of young boys had pooled money together to run the video theater under a different name. The first time I visited Anand Video Theatre was to pass time in between my interviews and avoid heat in its dark screening hall. But I became a frequent visitor over time. A short man in his mid-forties, Hasan used to sit outside the theater selling tickets while shouting "*Double dekho! Tees ka double dekho. Pet bharke dekho. Khana mat khao, film se peth bharo!*" "See two movies for 30 Rupees only. Fill your appetite with films, forget the food." He had been managing theaters for the past 20 years in different slum localities in Mumbai. Hasan was intrigued by my presence and inquired about my visits to the locality. During one of our conversations, Hasan, trying to make sense of my interest in his theater, asked me the "real intent" of my visit to his theater: "Are you *planning* to start a video theater?" My immediate response was "No!" Over the next few months, Hasan's question distracted me from my own conception of planning. As I thought about his question, I wondered why does an intervention always address the basic needs of development? Why do we never *plan* a video theater in a slum? Why intervene through "megaprojects" and not "minor-projects," such as a video theater that affords its residents the pleasure of seeing, experiencing, and connecting times and places? And how would this "minor-project" differ from megaprojects such as mall-multiplexes that are proliferating across Indian cities?

"Double Dekho": A Dialectical Standstill

The phrase "*double dekho*," circulating in the space outside Anand Video Theater, can be understood in two senses. On the one hand, it connotes a capitalist economic relationship between the activity of watching films and money: "*double dekho*" as in "get the full value of your money." This capitalist relationship between the full value of money and watching films underlies the proliferating new urban leisure economy that is replacing the older single-screen theaters and the deindustrialized spaces in Mumbai. And it finds its concrete manifestation in the urban type of "mall-multiplex."

The history of the multiplex in India, as Adrian Athique and Douglas Hill show in their book, is closely tied to the big corporate retail economy as well as the corporatization of film exhibition practices (2009: 73). Both sectors gained prominence in India post-1990s due to a shift towards a service-oriented economic paradigm in the state's economic policies at the national level. At the city level, this shift resulted in urban authorities adopting entrepreneurial policies that would transform urban environments to meet the needs of investment capital and of those able to actively participate in a lifestyle centered upon rising consumption. A significant aspect of the multiplexes, Athique and Hill note, is the tax benefits they receive from the state (ibid.: 61–65). In their desire to foster prestige commercial development projects, a number of economically central states, including Maharashtra, elected to give multiplexes complete entertainment tax exemptions for the first five years and allow for dynamic ticket pricing, while leaving the high entertainment tax on single-screen theaters intact (45 percent in Maharashtra).[31] This uneven tax system has created a boom of multiplexes in major and smaller Indian cities, while making it difficult for family-owned single-screen theaters, which cater to a mass audience consisting of families and single male subjects, to compete with the multiplexes and sustain in cities. This has resulted in frequent closures of single-screen theaters or their redevelopment into multiplexes. Moreover, the multiplex business in most cities has been dominated by a handful of players who aspire to build a chain of exhibition spaces at the urban and national levels in order to achieve economies of scale.[32]

Another significant aspect of the mall-multiplex phenomenon, Athique and Hill further note, is the coming together of retail, film exhibition, and real-estate development as an organized sector.[33] At the scale of an individual urban typology, the mall-multiplex complex is constituted by four major players: first, the mall developer, who puts up the property and collects rents; second, the multiplex operator, who gains access to infrastructure and a public suited to the staged showtimes and small auditorium model;[34] third, the retail chains who avoid infrastructure costs by moving into the malls and benefit from the crowd-pulling power of the multiplex; and fourth, the food courts that service the mall and capitalize on dining-out practices. All four players share the footfalls from each other's activities. In contrast to the mass in-and-out crowds in older cinema halls, the mall-multiplex format, they suggest, is based on a continuous flow of mobile high-value consumers, specifically young upwardly mobile people with high disposable income looking for quality as well as good value for money (ibid.: 65). In so doing, the mall-multiplex culture, Ravi Vasudevan argues, entwines film viewers into a network of branded consumer culture that is representative of the contemporary multinational-driven constellation of the commodity world (2010: 406). However, to gauge key contests and differences in film cultures and publics, he notes, we need to pay attention to the differentiated circuits and exhibition forms of cinema that rest alongside the mall-multiplex culture. These other circuits, he suggests, challenge the theatrical trade and reconstellate publics by copying and dispersing viewing from its desired temporal sequence into a simultaneity produced through another regime of technological relay and access (2010: 410).

In a city experiencing rapid growth in an organized and corporate form of urban leisure economy, alongside the closures and redevelopment of older affordable single-screen cinema theaters, small video theaters in slum localities are one of the few spaces for some of the residents of Toba Tek Nagar to experience films in an affordable and public format. The price affordability (INR 30 or USD 0.8 for two consecutive shows), the anachronistic form of film exhibition, the screening of films from different genres, the openness to using the theaters in no particular way, and the mixing of men from different social worlds, all afford slum residents a space to experience films, connect different cinematic elements to their own particular situations, and a medium to space out. It is in this audiences' spacing out in video theaters that we arrive at the second sense of Hasan's phrase "*double dekho*" to attract audiences into the video theater. In this spacing out, the temporal distance between the past and the present, as well as the spatial distance between the multiplex and the residents—what Benjamin refers to as the aura—is short-circuited to produce a time of simultaneity, which is also time at a standstill. Simultaneity because temporal elements of present and past, real and virtual, near and far, are brought together in the interplay between the different films and its different audiences. And standstill because the short-circuiting interrupts the time of work, of migration, of everydayness, and of historical progress, it brings it to a standstill, while allowing the viewers to depart—to space out. In this extended space, which is created in the video theater, urban residents are freed from the constraints of time and afforded a leap into other worlds, particularly memories, fantasies, and anticipations. This leap beyond what is, however, is predicated on the coming together of the disparate elements in the local video theaters.

Notes

1 Translation: See two at the price of one.
2 Played by the popular Hindi film actor Anil Kapoor.
3 The role was played by the popular Hindi film female actor Madhuri Dixit. Mishra plays with the contrast between fantasy on-screen and reality in his choice of actors too. The "real" slum residents are portrayed by actors such as Om Puri, Shabana Azmi (who then went on to become a real-life housing rights activist of slum dwellers in Mumbai), and Raghuvir Yadav, from the "parallel cinema" realm, while popular Hindi film actors portray the "fantasy" characters. In this regard, the first scene portrays slum residents as an ideal spectator, one completely interpellated by the film.
4 Tangella 2005: *Sagar Cinema: A Poor Man's Multiplex*, Sarai Independent Fellowship Project.
5 In saying so, I do not want to generalize that films are an important part of slums everywhere. If films and film theaters are of significance in Mumbai, there exist similar spaces in other cities.
6 The video theaters in slums do not fall within the hierarchies of A to D circuit cinema exhibition spaces. However, they do reflect some of the older hierarchies in colonial Bombay, when cinema was becoming a popular form of mass entertainment. As Kaushik Bhaumik shows in his history of cinema in colonial Bombay from 1896 to 1928, the theaters in older parts of Bombay would be used by the Europeans, Eurasians, and upper-class Indians, while the theaters outside of it, which came up with the expan-

sion of the city, would cater to students, lawyers, clerks, shopkeepers, petty-traders, and workers living in the now inner city (Bhaumik 2011: 54).

7 During the interview, Sagirbhai reflected a lot on the exclusionary nature of certain religious practices, both Hindu and Muslim, and undoing them, he suggested, was one of the biggest challenges of organizing in the locality. He was involved in a number of projects that ranged from small infrastructure projects, to expanding activities of the CBO during moments of emergency such as floods, to programs for youth in the locality.

8 Films, particularly so, because they depend much on the play of light and shadows.

9 This section is based on interviews with the group as well as a study of their YouTube series, which is available here: https://www.youtube.com/channel/UCBdNj7qrJh BtlWW6POk-v3Q, Accessed August 2014.

10 Afzal, the director of the show, had graduated with a bachelor's degree in Mass Media from the Zee Institute of Media Arts and was well versed with the technicalities of filmmaking.

11 After two episodes, the youth group stopped producing the crime show and moved on to recording and filming a music album.

12 When I asked the members about their favorite films, they all unanimously claimed that they like films with a message—which meant films that revolve around a social issue. So, their favorite films included classics such as *Mother India* (1957) and contemporary films such as *Chak De* (2007) and *Three Idiots* (2009).

13 In the end section on "making of the film," one can hear Afzal, the director and scriptwriter, shout out to others to follow his instructions and admonish them, as well, for screwing up despite rehearsals the night before. The shots are shown in the main film, just muted.

14 Post-premier, the film was broadcasted on televisions in the locality through local cable TV networks.

15 The interview with the youth group also reflected the same disdain that the older residents have towards the video theaters and the temporary migrants.

16 The ethnography for this chapter was conducted in three different video theaters at different times of the year and at different times of the day. Anand Video Theater is presented here as an archetype.

17 Most window grills, ladders inside houses, boxes to secure water pumps, and furniture in Toba Tek Nagar are designed and manufactured by the iron-grill shops near the city highway. These shops procure iron from demolished buildings and settlements in Mumbai, as well as from abandoned industries in other cities.

18 Bhojpuri—a dialect of Hindi—is spoken in the eastern part of the state of Uttar Pradesh, the western part of the state of Bihar, and some parts of Jharkhand. Bhojpuri films, as the work of Akshaya Kumar shows, have been in production since 1963. The dramatic growth of the film industry, its star system, and its consolidation into a territory of Bhojpuri cinema is due to the spread of the Bhojpuri-speaking migrants, who travel in search of work all across the country, specifically, in cities such as Mumbai, Delhi, and more recently Bangalore, Hyderabad, and Chennai, among other cities. The main audiences of Bhojpuri films (as well as Bhojpuri music) in urban centers are construction laborers, porters, rickshaw wallahs, and taxi drivers (Kumar 2016).

19 Madhavi Tangella's work on Telugu video theaters shows the significance of the video theaters for migrants from Andhra Pradesh and Telangana in a slum locality in the western suburbs of Mumbai (2005).

20 "Films and cricket," as one of the manufacturing-unit owners told me, "are the only activities that they choose to spend money on. The rest of the money is sent to families back home" (Interview 2013).

21 The lack of moral boundaries refers to the mobility of temporary migrants, who move in and out of the locality without any familial attachments (family or property) within the locality. However, one of the common concerns expressed by the older residents was eve teasing by the younger migrants.

22 For example, see movies such as *Yamraaj*, directed by Raj Babbar (1998), and *Keemat—They Are Back*, directed by Sameer Malkan (1998).

23 See *Saugandh* (An Oath), directed by Raj N. Sippy (1991).

24 These Hindi films from the 1990s belong to the action genre but are hybrid in nature. The film moves through moments of comedy, action, crime, romance, and family drama. See, for example, *Ghatak: Lethal*, directed by Rajkumar Santoshi (1996).

25 This turn of events during a climax scene is a common motif in Hindi films. Sometimes, this turn is doubled or even tripled, wherein the hero and the villain keep getting an upper hand over the other due to some occurrences at the scene of action.

26 One of the most watched scenes is the fight between Akshay Kumar, a Hindi film actor known for his martial arts skill, and the World Wrestling Federation's wrestler undertaker in Umesh Mehra's 1996 film *Khiladiyon Ka Khiladi* (*Player of Players*).

27 I have not figured out if it is coincidence or a cinematic aspect that I would have a great interview with the two resident-cinephiles (who together form Khalid here) after we had all watched the movie *Khel Khel Mein* (*All in the Game/Play*) and that I would use Hansen's ideas on "cinema as a *play-form* of second nature" a year later.

28 Kamathipura is the historical as well as present-day red-light district in the inner city of Bombay. The film theaters he refers to were one of the early film theaters that were built in Colonial Bombay during the 1920s in the Grant Road-Lamington Road area (Bhaumik 2011: 50).

29 Writing on the inability of the traditional tools of film theory scholarship to understand the relationship between films and society in the case of Bombay cinema, Kaushik Bhaumik emphasizes the sonic elements of films: "the Bombay film is predominantly built in terms of its sonic structures with the main impact of the film depending on a complex layering of sounds that encompass dialogue, music and songs. The sonic map of the film sets up the rhythm of the film, acting being subsidiary to sound" (Bhaumik 2004).

30 Most video theater managers ascribe the absence of women in the audience to the lack of a separate seating section in the screening hall. The quest for pleasure, the struggle against sexual and gendered violence, and access to public spaces, feminist scholars Shilpa Phadke, Sameera Khan, and Shilpa Ranade have argued, are deeply connected (Phadke 2007a and 2007b; Phadke, Ranade, and Khan 2009). One of the common ways in which urban policies in Mumbai have attempted to resolve the issue is through segregation—avoiding contact between men and women in public and semipublic modes of transportation. However, this strategy of segregation, the scholars show, also ends up arresting their movement under the trap of protection and, in turn, denying them their right to public spaces. In the case of leisure and pleasure as nonpurposeful activities in public spaces, they write, if women cannot manufacture a sense of purpose for which their presence is mandatory in the public space, they must instead be where they really belong, that is, in the domestic spaces. The significant issue here, they argue, is one of rights rather than of protection—the right to pleasure thus includes the right to public spaces. The relationship between leisure, gender, and stratification of public space can be seen explicitly in the case of film exhibition spaces in Mumbai. The figure of the single woman audience has been absent in the realm of film exhibition as well as film genres. Women were and are always seen as a part of a family or as accompanied by men. In the case of film theaters, the balcony sections, seating sections elevated above the stall sections, which were divided based on class segregation also became "safe spaces" for women. In other instances, theaters would house a separate "family-box section" that would be located behind the balcony sections. In recent years, one of the major appeals of viewing films in multiplexes has been their portrayal as "safe spaces" for women (Kumar 2016: 158).

31 Athique and Hill argue that the states have provided tax exemptions for the first five years in order to allow multiplexes to develop a strong business in that period, which can then be taxed at the regular rate. This is a long-term strategy on the part of the state.

However, a number of multiplex operators, their study shows, believe that they would continue to receive tax benefits even after the five-year period (ibid.: 63).

32 In 2009, five companies operated two-third of India's multiplexes, which is a marked departure from the disaggregated form of film exhibition sector that existed in India up until the 1970s (ibid.: 58).

33 Their study shows that most multiplex operators are either subsidiaries of private housing developers, mall developers, and/or multi-media conglomerates or are transiting towards becoming one of the three.

34 The small auditorium format has also changed the genre of films that are being produced as well as the proliferation of independent filmmakers. The older and larger single-screen theaters primarily screen Bollywood masala films that attract a mass audience alongside English films (dubbed Hollywood films) and pornographic films during the matinee or the morning show.

References

Athique, Adrian, and Douglas Hill. 2009. *The Multiplex in India: A Cultural Economy of Urban Leisure*. London, UK: Routledge.

Babbar, Rajiv. 1998. *Keemat-They Are Back*. Abha Films.

Benjamin, Walter. 1969. "Theses on the Philosophy of History." In *Illuminations: Essays and Reflections*, edited by Hannah Arendt, translated by Harry Zohn, 253–64. New York, NY: Schocken Books.

Benjamin, Walter. 2010. "The Work of Art in the Age of Its Technological Reproducibility [First Version]." Translated by MICHAEL W. JENNINGS. *Grey Room* 39 (Spring): 11–38.

Bhaumik, Kaushik. 2004. "A Brief History of Cinema from Bombay to 'Bollywood.'" *History Compass* 2 (1): 1–4.

———. 2011. "Cinematograph to Cinema Bombay 1896–1928." *Bioscope: South Asian Screen Studies* 2 (1): 41–67.

Dickey, Sara. 1993. *Cinema and the Urban Poor in South India*. Cambridge, UK: Cambridge University Press.

Hansen, Miriam Bratu. 2011. *Cinema and Experience: Siegfried Kracauer, Walter Benjamin, and Theodor W. Adorno*. Edited by Edward Dimendberg. Berkeley, CA: University of California Press.

Horkheimer, Max, and Theodor W. Adorno. 2002. *Dialectic of Enlightenment*. Edited by Gunzelin Schimd Noerr. Translated by Edmund Jephcott. Stanford, CA: Stanford University Press.

Kumar, Akshaya. 2016. "Bhojpuri Cinema and the 'Rearguard': Gendered Leisure, Gendered Promises." *Quarterly Review of Film and Video* 33 (2): 151–75.

Larkin, Brian. 2008a. *Signal and Noise: Media, Infrastructure, and Urban Culture in Nigeria*. Durham, NA: Duke University Press.

———. 2008b. *Signal and Noise: Media, Infrastructure, and Urban Culture in Nigeria*. Durham, NA: Duke University Press.

Liang, Lawrence. 2010. "Beyond Representation: The Figure of the Pirate." In *Access to Knowledge in the Age of Intellectual Property*, edited by Gaëlle Krikorian and Amy Kapczynski, 167–80. New York, NY: Zone Books.

Malkan, Sameer. 1998. *Keemat-They Are Back*. B4U Films. Mumbai.

Mehra, Umesh. 1996. *Khiladiyon Ka Khiladi*. DMS Films. Mumbai.

Mishra, Sudhir. 1991. *Dharavi*. NFDC-Doordarshan. Mumbai.

Nandy, Ashis. 1998. "Introduction: Indian Popular Cinema as Slum's Eye View of Politics." In *The Secret Politics of Our Desires: Innocence, Culpability and Indian Popular Cinema*, 1–18. London, UK: Zed Books Ltd.

Phadke, Shilpa. 2007a. "Dangerous Liaisons: Women and Men: Risk and Reputation in Mumbai." *Economic & Political Weekly* 42 (17): 1510–18.

———. 2007b. "Re-Mapping the Public: Gendered Spaces in Mumbai." In *Gender and the Built Environment in India*, edited by Madhavi Desai, 53–73. New Delhi: Zubaan.

Phadke, Shilpa, Shilpa Ranade, and Sameera Khan. 2009. "Why Loiter? Radical Possibilities for Gendered Dissent." In *Dissent and Cultural Resistance in Asia's Cities*, 199–217. London: Routledge.

Rao, Vyjayanthi. 2006. "Slum as Theory: The South/Asian City and Globalization." *International Journal of Urban and Regional Research* 30 (1): 225–32.

Razvi, Afzal. 1996a. CASE *01: Khoon Paani*. SVJ Bozz. https://www.youtube.com/watch?v=ytlT7Rybn1M.

———. 1996b. CASE *02: Laapata Bacha Shivaji Nagar Ka*. SVJ Bozz. https://www.youtube.com/watch?v=ytlT7Rybn1M.

Roy, Ananya. 2011. "Slumdog Cities: Rethinking Subaltern Urbanism." *International Journal of Urban and Regional Research* 35 (2): 223–38.

Santoshi, Rajkumar. 1996. *Ghatak: Lethal*. B4U Films. Mumbai.

Sippy, Raj. 1991. *Saugandh*. Tridev Films. Mumbai.

Tandon, Ravi. 1975. *Khel Khel Mein*. R.M. Films & Rose Movies. Mumbai.

Tangella, Madhavi. 2005. "Sagar Cinema: A Poor Man's Multiplex." Sarai, CSDS. http://www.sarai.net/fellowships/independent/archival-submissions.

Vasudevan, Ravi. 2003. "Cinema in Urban Space," *Seminar*, 525 (May). https://www.india-seminar.com/2003/525/525%20ravi%20vasudevan.htm.

———. 2010. *The Melodramatic Public: Film Form and Spectatorship in Indian Cinema*. Ranikhet, India: Permenant Black.

Weber, Samuel. 2008. *Benjamin's-Abilities*. Cambridge, MA: Harvard University Press.

Willemen, Paul. 1994. "Through the Glass Darkly: Cinephilia Reconsidered." In *Looks and Frictions: Essays in Cultural Studies and Film Theory*, 223–57. Bloomington, IN: Indiana University Press.

Figure 3.1 On the lookout

3   On Toilets, Deceptions, and Citability

Kaminey, A Tragic Play

Kaminey

> *Beta Charlie, life badi kutti cheez hai, aur is duniya mein kutton ka sirf ek hi jawab hai ... Kaminey.*[1]

As he stands amidst the railway tracks and a local suburban train speeds by, Charlie reflects on the city by recollecting the words of his dead father: "Life here is a bitch and the only answer to the dogs of this world is a Scoundrel." The film *Kaminey* by Vishal Bharadwaj (2009) is situated in Mumbai and most of its characters are migrants. The film's main protagonists, twins Charlie and Guddu, are sons of an Uttar Pradeshi migrant. Charlie is a small-time gangster. He fixes horse races and dreams of having his own betting counter at the racecourse. Guddu, on the other hand, is a college student and volunteers in his free time at an NGO. Both have speech impediments, an expression of not theirs but the city's inability to understand the speech and desires of the outsider. Guddu's girlfriend, Sweety, on the other hand, pretends to stutter and hides her family background to build a romantic relationship with Guddu. She is the sister of a nativist ("Mumbaikar") gangster cum politician Bhopebhau (Brother Bhope), who is trying to marry her off to a real-estate developer's son in return for election funds. The other characters of the film include three Bengali brothers who are bookies and arms dealers; a drug kingpin named Tashi and his two African brothers-in-law who have arrived in Mumbai to exchange diamonds for drugs;[2] and lastly, two corrupt Indian police officers from the anti-narcotic department: Lobo and Lele. The film moves incessantly through a series of twists and turns in the plot, which unfolds over the course of a single day. As the plot advances, every character, at every turn, is trying to deceive and outdo the others for drugs, money, power, or love. This movement, however, also holds within it intervals, where a choice opens up between getting more deeply involved in the plot and walking away from it. At these intersections, Charlie, conscious of the fact that getting involved might be a huge risk, cunningly reasons: "The choice is not between a right way and a wrong way (...) We get screwed not by the path we choose, but the path we leave behind."

DOI: 10.4324/9781003051848-5

The Black Sheep, Tricksters, and Scoundrels

In his surreal short story, "The Black Sheep" (1995), Italo Calvino tells a tale about a nameless city where everyone, absolutely everyone, is a thief. They all work during the day and steal at night from each other. Here trade involves cheating on the part of both, the buyers and the sellers. Even its city government is a criminal organization; it steals from its subjects, and the subjects, for their part, defraud the government. The "Black Sheep" of Calvino's short story is an honest man, who arrives in this larcenous city but refuses to steal from anyone. His honesty, over time, creates a societal imbalance in the city and transforms it from a place of thieves into one divided into rich and poor.

In sharp contrast to the Black Sheep—a figure with utmost honesty as its only characteristic, are the tricksters, whose stories circulate among different West African and North American First Nations communities. Often, these figures are polymorphic and shape-shifters. For instance, Anansi, a trickster from Ghana, whose stories traveled with plantation slaves to Caribbean islands and were significant to their antislavery struggles, is a spider-spirit-human that takes on different avatars based on the situation. The Anansi, they say, lives on the ceiling, looking at everything upside down, inverting life and spinning webs of intrigue (Hecht and Simone 1995: 79). Similar to Anansi, is Eshu, a deity of the Yoruba people in West Africa, who, they say, can turn shit into treasure, and just as often turn treasure into shit (ibid.: 91–92). The trickster is two-faced, is mischievous, is unpredictable, and converts into an agent of chaos when things get too identical. Scholars writing about such figures suggest that these figures are conjured and mobilized by individuals or communities in specific historical moments using stories (Fagan 2010). The role of these stories is manifold: to pass on intelligence in times of need, to set peace in the community using gifts from gods, to set and transgress moral boundaries of the community, and to pass on tricks so as to avoid "ends" in precarious times (Sinclair 2010). The ways in which these tricksters come to possess these gifts are also stories in themselves. Often, for individual reasons such as pride, arrogance, and even selfishness, they rescue divine gifts by tricking both fellow animals and gods. They exploit their own wisdom as well as the folly of their co-animals to wriggle out of the tightest corners. Through these acts, the trickster "shows that the 'really real' is incessantly multifaceted and ironic." And any and all attempts at closure, which "determine what's in or out, what's incorporated or 'free,' must eventually burst out (Hecht and Simone, 1995: 91–92)." The tricksters, M'Baye Babacar thus argues, epitomize behaviors and identities that defy the good versus evil binary that characterize the European concepts of morality and order. Thus, rigid oppositions or speculations about their honesty, morality, or religiosity are unnecessary, because they all have flaws that play an equally important role in stories (2010).

In his 1921 essay "Fate and Character," Walter Benjamin analyzes and critiques the deterministic relationship established between guilt and fate in the religious world, and character and judgment in the modern world, along similar lines. Character, he argues, should not be seen and perceived as the core or moral nature of an individual, based on which an individual should be judged and their fate determined. Instead, characters are basic concepts that are morally indifferent, and which point towards different life-worlds and thought figures. An exemplar of the latter, he notes, are two ironic figures: the comic figure on stage; and the scoundrels in the real world. Both possess anonymity as individuals and ambiguity in moral terms, which make their actions both tragic and comic and free them from judgments of guilt, empathy, morality, and fate (1978 [1921]). In other words, the comic and the scoundrel, as characters, point towards an impossibility of fixing them within frames and the possibility of other forms of life.

Deceptive Playacts

What is common to these figures across the different contexts is not just their polymorphic nature or their ability to wriggle out of frames and categories but also the possibility of reading the city itself as a make-believe theater, where inhabiting involves playing different roles at different times (Benjamin and Lācis, 1978[1925]). But what possibilities does such playacting open up? Samuel Weber's essays, which explore Benjamin's writings on the city itself as a theater and the latter's fascination with theater, particularly Bertolt Brecht's "Epic Theatre," are insightful in this regard (2008: 95–114; 227–39).

In these essays, Weber draws attention specifically to the "citability (cite-ability) of gestures" in playacting. To gesture, he writes, suggests two actions at once: to bring (about) or carry a movement by repeating and imitating it; and second, to interrupt and contain that movement by giving it a form—a gesture (ibid.: 100). Similarly, to cite too connotes two things at once: first, to arrest a movement, a sequence, or a goal-intended action, like a cop arresting a car speeding towards its destination by handing out a citation; and second, to ex-cite or in-cite, that is, to stir things up and bring about a movement (ibid.: 99). Although gestures and citing imply this tension between acting and interrupting the action, actors, he notes, "make gestures citable." And in making gestures citable, actors gesture towards the possibility of interrupting intentions, judgments, and identities implied in the gesture (citing gestures), as well as the possibility of carrying them elsewhere (gesturing towards their citability). This pretension of being something or someone, only to deceive it (interrupt and alter) is the cunning ability in playacting.

Drawing on lessons from the different figures cited above (tricksters, scoundrels, and *kaminey*) and Benjamin's cunning theorization of performance, this chapter explores deceptive playacting as a form of operating in cities. To do this, it narrates ethnographic stories of three neighborhood toilets projects that were implemented under the Slum Sanitation Program (SSP) in Toba Tek Nagar. The program was initiated by the Mumbai municipality in partnership with the World Bank in 1997 to improve sanitation in the city's slum localities through a model of community participation that would bypass the older model of political patronage. The ethnographic stories attend to on how the individual toilet operators got these toilets built (or not built), the material details of the toilets, how the toilets work (or not work), as well as their relationship to the SSP model. Each of these toilets,

I show here, were not just built by deceiving others involved in the program, but were also in themselves deceptions of the model envisioned by the program. In doing so, this chapter hopes to show how, in deceptive playacts, other forms of inhabiting are possible in a city, despite its territorialization by religious communalism, state power, and capital.

A Toilet: An Exact Fantasy

"Could you tell me about any one thing in your neighborhood that you find beautiful?" Siraj, a resident of Toba Tek Nagar answered: "Our toilet."

Built in 1998, the toilet in Siraj's neighborhood was one of the first toilets to be built under the Slum Sanitation Program in Toba Tek Nagar. The new toilet replaced an older toilet that was built in the 1980s using funds distributed to elected municipal councilors under the Slum Improvement Program, which had aimed to upgrade basic infrastructural facilities in Mumbai's slum settlements. But the old toilet had been in a state of constant disrepair for various reasons. It had only eight seats for men and women each in a neighborhood of 15,000 residents. It was connected not to the city's sewerage system but to an overburdened belowground septic tank. And to add to it, it was built as a load-bearing structure on reclaimed marshy land and had begun to sink slowly into the ground, further reducing the capacity of the septic tank. This meant that the sludge and its putrid odors regularly overflowed into the neighborhood. Furthermore, in the absence of municipally provided water and sewerage infrastructure, the local residents were forced to depend on private tankers to supply water and on private truck operators to pump out and cart away the sludge. These were huge expenses for most local residents, particularly those below the poverty line. Every few years, just before a municipal, state government, or central government election, residents would deposit letters and file petitions with different politicians, requesting the rebuilding or repair of the toilet but without much success. Pink in color, the old toilet had come to stand for an eternally recurring, circular time of development governed by electoral politics among residents.

Then, in 1997, the Slum Sanitation Program (SSP) was launched by the Mumbai Municipal Corporation as part of a broader umbrella initiative called the Bombay Sewerage Disposal Project (BSDP).[3] Funded by the World Bank and the Maharashtra government, the BSDP aimed to strengthen Mumbai's sewerage infrastructure. The implementation of the SSP was recommended by the World Bank as a mandatory condition for funding the BSDP. The SSP aimed to address four key areas: providing sustainable sanitation facilities in Mumbai's slum localities and connecting them to wider city sewerage networks; reversing "clientelistic" relationships between politicians and slum residents by changing the older "supply-based" model to a "demand-based" model; encouraging community participation by involving nongovernmental organizations (NGOs) and forming community-based organizations (CBOs); and lastly, instituting a new financial model that could foster a "sense of ownership" among slum residents and help them maintain and operate toilets without external funds. To institute the last goal, the SSP mandated an initial household contribution of INR 100 per individual (USD 1.50) or a maximum of INR 500 (USD 9) per family. In return, these individuals or households were to be provided a family pass for a minimal yearly cost of INR 120 (USD 2). The SSP also required participation of at least 50 percent of households in order to assure the financial sustainability of any project.[4]

In sharp contrast to the old dilapidated toilet, the new SSP toilet in Siraj's neighborhood is an aesthetically striking structure. It is built with a raft foundation whose reinforced concrete piles travel 30 feet below the ground to find stability in the hard rocks below the marsh. The building's surfaces are carefully and attentively adorned: the outsides are clad with rough off-white ceramic tiles and the inside walls with glossy gray, brown, and off-white tiles. Furthermore, the sludge is disposed into the septic tank and from there into a *nallah* (small stream) using an ad hoc pipe that was absent in the plumbing drawings submitted to the municipality. The toilet boasts metered electricity and billed water connections, although a suction pump purchased using residents' contributions is used to offset the low-pressure municipal water supply.[5] The presence of these different elements helps avoid the residents from depending on local politicians. However, this does not mean that the toilet was built without the local councilor's involvement. She was invited as the guest of honor for the project's *bhoomi poojan* (a ritual for inauguration). In addition, a black granite tile with her name engraved in golden letters was installed at the toilet's entrance. Thus, despite her efforts to impair and stall the project, her blessings were taken so that the residents could collaborate with her on other issues.[6]

A cast-iron staircase at the back of the concrete structure leads up to a terrace, which is used by residents for various non-toilet-related activities (tuition classes, stitching classes, etc.). The terrace floor is decorated with colored ceramic tiles and lined with potted green plants. A small channel around the edge of the terrace floor carries rainwater to the underground water storage tank. The tank is connected to a metered municipal water connection, out of which pressurized water flows between 6 and 8 am each morning. Mehmoodbhai or his son Sajid switch on the electric pump that lifts the water from the underground tank into the overhead tank. A short stout man with a cropped beard, Mehmoodbhai is the new toilet's caretaker as well as the head of the CBO that operates and maintains it. He migrated from Muzaffarnagar, Uttar Pradesh, to a slum settlement in Byculla, Mumbai, in 1972. He was relocated to Toba Tek Nagar in 1975 as a result of the Emergency-era slum demolitions and evictions. His office is located up on the terrace next to the overhead tank, and he resides with his wife, son, daughter-in-law, and their two children in a two-room structure at the other end of the terrace. The family also owns a vegetable stall in the wholesale market in Navi Mumbai. Mehmoodbhai had played a key role in getting the SSP toilet built: he organized the residents to form the CBO, liaised between the residents, the NGO, and the municipality, and more importantly, gave up his own house to make space for the new toilet. His old house, as he told me, had been situated just next to the old pink toilet. Rather than being relocated, he opted to take on the role of the caretaker, which provided him with a rooftop home. In recent years, Mehmoodbhai's son Sajid has taken over as the caretaker.

Access to the new toilet works like this: older residents—those who can provide documentary proof that their tenure in Toba Tek Nagar precedes the cut-off date of 1 January 2000, avail a prepaid monthly pass against the payment of INR 500. Residents who migrated *post*-2000 are allowed to purchase monthly prepaid toilet passes as and when they are able to avail documentary proof of legal residence (electricity bills, power of attorney certificate, children's school fee receipt, water-supply bill, etc.). Allowing post-2000 residents to purchase monthly passes is a unique feature of Mehmoodbhai's toilet; this is not a part of the SSP program, which explicitly excludes post-2000 residents. Newer migrants living as subtenants are not provided a monthly pass. They pay INR 2 (USD 0.025) per visit. The new migrants, mostly single men who work in manufacturing workshops in Toba Tek Nagar form the largest group of "pay-per-visit" clients. The income from these "pay-per-visits" is the primary income source for the maintenance and upkeep of the toilet. Conversely, relatives of local residents visiting them from outside Toba Tek Nagar are allowed to use the toilet for free. For Mehmoodbhai, it is a matter of pride when visitors express their awe of the beauty and cleanliness of the toilet or become envious of their relatives who are its members. Every year, he celebrates World Toilet Day. The toilet gets covered with colorful lights, music is played on hired speakers, and a chief guest, such as a well-known builder, a senior municipal official, or a local politician, is invited. The toilet becomes a space for a festival and the festival a space to develop affiliations with prominent actors of urban development.

During one of our many conversations, Mehmoodbhai explained his renovation plans to me while arranging the tile pattern for the outside walls on his desk. "The tiles will be glossy on the inside and rough on the outside. It will give the toilet a posh look on the inside and a natural look on the outside." I nodded in agreement. "I will also install speakers—you don't see that often in toilets, right?" I suggested he could play songs. "Not songs," he insisted but "news, melodies, and instrumental music. It will help people relax while using the toilet." He wanted the toilet to be not just pleasurable for use but also a spectacular object and an object of everyone's attention—what an exact fantasy.

Exact Fantasy and Playing Mimetic Tricks

To mime, as Benjamin suggests, is not to reproduce sameness but to produce a different copy—give it another form. And for Theodor Adorno, to mime the original in a new modality requires the organizing principle of "exact fantasy" (in Buck-Morss 1989: 85). The concept of "exact fantasy" in Adorno, Susan Buck-Morss elaborates, connotes a fantasy that is guided by the object or the materials presented to experience by a phenomenon, as well as the subject's drive to rearrange the elements of the phenomenon, with the aim of bringing the later into different possible relationships, until they crystallize into a new cognitive configuration that reveals the truth (ibid.: 86). In this process, one moves back and

Figure 3.2 Beauty

forth between the elements of the phenomenon and one's intentionality, without allowing either to take over completely. And in doing so, rather than being merely duplicated, elements are transformed through a mimetic rearrangement to reveal the truth. This revelation, for Benjamin, is nothing but the impermanence of the original and the possibility of its betrayal through its infinite reproducibility in different mimetic mediums. Mimetic play is this trickery of producing difference and sameness. On the one hand, mimesis, driven by an exact fantasy, involves producing something that appears the same but is different; and on the other, mimesis, driven by the desire to produce identity, is instrumental to producing difference (identify an alien other) in order to maintain sameness (Taussig 1993: 129). These trickeries are very much at play in the implementation of the Slum Sanitation Program in Toba Tek Nagar.

Toilet Tricks: Different and Same

Nizambhai, another toilet operator in Toba Tek Nagar, had a somewhat different story to tell about Mehmoodbhai's toilet. According to Nizambhai, Mehmoodbhai is a *kamina* who had deceived the local residents, particularly those who were unable to afford the initial contribution towards the toilet. Mehmoodbhai had convinced them to sign up for the program, Nizambhai explained, by offering to pay their part of the contribution. The plan was to get approvals from 50 percent of households to get the project approved. However, once the toilet was built, Mehmoodbhai refused to hand these residents their family passes and demanded per visit payments until they repaid him for their initial contribution. Furthermore, Nizambhai continued, Mehmoodbhai never actually owned a house next to the old toilet; it was a story he made up to justify his living above the toilet.

Over the years, Mehmoodbhai's SSP toilet has become renowned in international development circles as an instance of "best practice" of slum sanitation in the developmental world. Photos of award ceremonies, certificates from international organizations, travelogues of international conferences, newspaper cuttings, and photographs of visits by NGOs, researchers, and foreign visitors, all are archived on his computer, walls of his office, as well as social media. Mehmoodbhai has used the celebrated SSP toilet as a conduit to develop strong relations with different actors, including municipal bureaucrats and myriad national and international development agencies. For instance, he allows specific NGOs to showcase "his" toilet to international donors as "their" best practice model in order to attract more funding. In turn, Mehmoodbhai calls upon these NGOs when he needs funds or favors. A few years after the toilet was built Mehmoodbhai set up a citywide NGO to coordinate among different city's slum-based CBOs and the city municipality. Furthermore, given his affiliations and knowledge, residents from Toba Tek Nagar come to him for help in navigating all manner of bureaucratic procedures: getting themselves onto the Below Poverty Line list, resolving issues of informal land occupancy, availing formal water and electricity connections, or using his networks in various government offices for timely completion of paperwork.

Mehmoodbhai assists the residents in every which way without expectations of any returns. Unfortunately, the NGOs had refused to fund his renovation plans, to which Mehmoodbhai politely responded by refusing to allow his toilet to be showcased to donors.

Such instances of seizing developmental opportunities aren't peculiar to Mehmoodbhai's toilet. In another slum locality, in the Southern part of Mumbai, the situation was similar, but also different, in many ways. Here, the local CBO in charge of leading and managing the SSP toilet was formed in 1995 under the tutelage of the local councilor and in partnership with the NGO that was in charge of liaising between the CBO and the municipality (WSP/World Bank 2005). In its initial phase, the CBO had collected the consensus and the basic membership payment from the residents. But once the toilet was built, they refused to issue monthly passes to the residents. They had to pay per use. The only members with monthly passes were the members of the CBO and their families. In instances where the neighborhood residents refused to pay per use or challenged the authority of the CBO by filing complaints, the members of the CBO threatened and beat up the residents individually (Interviews 2006). Furthermore, the CBO had outsourced the daily operations to a private contractor, who earned a daily income of around INR 2,000 (USD 29) and paid a part of it to the CBO as rent. The NGO assigned to ensure the community's participation in the workings of the toilet was well aware of this but refused to pay heed to the residents' complaints since the toilet was one of their "model" toilets that helped them acquire funds from international donors. Such foreclosing of toilets wasn't peculiar to this particular SSP toilet in the locality. Two other toilets, which had been built under the older Slum Improvement Program, had also been "captured" by the CBO. Thus, despite the goals of the SSP to break away from the older dependency model, the toilet had been enclosed by the NGO, the CBO, and the councilor, completely. Unlike in Mehmoodbhai's case, here the toilet tricks merely reproduced the older forms of relationships in new ways through the means of the SSP.

Working the Model

Residing at the other end of Toba Tek Nagar, Nizambhai, who told me Mehmoodbhai's "true" story, too has a toilet story. He had migrated from a village in Western Maharashtra to a slum settlement in South Bombay during the droughts of 1970–1973. He too was relocated to Toba Tek Nagar during the Emergency-era demolitions. His neighborhood lacked most services in those days. Nizambhai and some of his neighbors, he recalls, were instrumental in assembling some of the infrastructures: an access road, electricity lines, bus routes, and so on. A few years later, he left his job as a private security guard and began working with a local NGO that had recently set up an office in the locality. As months passed by, Nizambhai grew frustrated with the NGO's ethical stance, which prohibited interventions outside the fields of health and education. He began organizing informal waste pickers and textile workers in his free time. Eventually, he quit the NGO and started his own NGO with a few friends, most of whom earned their incomes by renting the additional floors of their housing units.

For the first project, they planned to obtain an SSP contract and continue working in Toba Tek Nagar. They thus applied for a contract to implement the community awareness and community organization component of the program. The NGO was awarded the contract, but unfortunately, they were assigned to work in slum localities in other parts of the city. Despite the disappointment, Nizambhai and his friends went on to work in these localities and built relationships with municipal officials, local politicians, contractors, and local leaders. A few months later, drawing on the relationships with municipal bureaucrats and contractors he had built through the SSP, he managed to divert funds from a failed SSP project to build a 24-seat toilet in a post-2000 neighborhood in Toba Tek Nagar that lacked any toilet facilities. On its completion, the toilet was handed over to Nizambhai's NGO for operation and maintenance on a five-year lease. This arrangement occurred outside the ambit of the SSP but Nizambhai operated it as per the SSP rules. This replication of SSP rules in a non-SSP toilet wasn't peculiar to his toilet. A number of toilets built under the older sanitation model were being maintained and financed by communities using the SSP model. A few months later, the SSP contract awarded to his organization came to an end and Nizambhai stopped being actively involved in it due to ill-health. The lack of leadership led to the organization becoming inactive soon after. However, Nizambhai continued to operate the toilet as per SSP rules and collect dues from its users.

A few years later, the NGO that was eventually awarded the contract to build an SSP toilet in the neighborhood where Nizambhai's toilet was located, approached him. They wanted to demolish his toilet and rebuild a bigger, forty-seat SSP toilet in its place. The NGO, like most involved in the SSP, ran a private for-profit construction company that had been awarded the contract to construct SSP toilets. Both the NGO and its associated construction company had much to gain from demolishing and rebuilding the toilet in the form of international development funds and contract awards. After a few informal exchanges, a face-to-face meeting was organized at the local youth center between the NGO, the contractor, and Nizambhai. After some initial disagreement, Nizambhai, who was in need of money due to ill-health, agreed to sell the toilet for a price that included its cost of construction and his expected income over the next three years. When I ended my fieldwork, the NGO and its construction company were deliberating how much they would gain and lose in the deal.

A Toilet Lesson

Seeing Mehmoodbhai's SSP toilet, Kasim, a youth group leader from the adjacent neighborhood, decided to initiate a similar toilet project in his own neighborhood. With the help of Abdulbhai,[7] previously a tout and now Kasim's mentor in reclaiming land, a piece of land was identified. Over the next few months, all the required paperwork for the land and the project was acquired from the municipality. The process of excavating land began a few days later. But the older residents of the neighborhood stopped the excavation and opposed the project the very next day. They claimed the land was theirs. The matter was taken to the community hall. To make the discussion peaceful, the Quran was placed at the head of the community hall and *maulvis* (Muslim religious scholars) were invited to give their blessings. The local politician, municipal officials, and NGOs were all kept out of the meeting to avoid external interests influencing the discussion and to conceal the internal dynamics between the inside and outside actors. The discussion at the meeting was peaceful, but the participants never arrived at an agreement. That night, a set of anonymous people attacked Kasim at his house. As violence ensued, tensions rose in the community.

The next day, an ad hoc discussion began in a neighborhood street where all the men involved had assembled. Both sides had already called upon their henchmen in the political party offices, who in turn contacted their acquaintances in the police, to stay alert. No one took responsibility for the attack openly. The discussion on the street was a way of figuring that out. Abdulbhai had arrived to support Kasim and make sure the argument didn't turn violent. The discussion went on for a few hours, and individuals began leaving the scene intermittently. With the departure of each individual, the discussion would change to evaluate the stakes of the person who had just left. The sides somehow dissolved into a series of individual actors, each trying to read the scenario and speak accordingly. This went on until Kasim and Abdulbhai were the only ones left. Their conversation turned into a dialogue about the ownership of land in Toba Tek Nagar. As per the municipal records, the land belonged to the district collector from whom the municipality had leased it on a fifteen-year basis to rehabilitate the pre-1995 slum residents. But locally, the older migrants were claiming a stake in the land. To recap, Toba Tek Nagar was built on marsh. There was no land until the touts and politicians reclaimed the marsh with debris and sold the reclaimed land as small parcels to existing residents. During this reclamation process, the touts had also reclaimed a bridge that connected the neighborhood to the main road across a *nallah* (small stream). The toilet project was located at one end of this reclaimed bridge. The older residents and the kin of those who were involved in reclaiming that piece of land were now claiming a stake in it. They wanted half the land to build housing units and sell them. The matter couldn't go to the local politician in power because he had struck a deal with the older residents for a share in those houses. The *Maulvis* couldn't be called upon to intervene because they had a deal with the politician for building a new mosque in the area, a part of which would be converted into housing units and sold off by the politician. Religion, land, and money, Abdulbhai and his friends argued that evening at the Human Rights Commission Office, have become so intertwined in the city that it's difficult to differentiate touts from religious leaders, Hindus and Muslims alike. They were referring not just to the toilet dispute but also to the land behind Abdulbhai's home, which was being physically fought over by the Naga Sadhus from Uttar Pradesh and disciples of a demi-god (Asaram Bapu).

The attack that night had shaken Kasim, but the visible support from Abdulbhai had put the older residents on a back seat. As tensions rose, the toilet project was stalled. It was a moment where the conditions of development had been rear-ranged, but not necessarily for the better. The situation had reached a standoff, where any move from any of the participants would turn the situation violent. A few weeks later, gossip began circulating in Toba Tek Nagar that news of the violence over the toilet land had reached the municipal office. The ward officer would soon send a team to verify everyone's paperwork so as to distinguish legal from illegal occupations. The fetish of land and money, Abdulbhai and his friends argued, has taken over everyone and may lead to demolitions.

The Developmental World of Slum Sanitation Program

Since its inception, there have been polar responses to the different components of the SSP, including the program's broader framework, its political form, and its implementation. R.N. Sharma and Amita Bhide, who were involved in the prepa-ration of its "Monitoring and Evaluation Report," highlight some critical issues regarding the SSP's "participatory approach" (2005). The latter was enforced by the World Bank on to the municipality to put a check on the corrupt, inefficient, nonaccountable, and manipulative state machinery. This insistence, they sug-gest, resulted in the municipality being pressured to create a space for NGOs by forgoing significant rules of tendering and implementing the program. Despite these changes, most NGOs lacked the required resources, skills, and ground pres-ence, which led to a single Giant NGO (GINGO) with considerable presence in Mumbai's slum localities monopolizing the program in its second phase. The GINGO became the "super contractor" that had direct access to higher bureau-crats, politicians, and actors in the international donor agencies, and could change the terms of the program to fit its needs and capacities. At the locality level, the authors write, the municipality and the NGOs were ill-equipped to mobilize a "community" across internal divisions based on religion and caste. And rather than work with the conflicts, the NGOs often bypassed the mobilization and participation stage by working with already active CBOs, individuals, or local politicians. This led to the further exclusion of already excluded slum residents, and in some cases reproduced the older patronage system between residents and politicians.

Other scholars writing on the SSP have pointed out a range of other issues, including the siphoning of money by different actors (contractors, NGOs, poli-ticians, CBOs), a lack of accountability between residents and NGOs, the pri-vatization of SSP toilet blocks by CBOs with a close relationship to NGOs or local politicians, the replacement of a state body by a GINGO, and use of fraudulent ways to bypass monitoring and evaluation process, among others.[8] Colin McFarlane's recent scholarship on informal sanitation in slum localities of Mumbai expands these critiques (2008a, b, 2012; McFarlane, Desai and Graham 2014). Based on ethnographic research, he argues that the techniques (approaches and practices) and models (representations and formal arrangements) employed by programs such as the SSP are instrumental to creating neoliberal subjectivities by devolving state responsibilities onto slum residents and encouraging urban entrepreneurialism (2008b and 2012). "The privileging of partnership, participation, empowerment and cost-recovery that promotes the thrift of the few over the implied passivity of the many, generates new forms of marketization and values particular forms of disciplined subject (2008: 2801)." This is facilitated by the shared ideological interests among international funding agencies such as IMF and the World Bank, specific civil society groups, corporate groups, and entrepreneurial slum residents. The convergence of ideological interests through networks between actors produces, McFarlane argues, what James Ferguson and Akhil Gupta (2002) have called "transnational governmentality" (ibid.: 2807–808). McFarlane's broader argument is that these dominant actors see urban informality as a form of social and economic capital, and poverty and sanitation as potential sites for entrepreneurialism. Despite these problems, the World Bank has continued the program by forgoing some of its core principles and influencing key changes in slum-related policies. One of these significant changes was the Maharashtra state government's decision to stop all other forms of toilet provision systems to make SSP as the only possible way of accessing toilet blocks in slums. The decision was made under pressure from the World Bank, influential NGOs, and higher-level bureaucrats.

Another response to the SSP model has been its celebration as a democratic model. Arjun Appadurai's essay on Alliance, a GINGO in Mumbai that is composed of three affiliated organizations, has been influential in this regard (2000a). In a context characterized by the failures of big plans to provide a voice to the urban poor or address their issues,[9] the political form, techniques, networks, and vocabulary of grassroots organization (described above), he argues, constitute "deep democracy," "globalization from below," and "counter governmentality."[10] In his account, some of the problems identified by the above scholars are overturned to connote the agency of NGOs to create a space within the state, form alliances with higher-level actors in the developmental world, implement programs in a participatory manner, hold a neutral position towards the religious ideologies of political parties, and use the governmental tools of the state at the grassroots level to hold the state accountable. A good example of this upturning is the establishment of networks between different organizations from local to global scale. While in the earlier scholarly approach, this convergence is identified as a conduit for neoliberal transnational governmentality, for Appadurai, it highlights a democratic convergence of vertical collaborations (local and national) and horizontal learning (global) (ibid.: 17–18).

Deceptive Operations

My attempt in this chapter, and in relation to this debate, however, is neither to affirm the critiques or successes nor to identify a new category of subjectification. Besides, I am not really sure where the toilet operators like Mehmoodbhai, Nizambhai, and Kasim, and their toilet models fit within these critiques and categories.[11] Nor am I sure of the veracity of the stories they narrated to me, since most stories about the latest deals and alliances circulating in Toba Tek Nagar are always in question. However, what these stories and toilets draw attention to is deception itself as a mode of operating in the city. I dwell on these toilet stories with some elusive "thickness" not because they are unusual or unique or betwixt or deviations but because they are ordinary and exemplify how most urban forms in the city get built. In that sense, they are rather extraordinary in their ordinariness. They demonstrate how the SSP program has been imitated differently in each scenario, how it has taken on new lives, and how these toilets, like many others, don't necessarily fit clearly into the discursive models of neoliberalism, entrepreneurialism, or grassroots democracy, despite emerging from them. In that sense, these operators and their toilets are "deceptions"—that is, they deceive our analytical frameworks and the critiques and categories which these frameworks assign to them. They demonstrate how urban residents often deceive the proper roles and identities appointed to them, and how urban residents, like tricksters, use each other in deceptive ways to try out different roles and positions in order to create spaces in the city for themselves and for others to make moves. Thus, rather than check the veracity of stories or recategorize subjects and models according to discursive frameworks, I feel a more productive path would be to look at the amount of attention the urban residents pay to the policies, discourses, deals, and stories circulating in the city, and what they do with it. In other words, to look at deception itself as a heuristic device for knowing the city; as a form of performative operation through which urban residents partake in order to play the game of urbanization; and as an invitation to palpate what possibilities deceptions generate in cities (Goldberg 2012). This involves, as Judith Butler notes, paying attention to how the subject performs the discourse, rather than being a preformed by it (1990). And to do this requires seeing things as situated and in-process, and paying attention to the many mimetic circuits through which discourses are formed and performed.

Partitions, Identities, and Aliens

Toba Tek Nagar, where these toilets are located, is a constellation of individuals and objects, which do not necessarily belong together as some form of an ideal "community." Nizambhai is one of its older residents. He migrated to Mumbai (then Bombay) in the 1950s. The city then was an industrial center. Like many other older residents of his neighborhood, he migrated from rural parts of West India to slums around the textile industries in South Bombay (Byculla, Parel, Worli, and Sion, among others) in search of work (Interviews 2013). These residents were relocated to Toba Tek Nagar in 1976. It was the year when the first census of slums was conducted and those found eligible were given a photo pass and an alternative site for rehabilitation in the city's peripheries. The relocation of Nizambhai and the other residents was part of a sustained and disciplined move to control the growth of slum localities in prime areas of the city by moving them to peripheral lands. They were brought in trucks en masse onto the marsh of Toba Tek Nagar and asked to rebuild their houses on ten-by-fifteen-meter plots of a sites-and-services scheme. The smaller blocks within these neighborhoods were divided and named after the older areas from where they were relocated. In a few years, the locality expanded around this sites-and-services scheme. Twelve new neighborhoods were created by newer migrants using the infrastructures set up for the sites-and-services scheme while simultaneously developing their own infrastructure through various means. While the new residents migrated from rural areas in search of work or to get away from crises in their villages,[12] the older urban residents of the city moved to Toba Tek Nagar to break away from joint families or due to demolitions. Mehmoodbhai had migrated to Byculla (in South Bombay) from Muzaffarnagar, UP, in the 1950s. In the 1970s, he moved to Toba Tek Nagar due to demolitions. He, like with many others, bought a small plot of land from touts, who in partnership with local politicians had reclaimed marsh with urban debris.

The 1970s was a peculiar time for the city. Textile industries across the world had begun using better manufacturing technology and producing cheaper textiles. Unable to compete with cheaper manufacturing costs, the industries in Bombay began fragmenting into smaller units and moving out to the city's peripheries. This flight and fragmentation of industries triggered a number of shifts: the dispersal of the working class and their unions; a rise of service and finance industries with high-skilled jobs; the rise in real-estate markets, and so on.[13] During the same time, the discontent over food shortages, rising prices, growing income disparities, and asset disparities between regions translated into state and industrial workers' strikes as well as protests across India (Lele 1996). Caught in a force field of migration, inflating real-estate prices, a growing civil society of upper-middle-class people and multinationals, and newer non-regulated economies, the urban space became a contested realm for territorialization by different actors.

One of these many actors was Shiv Sena, a populist nativist political group in Mumbai. It established its dominance over the city by deflecting the attention of the masses away from the consequences of unchecked capitalist development in industry and the state-assisted distortions of land, housing, and jobs to regional politics (ibid.: 190).[14] This involved identifying itself as a group of Marathi-speaking "sons-of-the soil" as opposed to the city's "outsider" or "traitors"—the South Indians, the Communists, and the Muslims (Hansen 2001: 49–68). On the one hand, the Shiv Sena sutured "a specific form of regional chauvinism with a message about Hindu power through the deployment of the figure of the Muslim as the archetype of the invader, the stranger, the traitor"—an alien other (Appadurai 2000b: 646); and on the other hand, it forged complex links and collaborations with three groups: the cleaner capitalists (big and small industrialists and service and film industry magnates), the under-sided chaotic capitalists (builders, import-exporters, smugglers, bootleggers), and underemployed and unemployed youth (Lele 1996: 199). In his work on urban violence in Mumbai, Thomas Blom Hansen theorizes Shiv Sena as an expression of "vernacular modernity" (2001). Through hyper-masculine gestures, everyday practices of matriarchal patronage, and assertion of plebeian identities, Shiv Sena has been able to fashion a new mode of urban politics in Mumbai (Bedi 2007; Hansen 2001). Its alliance with the Bharatiya Janata Party (BJP) in 1984 publicly pronounced its turn towards *Hindutva* and Hindu nationalism. These territorial assertions of identity and politics were consolidated into a spectacle of violence in 1993—the Hindu–Muslim riots in Bombay. The 1993 riots, for Appadurai,

> marked a conjuncture between the violent efforts to create Hindu public spheres and spaces, to depopulate Muslim flats and neighborhoods, to destroy Muslim bodies and properties, and an ongoing form of civic violence directed against Mumbai's slums and street dwellers.

As Appadurai describes the riots, "Muslims were cornered in slums and middle-class areas. With lists of names in the hands of organized mobs Muslim businesses and properties were relentlessly put to the torch" (2000b: 648).

Toba Tek Nagar was one of the many localities where the 1993 Hindu–Muslim riots unfolded violently. It was the second in a series of religious riots and left its mark on the neighborhood. During and after the riots, most non-Muslim residents left the locality to return to their villages or moved to non-Muslim-dominated slums. These outwards movements made the locality a Muslim-dominated locality. This change in demographics raised concerns among other non-Muslim groups, redrawing new lines of fear, abjection, and identity with respect to Muslims. It is not an uncanny coincidence that in a city being territorialized by nativist myths of "sons of the soil," a local Muslim poet at an event in Toba Tek Nagar incites his audience to carry the "burden of the soil" to address Muslim minoratization.

> Why do you walk with your head up in pride, when the reality lies down there in the soil? The Muslim head is not to raise, but to carry the burden of this soil. It is in this soil that the flowers bloom.

Pointing to the Khilafat Movement as the flowers of past Muslim leaders on Indian soil enjoyed by present-day Muslims, the poet enjoins his audience to follow in their footsteps and continue that work for future generations.[15] Situated in a city where Muslims are being continually alienated as outsiders, traitors, and abject citizens, such self-reflective discussions on Muslim ethics and locating and identifying oneself within the larger schema of religious territorialization have attained an everydayness in Toba Tek Nagar.

If the 1993 riots marked a conjuncture of ethnic urban cleansing, post-riot slums became vulnerable to the assertions of the market and its violence. The liberalization of state policies shifted the state's role from provider of public necessities to facilitator by the early 1990s. This shift resulted in the adoption of market-based mechanisms to provide mass housing in Mumbai. The city's slum policies followed the same route soon after. In 1995, Shiv Sena formulated the populist Slum Redevelopment Scheme to address its own unpopularity in electoral politics. It instituted an in situ free-housing program, where the cost of rehousing slums would be cross-subsidized through private-sector development and controlled through land regulation policies. This meant that private developers could redevelop slums that had been established prior to 1995 and recover their cost by building an equal amount of floor space in situ and selling it on the market for profit, or could carry the floor space to more profitable parts of the city in the form of Transferable Development Rights. This change occurred concurrently with the decentralization and devolution of governance to the local level and resulted in the increased participation of local and international NGOs in the implementation of developmental programs in Mumbai. In an island city with limited land resources, slum-occupied lands became one of the biggest sources of profit for developers.

This exposure of slum localities to market mechanisms provided the means to alienate them and reify them into land parcels with a developmental value. This history, as a housing right activist narrated to me, has resulted in a threefold alienation[16] of slums: first, the alienation of slum residents from their life-work, memories, and desires that are embedded in the locality; second, the alienation of residents from the physiognomic experience of heat, rain, and social life in the new high-rises where they are rehabilitated; and third, the estrangement of Muslims in slums through their identification as traitors and abject citizens. It is this movement in the city's history that connects Hansen's conception of Shiv Sena as an expression of "vernacular modernity"; Appadurai's elaborations on "urban cleansing" and the growing liberalization of the housing and land markets since the riots; and Lele's argument that the project of *Hindutva* under Shiv Sena has been to homogenize and proliferate predatory capitalism in spaces that were previously occupied by "others." With the convergence of capitalism and fascism, experience, as Benjamin predicted, has fallen in value. Lived experience, the raw material necessary for engaging in a mimetic play of telling tales, stories, and proverbs to hand down wisdom across generations, has lost its value today—we have been impoverished. It is no surprise, then, that the film begins with Charlie, the film character, repeating a saying passed on by his father on his death bed: *"Beta Charlie, life badi kutti cheez hai, aur is duniya mein kutton ka sirf ek hi jawab hai—KAMINEY."* "Life here is a bitch. And the only answer to dogs of this world is a Scoundrel."

Making Models Citable in Deceptions

This detour through the turns and twists in the city's plot as well as other stories and figures was to situate Mehmoodbhai, Nizambhai, and their toilets at the intersection of different movements in the city's history: movements of finance, spectral real-estate inflation, religious territorialization, state privatization, nation building, urban alienation, and the dominant discourses circulating in the city. Here, the aesthetic experience of beauty and pleasure is an exclusive one. One simply needs to look at the real-estate advertisements in public spheres. They speak of the beauty of green nature; of the panoramic view; of leisure and silence, where music can be enjoyed in privacy; of the shiny vitrified tiles and the German-manufactured taps and flushes that require only the slightest movement of a finger. This whole aesthetic experience of technology, beauty, and pleasure, as well as their social meanings, is partitioned, despite being identified as "World-Class" (Ghertner 2015). Such partitioned urban imaginaries are increasingly enmeshed in the territorial urban politics and ideologies of *Hindutva* today. As the work of numerous scholars over the past decade shows, Muslim slum localities across Indian cities are being exiled from both material forms of infrastructure connections and new urban imaginations through inscriptions and performances (Jaffrelot and Gayer ed. 2012; Chatterjee 2011).[17]

Another significant aspect is the toilet's historical relationship to colonialism. Toilets, hygiene, and proper control of bodily excesses were intimately tied to the colonial narrative of development and progress through colonial rule (Anderson 1995; Horan 1997). In Mumbai specifically, toilets are located at the juncture of three historical phenomena. First, sanitation and public health as the basis for segregating the city between the colonized and colonizer, as well as the justification for carrying out paternalistic and violent urban renewal programs (Kidambi 2007). Second, as Nikhil Rao's historical account tells us, "private toilets" first entered colonial Bombay with the emergence of "self-contained" apartment units in suburbs and became integral to the creation of class and caste identities by the native urban middle-class (2013: 98–107). The inclusion of the toilet within the home established the "self-contained" flat as the symbol of modernity, middle-classness, and upper-casteness. And the third phenomenon is the synthesis of the earlier two, where the lack of toilets, hygiene, and open defecation in slum localities have become a justification for their inhabitability and their erasure in the World-Class city, while the "self-contained" flats in "pigeon-holed" high-rises have become the ideal housing typology for the slum rehabilitation projects.[18]

The toilets and their operators, discussed earlier, stand at this political and historical intersection of urban politics and aesthetic impossibility—the impossibility of creating and experiencing beauty and pleasure in slum localities, undoing the abjection by making one's locality beautiful, and the alienation of Muslim residents from urban imaginaries. To draw on the poet's provocation: How does one then make flowers bloom in the soil without othering or self-identification, as well as without an origin, an end, or a partition? This impossibility, I argue, breaks down when slum residents such as Mehmoodbhai, Nizambhai, and Kasim make the choice to go deeper into the plot, to deceive the "community" and build a common toilet. In building the toilet, the operators mimic, on the one hand, the shiny tiles, the music, the beauty, and pleasure, and on the other, the politics of the developmental world, where NGOs and their sister construction companies look for ways to route international and governmental funds through their own toilet projects. Here, mimetic play connotes not the bourgeois duplications such as the "Singaporisation" of Indian cities, but a performative operation guided by the individual's exact fantasy and the reality of the SSP's developmental world. Thus, the toilet operators do not just mime the World-Class city aesthetics (Ghertner 2015) but also deceive its aesthetic order by creating them in spaces where they aren't supposed to be—in toilets in slum localities. On the other hand, these operators also mime the discourses and practices of the SSP and play the roles assigned to them in order to learn how to navigate their way through the developmental world and

Figure 3.3 Beauty 2 (At Mumbai Real Estate Expo 2014)

its twists and turns. This navigation involves moving between multiple worlds—oneself, one's locality, the city's identity politics, and the developmental world of financial and political transactions, and trying on different roles and different routes, but never belonging to any completely—always deceiving each of them. This staying in contact with, and at the same time moving between different worlds, without allowing either to take over, is what I take Adorno to be arguing in his elaboration of the relationship between exact fantasy and mimesis (Buck-Morss 1977: 186). Thus, the mimicking subject moves back and forth between different worlds—one's fantasy and the phenomenon. And in this movement, the elements are not merely duplicated or reproduced but deceived in their mimetic rearrangement to reveal the truth—the truth being the ability to deceive the original by reproducing them as different iterations. Furthermore, this movement is manifested in the creation of a new space—a toilet—that is not an ideal "community toilet" in the sense intended by the SSP based on ideas of inclusion and sense of ownership, nor is it based on the ideals of neoliberal thrift, as seen in the excessiveness of the built form and its sonic aspirations. Yet, it's neither a toilet based on notions of equality and collectivity nor a subaltern resistance. Instead, they are deceptions that continuously deceive the categories, identities, roles, and models that analytical frameworks usually assign to them. But what possibilities do such deceptive operations and of the figures (tricksters, scoundrels, and *kaminey*) gesture towards?

On Urban Deceptions

In their essay "Urban Charisma," Thomas Blom Hansen and Oskar Verkaaik theorize such figures as a locus of "infra-power" (2009: 20–23). These figures take on different avatars. They can be figures who are mediators, charismatic diviners, and competent translators, such as hustlers and tricksters as well as historical myths and narratives. By "infra-power," the authors refer to a web of connections and structures that traverse neighborhoods and communities and facilitate economic and political exchanges in cities marked by radical discrepancies and disconnections. These connections are unpredictable, unlikely, and improbable. They are neither fully visible to the outside gaze nor officially codified, but also neither concealed nor secret. Furthermore, Hansen and Verkaaik propose two ways of understanding infra-power: potentiality and emergence. The earlier refers to infra-power as the enactment of one's potentiality to "read, master and 'work' the city to make it yield benefits, magical power and eros, if one runs the risks and has the courage to 'play'—the central trope in urban politics, exchange and pleasure" (ibid.: 22). The latter, emergence, refers to infra-power as a form of power that is unstable and unpredictable and becomes visible only through performative action and exchange. This play of visibility and invisibility, of keeping secrets and secreting information, of becoming a sovereign in the slippages of sovereignty, and of putting on different faces at different times is at the heart of deception and deceptive performances, which often remains undiscerned in cities.

David Theo Goldberg, in "Epistemologies of Deception," asks us to attend to deception as a heuristic and epistemological device (2012). The latter, he writes, is a way of knowing things at an angle, in and through denials and misdirections; seeing not just behind and beneath those older structural models but as a way around the analytic and conceptual inadequacies of the critical terms currently available to us. In his study of three urban development cases in and around Lebanon, Goldberg demonstrates how deception points to not just the generalizability of precarity but also the proliferation of precarious possibilities and anachronistic and catachrestic urban forms in a "neo-con-liberal" context (ibid.). Written with a similar vibe is the collection of texts, conversations, short stories, and diary entries titled, *Trickster City* (Tabassum et.al. 2010). In this book, the city of Delhi emerges as this space of violent urban demolitions and state power, within which a range of multi-faced and multifaceted *behrupiyas* engage in a fragile play of love and care with others, of experiencing the pain and beauty of uncertainty, and of enacting and performing trickery. Here, the *behrupiya* takes on a ludic multi-face, with one that looking at the life in the settlement that has passed by, one looking at the movements in the city and making its moves, another one anticipating a life that is not here, and many more.

Similar to the tricksters, the *bahurupi,* the Raqs Media Collective write,

> "is a person of many guises, a polymorph, a shape-shifter, a fantastic masqureder and pantomime … (They) make their living by masquerade, by the performance of different roles by iterant practitioners, for the entertainment, edification and occasionally, defrauding the general public. They might dress up one day as god, another day as a monkey, and a third day as a comical police constable—and expect to earn money by merely turning up at doorsteps, or hanging around.
>
> (2010: 74–75)

For the Collective, the *baharupi* is an "exemplar for a kind of performative agency" and a strategic method to meet the intensification of security and scrutiny of power with guises, guile, and multiple expressions of the self (76). Disguise and deception, the Collective notes, is a means to travel to a "liminal zone where roles can be rehearsed, different patois perfected, the various grades of personhood can be tried on for size (…)" [75; also see Abbas, 2008]. In cities, Simone notes along similar lines, where there is a compulsion to "fix" things—that is, to see the city as something to be fixed through interventions and regulations, as well as where things already seem "fixed in advance," deception entails trying out

> various tactics of hedging and arbitrage by the majority of people—of playing with and against the differences of possible outcomes, of showing various faces and facets of oneself to different audiences on different occasions, in order to construct some sense of movement without making it visible
>
> (2014: 129).

Waiting rooms everywhere, write Raqs Media Collective, "are full of impostors trying out different acts in order to pass through the intense scrutinies in order to arrive at the stage of history" (2010: 76). However, deception, they further note, is double-edged. It is also an accusation; one that power often filings at anyone it chooses to place under scrutiny and to certify its own authenticity. So, one could read the toilet as an ideological object, a spectacle of shiny things, a deceiving of the community, or a realization of a neoliberal regime that transfers state responsibility onto the community and creates state subjects (McFarlane 2012: 2802–807). But to read the toilet projects and the toilet operators in such a way is to fall, on the one hand, into the undialectical teleology of enlightenment, where things and beings are essentialized into abstract categories, and on the other, into the space of the sovereign, where the city idealized as a "community" is always founded on an alien outsider—the migrant, the Muslim, the slum dweller. Sovereignty, as Simone suggests, is "a means of completion, of finishing the identity of territories and subjects ... and converting them into an immutable reference" (Simone, 2012: 363). A city, however, is not the sovereign, rather a ruse that is given a form of "the city" to identify it as such and to make things work. But this form is also being cited, worked upon, and played with, by urban residents in indiscernible ways. A city, in that sense, is an accretion of deceptive operations that appears to be spatially fixed in its appearance and form but is always moving towards somewhere else.

A deceptive city, like Calvino's larcenous city, demands a different mode of inhabitation—one that requires paying attention to the elusive thick details of deals and stories; to the movement of others across different worlds and roles, despite being localized; an indifference to morality and judgments; and above all, averting forms of foreclosures so that life can take on other forms. In my observations during the fieldwork, Mehmoodbhai's fellow residents or other toilet operators never refused to seek his assistance or collaborate with him, despite knowing his deceptive nature. Likewise, the fellow resident Siraj's identification of Mehmoodbhai's toilet as "our toilet" at the beginning of the chapter points to a continual claim that leaves the toilet's ownership open-ended. Here, the desire for identification, for empathy, and the rush to judgments are interrupted to keep things in play. Thus, urban residents don't attempt to fix the city or each other so as to make things work but play each other and play at being others so that things and the self can take on other forms. In doing so, deceptive operations render the attempts to model and identify in cities as inoperative, while gesturing towards the possibility of citing models and identities infinitely in deceptive ways. In this deceptive city, residents such as Mehoodbhai, Nizambhai, and Kasim play different parts and roles. They inhabit cities as the spider-spirits who spin webs, circulate stories, pass on intelligence in dire situations, create objects by stealing from others, and disturb boundaries of communities that otherwise seem immutable. And while the SSP and the toilet offered them a medium to insert themselves into the game of urbanization, the other residents of Toba Tek Nagar spend a lot of time waiting, observing, and paying attention to thick details, despite their elusiveness, so as to make their move. But this is not to say that deceptions always work or succeed. As the many stories of Anansi, and the story of Kasim (above), show, the spider-spirit also often fail or make a fool of themselves. But there are

Figure 3.4 Deception

lessons there too: "Forgive the trickster and the tribe will be happy. Kill the trickster and the tribe will be ruined" (Hecht and Simone, 1995: 79).

Notes

1 *Kaminey*, directed by Vishal Bhardwaj (2009). For lack of a better translation of the word *Kamina* or *Kaminey*, I use the word scoundrel. However, as I argue in this chapter, the figure of the *Kamina* is a strange mixture of trickster and scoundrel.
2 The movie never specifies which part of Africa.
3 A survey conducted in 2001 found that 63 percent of the city's informal population or 3.92 million people were dependent exclusively on public toilets for their sanitation needs. The average ratio of persons per toilet seat in informal settlements was 81:1 often resulting in queues lasting two hours or more (MW-YUVA 2001: 4; cited in McFarlane 2008: 90).
4 The original plan was to get consensus from at least 75 percent of the residents, which was then scaled back to 50 percent. See Sharma and Bhide 2005: 1784–89.
5 For a more detailed ethnographic study of how the politics of water connections get mitigated in Mumbai's slum localities, see Björkman 2015: 497–517.
6 During interviews, a number of members of CBOs spoke of lack of cooperation as well as resistance from local politicians and thugs to the building of a new SSP toilet. The reason for this is that the project bypassed their involvement in the projects.
7 We met him before in the first chapter.
8 These reflections are based on conversations with different scholars and researchers that were involved in funded evaluations of the SSP in 2004–2005. They are also based on my participation as an undergraduate researcher in some of these evaluations. One of the fraudulent ways in which the NGOs were known to cheat donor agency evaluations was by introducing the evaluators to the same set of slum residents, who also worked for the NGO, in different localities. Further, a number of toilet blocks that were built in the earlier phases of SSP now lie defunct. In some cases, the monetary contributions made by the local residents never concretized into a toilet block.
9 Appadurai locates his essay in a context characterized by three shifts: first, the exhaustion of Marxist vision to produce change; second, the failure of the modernization and development paradigm to address questions of poverty; and third, the constitution of a networked globalized economy, in which world cities increasingly operate independently of national and regional mediation, while poorer cities and populations seek ways of claiming space and voice.
10 See Roy (2009) for critique for Appadurai's notion of governmentality from below.
11 Most actors I interviewed for this research, such as the municipal officials, NGO workers, slum residents, and CBO members, were well conscious of the issues with SSP I have listed earlier. For them research inevitably involved gathering information to critique NGOs and the municipality. Such reactions from these actors forced me to rethink the argument of this chapter in terms of moving away from problems or celebrations of SSP and focusing on figures and forms of politics that lie between and dis-identify with any neat categories.
12 The migrant groups who moved into Shivaji Nagar and its adjacent localities included Dalits who moved from different parts of Maharashtra, Muslims from UP, and Konkani-Muslims and Christians from Konkan region along the West Coast. The Dalits moved to the city for different reasons. Some moved due to drought in their villages while the others moved to get away from caste discrimination (Interviews 2013).
13 There are many writings on this history of the city. See Patel and Thorner eds. (1996); Appadurai (2000); Hansen (2001); Patel and Masselos eds. (2003).

14 Jayant Lele's account is one of the more revealing narratives of Shiv Sena. He sketches the relationship between the rise of Shiv Sena in the urban space, Bombay's changing electoral politics, and the rise of capitalism. Such a narrative is often left out in other accounts that focus on Shiv Sena's regionalist politics and its religion-based violence. Shiv Sena played an important role in breaking down the lower-caste and class-based industrial workers' struggle as well as the communist movements in Bombay.

15 For an interview-based account of postriot migration in Mumbai, see Punwani (2003: 235–65).

16 I use the word *alienation* not in the sense of alienation from human nature but as a partition, separation, and process of making one a stranger in one's own place of belonging.

17 Nikhil Anand's recent work on municipal water connections shows how Muslim slums in Mumbai have become "abject spaces" within the life of city, where not just their classification as slums but as "Muslim Slums" has led to their disconnect from municipal water supply by the lower-level municipal workers (2012).

18 Rao argues that the aspiration for a "self-contained flat" often leaves residents with less space than they previously had in the slum localities.

References

Abbas, Ackbar. 2008. "Faking Globalization." In *Other Cities, Other Worlds*, edited by Andreas Huyssen, 243–64. Durhman, NC: Duke University Press.

Anand, Nikhil. 2012. "Municipal Disconnect: On Abject Water and Its Urban Infrastructures." *Ethnography* 13 (4): 487–509.

Anderson, Warwick. 1995. "Excremental Colonialism: Public Health and the Poetics of Pollution." *Critical Inquiry* 21 (3): 640–69.

Appadurai, Arjun. 2000a. "Grassroots Globalization and the Research Imagination." *Public Culture* 12 (1): 1–19.

———. 2000b. "Spectral Housing and Urban Cleansing: Notes on Millennial Mumbai." *Public Culture* 12 (3): 627–51.

Bedi, Tarini. 2007. "The Dashing Ladies of the Shiv Sena." *Economic & Political Weekly* 42 (17): 1534–41.

Benjamin, Walter. 1978[1921]. "Fate and Character." In *Reflections: Essays, Aphorisms, Autobiographical Writing*, edited by Peter Demetz, translated by Edmund Jephcott, 304–11. New York, NY: Schocken Books.

Benjamin, Walter, and Asja Lacis. 1978. "Naples." In *Reflections: Essays, Aphorisms, Autobiographical Writing*, edited by Peter Demetz, translated by Edmund Jephcott, 163–75. New York, NY: Schocken Books.

Bhardwaj, Vishal. 2009. *Kaminey*. UTV Motion Pictures.

Björkman, Lisa. 2015. *Pipe Politics, Contested Waters: Embedded Infrastructures of Millennial Mumbai*. Durhman, NC: Duke University Press.

Buck-Morss, Susan. 1977. *The Origin of Negative Dialectics: Theodor W. Adorno, Walter Benjamin and the Frankfurt Institute*. New York, NY: Free Press.

Butler, Judith. 1990. *Gender Trouble: Feminism and the Subversion of Identity*. London, UK: Routledge.

Calvino, Italo. 1995. "The Black Sheep." In *Numbers in the Dark: And Other Stories*, translated by Tim Parks, 93–95. New York, NY: Houghton Mifflin Harcourt.

Chatterjee, Ipsita. 2011. "Governance as 'Performed', Governance as 'Inscribed' New Urban Politics in Ahmedabad." *Urban Studies* 48 (12): 2571–90.

Fagan, Kristina. 2010. "What's the Trouble with the Trickster?: An Introduction." In *Troubling Tricksters: Revisioning Critical Conversations*, edited by Deanna Reder and Linda M. Morra, 3–20. Wateloo, ON: Wilfrid Laurier University Press.

Ghertner, D. Asher. 2015. *Rule by Aesthetics: World-Class City Making in Delhi*. New York, NY: Oxford University Press.

Goldberg, David Theo. 2012. "Epistemologies of Deception: Topologies of the Extra/Ordinary." *The Johannesburg Salon* 5: 51–62.

Gupta, Akhil, and James Ferguson. 2002. "Spatializing States: Toward an Ethnography of Neoliberal Governmentality." *American Ethnologist* 29 (4): 981–1002.

Hansen, Thomas Blom. 2001. *Wages of Violence: Naming and Identity in Postcolonial Bombay*. Princeton, NJ: Princeton University Press.

Hansen, Thomas Blom, and Oskar Verkaaik. 2009. "Introduction-Urban Charisma: On Everyday Mythologies in the City." *Critique of Anthropology* 29 (1): 5–26.

Hecht, David, and Maliqalim Simone. 1995. *Invisible Governance: The Art of African Micro-Politics*. New York, NY: Autonomedia.

Horan, Julie L. 1997. *The Porcelain God: A Social History of the Toilet. Secaucus.* Secaucus, NJ: Carol Publishing Group.

Jaffrelot, Christophe, and Laurent Gayer, eds. 2012. *Muslims in Indian Cities: Trajectories of Marginalisation*. New York, NY: Columbia University Press.

Kidambi, Prashant. 2007. *The Making of an Indian Metropolis: Colonial Governance and Public Culture in Bombay, 1890–1920*. Hampshire, UK: Ashgate Publishing, Ltd.

Lele, Jayant. 1996. "Saffronization of the Shiv Sena." In *Bombay: Metaphor for Modern India*, edited by Sujata Patel and Alice Thorner, 185–212. New York and Oxford: Oxford University Press.

M'Baye, Babacar. 2010. *The Trickster Comes West: Pan-African Influence in Early Black Diasporan Narratives*. Minneapolis, MN: University of Minnesota Press.

McFarlane, Colin. 2008a. "Governing the Contaminated City: Infrastructure and Sanitation in Colonial and Post-Colonial Bombay." *International Journal of Urban and Regional Research* 32 (2): 415–35.

———. 2008b. "Sanitation in Mumbai's Informal Settlements: State, 'Slum', and Infrastructure." *Environment and Planning A* 40 (1): 88–107.

———. 2012. "The Entrepreneurial Slum: Civil Society, Mobility and the Co-Production of Urban Development." *Urban Studies* 49 (13): 2795–816.

McFarlane, Colin, Renu Desai, and Steve Graham. 2014. "Informal Urban Sanitation: Everyday Life, Poverty, and Comparison." *Annals of the Association of American Geographers* 104 (5): 989–1011.

MW-YUVA. 2001. "*Slum Sanitation Project: Final Report.*" Mumbai: Municipal Corporation of Brihan Mumbai.

Patel, Sujata, and Jim Masselos, eds. 2003. *Bombay and Mumbai: The City in Transition*. Oxford, New York: Oxford University Press.

Patel, Sujata, and Alice Thorner, eds. 1996. *Bombay: Metaphor for Modern India*. New York and Oxford: Oxford University Press.

Punwani, Jyoti. 2003. "My Area, Your Area: How Riots Changed the City." In *Bombay and Mumbai The City in Transition*, edited by Sujata Patel and Jim Masselos, 235–64. Oxford and New York: Oxford University Press.

Rao, Nikhil. 2013. *House, But No Garden: Apartment Living in Bombay's Suburbs, 1898–1964*. Minneapolis, MN: University of Minnesota Press.

Raqs Media Collective. 2010. *Seepage*. Berlin: Sternberg Press.

Roy, Ananya. 2009. "Civic Governmentality: The Politics of Inclusion in Beirut and Mumbai." *Antipode* 41 (1): 159–79.

Sharma, R. N., and Amita Bhide. 2005. "World Bank Funded Slum Sanitation Programme in Mumbai: Participatory Approach and Lessons Learnt." *Economic & Political Weekly* 40 (17): 1784–89.

Simone, AbdouMaliq. 2012. "Ghostly Cracks and Urban Deceptions: Jakarta." In *In The Life of Cities: Parallel Narratives of the Urban*, edited by Mohsen Mostafavi, 121–33. Cambridge and Baden: Harvard Graduate School of Design and Lars Müller Publishers.

Sinclair, Niigonwedom James. 2010. "Trickster Reflections: Part I." In *Troubling Tricksters: Revisioning Critical Conversations*, edited by Deanna Reder and Linda M. Morra, 21–58. Wateloo, ON: Wilfrid Laurier University Press.

Tabassum, Azra et al. 2010. *Trickster City: Writings from the Belly of the Metropolis.* Penguin Books India.

Taussig, Michael. 1993. *Mimesis and Alterity: A Particular History of the Senses.* New York and London: Routledge.

Weber, Samuel. 2008. *Benjamin's-Abilities.* Cambridge, MA: Harvard University Press.

WSP/World Bank. 2005. *TARU and WEDC, Study of the World Bank Financed Slum Sanitation Project in Mumbai (Vols. I, II, and III).* Mumbai: World Bank.

Figure 4.1 Waste and Play

4 On Swelling, Containment, and Recyclability

Cocktail Mix

The City Is Built with Garbage

I had arrived early for my "official" visit to the Denoar landfill. Part of my eagerness was because it had taken four months of bureaucratic back and forth to get official permission and the other part was just a curiosity to see almost a century of the city's waste amassing in one place. As I stood at its entrance waiting, a continuous stream of garbage carriers—dumpers, compactors, tempos, and trucks—made their way to the landfill. They, like ants, carried their daily collection of waste from the city into the garbage hills for disposal. Except, rather than drive in smoothly, they clumsily bounced their way into the landfill. This movement caused some of the garbage to fall off the truck, particularly the lighter materials, like plastic bottles. Children from Toba Tek Nagar were well aware of this. They stood along the street waiting for the recyclables to fall off, which they then collected to sell and earn some cash for the day. The clumsy movement of the garbage carriers was due to the unevenness in the street. In some places, there were potholes, and in other places, the spilled-over waste, left unpicked for years, had become one with the street. This ability of waste to become one with the street was instrumentalized by the colonial state to build the city. The British used debris and waste to reclaim marshes, salt pans, mangroves, creeks, and the sea (Dossal 1991). What was once rendered waste was reemployed to create valuable land for urbanization. Stories of waste are thus integral to stories of a city, and yet, are wasted to keep the discourse of "the city" intact. This last chapter tells one such story of waste and a city.

Waste and Interplay

This chapter attends to urban waste for three reasons. One is its relationship to Toba Tek Nagar and the lives of its residents. As I have mentioned many a times before in passing, Toba Tek Nagar is located on the edge of one of Mumbai's oldest landfill: the Deonar landfill. The latter was established in the early 1900s by the British-run Bombay municipality. Every day, two trains with 25 wagons each would carry the city's refuse to this landfill (Mirza 2019). The decision to build the landfill in the city's periphery was made after much deliberations between the

DOI: 10.4324/9781003051848-6

municipal councilors, the sanitary engineers, the medical officers, and the propertied class who were part of the municipality then. They weighed costs: the costs of having waste carried over a large distance against the costs of continuing to dispose of waste in the heart of the city and its effects on the health and morality of the population. However, the affects of waste on the visual and olfactory senses played an important role too. Particularly, the stench of waste carried by the winds from the sea into the city; the sight of flies, mosquitoes, cows, cesspools, decaying carcasses, mice, silt, night soil all mixing in with each other; and the resultant "miasma" (McFarlane 2008). There was no Toba Tek Nagar back then, just marsh, half land and half water, hidden below mangroves where the creek met the sea. The marsh closer to the land was fertile and was used for farming vegetables. The farming activities continued into the late 1970s, which is when everyone began reclaiming the marsh with urban debris and waste. Everyone reclaimed land—the municipality, the politicians, the residents, the touts; no exceptions there. The garbage trains were discontinued sometime in the 1980s (Interviews 2013).

Today, many of Toba Tek Nagar's residents work in the landfill in different capacities: waste pickers, *bouncers* (security guards), *kabadiwalas* (scrap dealers), recyclers, waste workers, and machine operators. Furthermore, the biophysical processes of waste, particularly the release of methane gas and leachate, affect the lives of Toba Tek Nagar residents in different ways, including their health, livelihoods, and habitat. For instance, a major fire broke out in the landfill in 2016 causing the residents from Toba Tek Nagar as well as the neighboring middle-class residential complexes to come out on the streets and demand a response from the municipality and the police (Chatterjee 2019). The latter blamed the "waste mafia gangs" that were supposedly living among the residents of the locality for initiating the fire. The search for the source of the fire led to a few arrests, demolition of the neighborhoods on the edge of the landfill harboring the "mafia," and revocation of waste pickers' access to the landfill. Moreover, in recent years, governmental and nongovernmental organizations have been rallying to realize a "Zero-Garbage" Mumbai, which has changed the workings of the urban waste world. The city is to be both "Slum-Free" and "Garbage-Free." The life of Toba Tek Nagar and its residents is thus entwined with the life of waste in many ways. This chapter aims to understand these transformations in the waste world and its affects on the lives of Toba Tek Nagar's residents.

The second reason for focusing on garbage ties back to the overall story of this book: In the making of "the city," lives, energies, habitats, spaces, times, and experiences are often rendered as "waste" and then "recycled" to reproduce meanings and values in the city. And my interest in this book has been to highlight the potentiality of the "wasted" to affect cities in different mediums. This chapter attends to a more literal form of "waste," that is, the urban waste itself. There exists a wealth of scholarship on urban waste, which points out that waste is central to questions of value, labor, human, and nonhuman relationships, and space (Gidwani and Baviskar 2019; Muecke and Hawkins eds. 2002; Alexander and Reno eds. 2012). With regards to value, John Frow suggests that "waste is the degree zero of value, or it is the opposite of value, or it is whatever stands in excess of value systems grounded in use (2002: 25)." And this zero-degree value makes waste a dynamic and generative space for the formation and deformation of value regimes. Within a capitalist regime, "waste," Vinay Gidawni and Raj Reddy note, is the antithesis of value that is repeatedly domesticated or eradicated and then reemployed in the creation of positive values. This dialectical process through which waste acquires an exchange value and becomes a commodity, they argue, is central to capital's spatial histories of surplus accumulation (Gidwani and Reddy 2011; Blomley 2002).

In her seminal work, Mary Douglas tells us that "dirt," "purity," and "pollution" are not given concepts but values that are assigned to objects and bodies through cultural value systems and techno-scientific knowledge in order to restate themselves (1966). For instance, in the South Asian context, conceptions of "purity" and "pollution" have been integral to how the caste system has restated social stratifications, hierarchies, hereditary occupations, and itself, historically (Dumont 1970). The labor of waste is thus assigned to specific people—those whose bodies are marked by race, caste, class, and gender, whose lives are rendered as excess, and their work as degraded (Rao 2012; Prashad 2000). This labor, although stigmatized and invisibilized, forms a vital infrastructure through which dead matter becomes live (Fredericks 2018). Waste is collected, cleared, sorted, cleaned, broken down, recycled, decomposed, exchanged, transacted, or eaten by species other than human animals (Kumar, Singh, and Harris-White 2019; Reno 2014). It also interacts with air, water, soil, and other life-forms leading to multiple biophysical processes such as the release of methane gas that then affects humans and machines (Mirza 2019). Given the abilities of waste to interact and contaminate, these biosocial relationships between waste, machines, and life-forms in cities are to be ordered, domesticated, routed, or harnessed, which, in turn, demand the production and governance of urban space. For instance, Sudipta Kaviraj draws attention to how vernacular and modern notions of filth influenced ideas and uses of "public" and "private" space in colonial India (1997). Similarly, the geographical division of cities into "miasmatic environs" and "clean, safe spaces" (Legg 2007), the relocation of "obsolete" industries into the "hinterlands" (Banerjee-Guha 2002), and the location of landfills in proximity to poorer neighborhoods (Pellow 2002) speak to the spatial imaginaries and practices that are rallied around waste's ability to affect human lives. These conceptual and spatial boundaries also demarcate what is a "proper" city, how it is to be "properly" used, and who are its "proper" citizens. Thus, stories of waste can reveal how relationships between values, labor, machines, life-forms, and space play out in cities.

The third reason for focusing on urban waste is its association to play. Waste and play have a historical relationship—an obvious connection is toys. In one of his children's radio programs, titled "Berlin Toy Tour I," Walter Benjamin tells his young listeners an interesting historical bit about toy manufacturing in Germany (2014[1930]). Until the 19th century, he says, there didn't exist a specialized industry dedicated to making toys. They were largely by-products of workshops, where artisans made toys from waste material during their spare time. It was only after new rules and regulations for guilds were introduced that artisans were barred from making toys since it fell outside their designated craft. This specialization in manufacturing led to the rise of a specialized toy manufacturing industry. In another instance, in his essay on "The cultural history of toys," Benjamin draws our attention to children's interest in the waste created by adults in their workspaces and using them to play (1999a[1928a]; also see, 1999b[1928]). While playing in waste, he notes, children aren't interested in reproducing the world of adults but in creating another world through repetitions. In this parallel world, objects that are assigned specific values and meanings by a specific cultural milieu are put to other uses and assigned other meanings and values. Urban waste is no different. As Joshua Reno points out, waste is not dead matter but a living sign, that is, it is a semi-biotic material left behind by one species to be interpreted and played with by other species (Reno 2014). In both scenarios, the act of bringing material objects from one world into another world for playing also puts these worlds and their value systems into an interplay. In this interplay, Theodor Adorno notes, a possibility for catachrestical reobjectification opens up, which frees objects from the systems to which they've been beholden, particularly the utilitarian telos of instrumental reason, and are drawn out into a space of indeterminacy (in Bill Brown 2016). And in this space of indeterminacy, economies of meanings start to unravel and objects open up in a way that they are always up for grabs by others (Taussig 2009). Thus, stories of waste can tell us stories of inventive inhabitations in cities.

Given the centrality of waste to life in Toba Tek Nagar, as well as urban waste's abilities to charge, discharge, and create frictions, this chapter explores the following questions: How does urban waste that settles and flows in the city catalyze lives, values, labor, and spatial practices? What kind of spaces open up when these entities are brought into relationships with each other? What forms of inhabiting the city make appearances? What happens when rules and regulations are changed by the state and courts? How do they affect the entities and their relationships? And lastly, what does this tell us about the city itself as a medium? I explore these questions here through an ethnographic study of Mumbai's waste world and by attending to the latter's transformation since the 1980s. However, two caveats are due here. One, I focus on one form of live waste: recyclables—that is, discarded entities with the ability to be collected, sorted, cleaned, exchanged, broken down, and put back together into something new. And second, this chapter does not provide a detailed historical account of the urban waste world but a series of textual images that draw attention to the different relational and conceptual devices that are at play in the world of urban waste.

Measures

Unlike most Indian cities, where privatization of waste management is a more recent phenomenon, in Mumbai, it began in the early 1980s. The *Safai Kamgars* Union (Conservancy Workers Union) was on a strike demanding for an increase in wages.[1] While the strike did yield the intended results, the municipality complemented the raise with a "no more hiring" policy and privatization of waste collection and disposal in parts of Mumbai. In doing so, the municipality displaced the risk of workers' resistance and reduced its expenditures on workers' wages and pensions. Consequently, since the 1980s, the "official" on-ground garbage collection and disposal system in Mumbai is comprised of two sets of actors: one, municipal, which includes *muccadams* (supervisors), sweepers, waste collectors, and garbage truck drivers; and second, private actors, which include contractors, subcontractors, private waste collectors, and private garbage truck drivers. The task of these actors, both municipal and private, is to collect residential and com-mercial waste[2] and dispose of it at either the transfer stations or landfills. The municipal and private services are divided as per the municipal wards[3] of the city: the municipal garbage trucks and workers serve wards in the older (southern) parts of the city, while private contractors and their workers serve wards in the newer suburban areas. However, the municipal *muccadams* supervise both.

The contractors for different wards are selected through a bidding process and their payments are measured by the tonnage of waste that they collect and dispose of. The aim of connecting money to weight was to incentivize a maximum collection of garbage. Thus, to earn more money, contractors ask their workers to be aggressive and maximize the collection and disposal of waste. Often, contractors also ask their workers to add a bit of sand, silt, dust, or debris to the waste and increase its weight. The job of the *muccadams* is to police such activities. The garbage truck contractors, on the other hand, are paid by the number of trips their trucks make to the landfill. The securitized entrance to the Deonar landfill is thus cordoned with a weighing machine. It's a small booth with an iron ramp, where the trucks halt before entering the landfill. The weight of the truck, its ID number, the name of the truck driver, and the names of the contractors in charge of collecting and carrying the waste are recorded on a computer. The truck is then weighed again on its way out. The difference in weight helps measure the amount of garbage collected every day and pay the contractors.

The Deonar landfill is going to be shut down soon since it has reached its maximum capacity (in weight and height) for the amount of waste it can store safely. It is managed by a private consortium (of national and international companies) that was awarded a 25-year-long contract in 2009. Its task is to oversee the construction of a methane gas plant, cover the garbage with geo-membrane to avoid the generation of leachate that seeps into the nearby creek, and ensure proper closure of the landfill by covering it with geotextile. The fees of the private consortium are based on a "tipping fee" that is calculated by fixing a rate per tonnage of waste dumped into the landfill. Unlike the contractors, the municipal and private waste workers are paid by the measure of time. All private companies are meant to follow the minimum wage ordinance of INR 178 (USD 2.5) per day, but the contractors often breach the ordinance by paying merely INR 100 (USD 1.5) per day. Thus, these workers are not interested in the tonnage of disposed waste. They earn an extra income by working two jobs or selling recyclable waste. Some, however, earn money from cricket. Many private contractors run cricket teams that enter into city-wide competitions organized by political parties or private organizers. The private waste workers play for their employers and are sometimes traded to another employer's team for a small amount.

Breaking Things Down

Waste can be recycled—that is, collected, sorted, cleaned, processed, broken down, reconstituted, and then sold. And this recyclability of waste, in turn, has catalyzed the recycling of Mumbai's waste world. Thus, despite all the efforts to measure and take the right measures to contain, the urban waste world has always exceeded the "official" collection and disposal system. Many "unofficial" or "informal" actors participate and work in it. These include private sweepers, *kabadiwalas* (scrap dealers), waste pickers, recyclers, waste pickers' organizations, and wholesalers. Given the centrality to waste to caste-based stratifications and occupational hierarchies, each of these actors belongs to specific caste communities. However, in the past few years, Muslim migrants from North and East India have taken up the work of waste picking in Mumbai (Seabrook and Siddiqui 2011).

The private sweepers, who belong mostly to lower-castes from Gujarat and Rajasthan (such as Mahar-Patels, Chohra, Mehtar) operate primarily within residential societies or commercial complexes.[4] Their task is to clean these premises each morning, collect waste from shops and households and hand over the waste to the garbage trucks or dispose of it in the municipal bins.[5] However, before disposing, they pick out recyclables from the household waste and sell them to the neighborhood *kabadiwalas* (scrap dealers). The *kabadiwalas*, also known as *katewallas* (ones with the weighing scale), belong to different caste and religious communities from Rajasthan, Gujarat, West Bengal, and Uttar Pradesh. They deal in recyclables such as plastic bottles, glass bottles, magazines, metal cans, newspapers, plastic containers, wooden furniture, and even electronics. They travel door to door in urban localities to buy sorted recyclables that are in good condition and do not require any processing, just a bit of cleaning.[6] The recyclables are bought on a per/kg basis and then sold either to recyclers or as secondhand objects to regular buyers. The remainder of household waste is then disposed of by private sweepers into garbage trucks or municipal bins.

The municipal bins are located primarily in public spaces such as street corners, along public parks, next to residential boundary walls, or next to market areas. They are municipally assigned points for "official" workers to collect city waste. They are also the primary space where waste pickers source their recyclables. Besides municipal bins, waste pickers also collect recyclables in public spaces, such as railway stations, parks, streets, bus stands, de facto garbage dumps, and public squares. The collected material is then sorted on footpaths, along boundary walls, at street corners, or at any small, available public space. The sorting is done as per the technicalities of the recycling process: paper is sorted into newsprint, glossy magazine, and wet paper; plastic into wet or dry plastic bags and plastic articles; bottles into glass bottles, plastic bottles, and bottle caps; and then there is the "*cocktail mix*"—an industry term for materials that cannot be sorted into any of the previous categories. The aluminum and tin foils, referred to as *german*, are left unpicked at the bins since they have a lower exchange value compared to other recyclables. These and other unpicked recyclables are collected by waste pickers at the landfill. Sorting complete, waste pickers sell their recyclables to recyclers at a location specified by the waste picker.

The recycling process is structured into three tiers based on the infrastructural capacities of the recyclers, which include waste collection and handling capacity, storage capacity, and transport facilities. The first-level recyclers run their businesses in small units (thirty-two-foot-square), employ three to five workers, and handle between five and ten tons of garbage daily. They don't own any machinery as they are engaged in the initial level of waste processing, that is, cleaning and sorting recyclables by the quality and fixing up small damages. They then transport the sorted material to second-level recyclers in self-owned or hired *tempos*. The second level is involved in a higher level of sorting and cleaning and handling 30 to 40 tons of recyclables every day. They employ around eight to 12 employees and are housed in sixty-five-foot-square units (approx). These units also serve as living spaces for the employees, who are mostly seasonal migrants from West Bengal and parts of North India. Sorting at this level is based on color, size, shape, grain of the material, and potential use or reuse of the materials. The quality specifications are specified by the third-level recyclers. Recycling at this level involves preprocessing, including washing and repairing broken materials. Sorted recyclables are cleaned, dried, and then sent to third-level recyclers. A small portion of the processed recyclables is also bought by household enterprises within slum localities for manufacturing plastic articles, toys, and other household accessories.

The third-level recyclers are engaged in a much more rigorous and mechanized processing of waste that involves granulating, compacting, and baling. The waste is broken down into smaller particles, packed into bags, and sent to wholesale merchants. The third-level recyclers do not function out of a single unit but have specialized smaller units for separating, processing, and packaging. Each of the smaller units employs five to six workers who process around 80 to one hundred tons of waste daily. Third-level recyclers also receive waste directly from large commercial enterprises, medical facilities, and industrial clusters, where they often have informal arrangements with the heads of housekeeping companies. This waste is not mixed with the city waste and hence requires minimal processing. When a minimum amount, usually around five hundred tons, is processed, the third-level recyclers transport it to wholesalers. While most recyclers operate in slum localities, the wholesalers are located in the city's peripheries. They work primarily as traders or *vyaparis* between large manufacturing companies and third-level recyclers. All processed waste from various recyclers is stored in their large warehouses and then transported to manufacturing units that are located outside the city. Ownership of these facilities allows wholesalers to work as traders without getting involved in the day-to-day recycling process itself. They simply have to arrange for large amounts of recyclables by buying them in bulk from recyclers. Manufacturing companies too prefer dealing with *vyaparis* rather than individual recyclers. At every level of this hierarchy, the rate of recycled material increases by 25 percent. The merchants fix this rate based on the demand, which is then subtracted down all the way to the private sweepers and waste pickers.

Calculated Rhythms

As mentioned earlier, the recycling hierarchy is based on infrastructural capacities such as finances, storage units, employees, transport, and more importantly, waste collection and handling capacity. The waste pickers, who do not hold any of these capacities, have to devise calculated rhythms and movements in order to access recyclables and work their way into the economy. These calculations are made in relation to the rhythms of recyclables in the city, other actors and machines, and the abilities of their own bodies. For instance, waste pickers that collect recyclables from public spaces and municipal bins follow a particular daily route at specific times of the day within a demarcated territory. This rhythm is calculated in relation to the "official" waste workers and trucks. If a garbage collection truck is scheduled to pick up waste from a bin at 9.30 a.m., waste pickers begin sorting there at 8:00 a.m. Many work in groups of two or three so as to cover a larger area, collect more recyclables, and reduce individual workloads. The collected recyclables are then pooled together, sorted, and then shared among themselves. Despite the precarity and the risks involved, waste pickers prefer working as waste pickers rather than as private workers since it provides temporal flexibility in terms of daily working hours and rhythms of salaries, which are not found in jobs with private companies or domestic work (Interviews 2013). Such flexibilities are preferred more by women waste pickers, whose everyday time is far more restricted by family and household affairs.

The rhythms of waste pickers working at the landfill are calculated too. Most waste pickers from Toba Tek Nagar start their day at six in the morning. They make their way to the landfill with a sickle in one hand and a collection bag in the other. The waste pickers registered with different WPOs in Toba Tek Nagar, of which there are three, enter the dumping ground by showing their ID cards to the security guards at the gate (see Chapter 1). Those without ID cards enter through the holes made in the boundary wall that divides the landfill from the locality by paying a small amount to the security guards. The waste dumped the previous night lies unsorted till the morning. It remains unsorted at the source too and hence tends to contain more recyclables. The next round of garbage trucks starts at around 11 in the morning and starts covering up the unsorted waste. The waste pickers thus try to make the most of their mornings. They work till five in the evening and then take stock of their collections. If the stock is large enough to sell, they make their way to the recyclers to sell it and return home by seven in the evening.

Different waste pickers pick different objects: plastic bags, *german, phugga* plastic (plastic containers), wood, metal, or cocktail mix. Plastic bottles are a rare find as they tend to get picked at the source itself. As soon as a truck dumps waste, the waste pickers begin unearthing it with sickles to find recyclables. Its pointed edge pierces through the mound and loosens it up, then with light force, plastic bags and paper are pierced and picked up. The act of collecting depends not just on the materials that arrive on garbage trucks but also on the physical abilities and the economic needs of the waste pickers. Those who depend on waste picking as their primary source of income tend to collect more and specific recyclables. The prices for *german* and *phugga* plastic are higher at the landfill and hence preferred. Those with more body strength, usually the male waste pickers, push their way through a crowd of waste pickers and walk faster through the mounds of waste and marsh to reach the new stock of waste that is being dumped. Often, waste pickers get pricked and cut by needles, glass, or metal. In addition, they suffer burns from the heat of the gases that get released due to the compaction of waste by the garbage compactors. This means that most waste pickers end up working four days a week and healing their wounds the other three days. The rhythms of work are thus based on the body's abilities—how much the body can endure, how much waste it can carry, and how much it can walk, bend, and push. Those who aren't able to expend much energy tend to collect a *cocktail mix*, although it earns them less money.

Levers

Despite the enormous waste generated in Mumbai (2.4 million metric tons a year, 2019), the amount of recyclables available is never enough for everyone in the city. Given the limited amount of recyclables, relationships have to be devised within specific spaces in order to share and exchange recyclables. These relationships of sharing and exchanging are calculated based on one's position within the caste system, the "official" waste system, the "unofficial" recycling system, as well as calculations of savings, pooling, and more importantly, leveraging.

For instance, the private sweepers belong mostly to the Mahar-Patels, Chohra, and Mehtar castes and have been a part of the city's sanitation system since the precolonial period. They hold customary rights to territories, buildings, or neighborhoods, which are passed on to the next generation as an inheritance (*jagirdari*). In addition, they are also paid by residential and commercial complexes for their work and get "rewards" (*bakshish*) during festivals. Thus, their transactions with *kabadiwalas* are based on the competitive market prices offered by the *kabadiwalas*. The latter, who belong mostly to different caste and religious communities belong to a higher caste (not the upper-caste though) than the private sweepers, and yet have a lower hand in the transactions. In addition, the relationships between competing *kabariwalas* are weak and have further declined due to the proliferation of *kabariwalas* belonging to other communities.[7] Thus, *kabariwalas* have to draw loans from recyclers to guarantee the supply of recyclables from households and private sweepers. These loans, however, bind them to specific recyclers. They can't exchange their goods with other recyclers. These ties can be broken only if another recycler offers to buy out their loan and provide a higher market price. The first-level recyclers do sometimes buy out loans to strengthen and lever their position in their relationship with those in the upper tiers of the recycling hierarchy. In Mumbai, the recyclers belong to specific communities: Muslim migrants from Tamil Nadu, Gujarat, and West Bengal; Nadars from Tamil Nadu; and a few upper-caste Brahmins (Bhide and Spies 2013). The latter, however, do not "handle" waste but are primarily involved as businessmen. Most have been working in the recycling industry for the past 30 to 40 years. The relationships between these recyclers are based on communitarian lines, age of businesses, familial relations, personal favors, and trust. But more importantly, the transactions between them are based on their ability to mobilize and supply a substantial amount of waste. This mobilization is based on their ability to develop relationships of care, loans, and coercion with *kabadiwalas* and waste pickers.

The waste pickers at the municipal bins and the landfills are well aware of their position within these relationships. Thus, their exchanges with "official" waste workers and "unofficial" recyclers are calculated too. For instance, both municipal and private workers, as mentioned earlier, collect and sell recyclables from municipal bins to supplement their low wages. But most times, waste pickers pay the "official" workers a small sum of money (INR 30 a day or USD 0.4) in exchange for letting them access all the recyclables in the bins. Here, it is assumed that the municipal workers have rights over urban waste as they represent the municipality. This hierarchy of access to waste is also tied to the customary rights to work and property guaranteed by the caste system (Masselos 1982).[8] "Official" workers belonging largely to higher Scheduled Castes and Other Backward Classes get precedence over waste pickers who belong to lower Scheduled Castes and Muslim sub-communities.[9] The small sum is thus a payment to forgo rights to recyclables guaranteed by the caste system. This transaction saves "official" workers their time and efforts and provides waste pickers access to more recyclables. This payment is calculated too, since a larger amount of recyclables provides waste pickers leverage in their relationships with recyclers. In case of disputes over recyclables between waste pickers and workers, the *muccadams* are called upon to mediate. Most waste pickers maintain cordial relationships with *muccadams*. Whenever a new municipal bin is installed, which means newer waste pickers can be put to work, the *muccadams* contact the waste pickers, who, in turn, arrange for one of their family members or friends to collect recyclables at that bin. In the case that a new waste picker wants to collect recyclables within a territory, the primacy over recyclables is given to the older waste pickers, after which the new waste pickers get a chance (Interviews 2013). These exchanges provide recyclables to go around, despite being a limited resource.

Such calculated transactions are at play at the landfill too. The latter is divided into loops, and since most loops have reached their holding capacity, waste gets dumped in just one loop. The garbage carriers usually dump waste in a common space. However, waste pickers can secure access to an entire load by pooling money and paying the driver. Usually, they prefer to access loads of waste from areas with higher-income residents, where the amount of recyclables is more and the chance of finding valuable material is higher. Waste pickers also pay garbage truck drivers to dump at a distance from the bulldozers. This payment, as some waste pickers pointed out, is not to secure access or get rights over recyclables in that truck but to "buy time" to collect recyclables and to reciprocate the driver's empathy. Waste pickers in either location are not employed by the recyclers. In some cases, however, they become bound to a recycler if they borrow an advance payment. Such advance payments might range between INR 1,000 and 1,500 (USD 20–25) and are used by waste pickers to pay rent, for family or medical emergencies, or to send home to sustain farming activities. The amount of waste collected by waste pickers plays a significant role in shaping their relationships to recyclers. The more waste collected, the more leverage they have in accessing loans. But these bindings lead to violence as well. In cases where a waste picker is unable to collect waste for some reason or diverges into other jobs, recyclers beat them up over fear and insecurity that the waste picker may be selling recyclables to a different recycler offering a higher rate. Hence a number of waste pickers avoid taking advances or selling waste to just one recycler; they "branch out" and transact with multiple recyclers simultaneously to keep their options in play. This also helps them negotiate a better rate. There are times when certain waste pickers move up the ladder and become recyclers themselves. This requires a large sum of capital, which, in turn, demands saving and pooling resources with other waste pickers to rent out a storage unit and buy substantial recyclables.

Reduce, Reuse, Recycle

Since the 1990s, Mumbai's waste world has undergone modifications as a result of a series of rules and regulations related to the city's waste management (1993, 2000, 2006, 2016). The first, introduced in 1993, was the decentralization of governmental responsibilities onto Urban Local Bodies (ULBs), particularly municipalities. While the dream of a decentralized municipal Indian state was part of Nehru's vision in the 1940s, the dream didn't get actualized until the 73rd and 74th Amendments to the Indian Constitution. The amendment was a response to the ineffectiveness of Urban Local Bodies (ULBs) to perform as "vibrant democratic units of self-government," and its aim was "restoring power back to the people by legally encouraging local self-governance" (GOI 1992). More specifically, decentralization devolved financial, decision-making, and lawmaking responsibilities pertaining to urban planning (land-use), planning for economic and social development, and providing urban amenities onto municipalities. The latter, in turn, decentralized these responsibilities further down. At the ward level, ward committees were formed, which included elected councilors, the ward officer, and three nominated NGO/CBO members. The aim was to reform governance from a centrally run municipal government, wherein citizenship was built on ideas of demanding rights and dependency, to a more participatory governance mechanism, wherein citizenship was based on active participation in these forums. Another reason for the decentralization of powers was devolving financial responsibilities. The ULBs were to perform as efficient and entrepreneurial financial entities that would raise funds on their own and not rely on the center. The path charted out to achieve these goals was the privatization of municipal services through public–private partnerships. In many ways, as Aman Luthra points out that the municipalization of Indian cities was modeled on privatization rather than the other way around (2019; 2020).

The issue of urban waste "management" came to the forefront in the mid-1990s and resulted in a huge mobilization among civil society groups, who filed a number of litigations in different courts. Furthermore, a series of rules and regulations were introduced for the proper management of solid waste in Indian cities over the next few years. For instance, new rules for Management and Handling of Solid Waste (MSW Rules) were instituted by the Ministry and Environment and Forests in 2000. These set out procedures for the proper collection, segregation, storage, transportation, preservation, and disposal of waste at different scales of the city (MoEF 2000). Then in 2006, the Supreme Court of India introduced a committee report, which demanded that ULBs in Class-1 cities set up a separate Solid Waste Management Cell and "modernize" its solid waste management system (Supreme Court of India 2006). Modernization here meant strengthening and building municipal capacities by hiring experts such as environmental engineers and sanitation inspectors; building partnerships with public and private organizations, and training them; modernizing technical aspects, such as, improving machinery, eliminating municipal bins, setting up roles and rules for all actors, and documenting best practices; setting up management information systems that would consist of daily, weekly, monthly, and yearly reports on monitoring, workings, and budgeting from all actors; and lastly, fiscal disciplining by linking financial incentives to efficiency. The Mumbai municipality responded to these series of rules, regulations, and governmental transformations by setting up several initiatives over the years: *Mumbai Chakachack* (Spic and Span Mumbai), *Saaf Aangan* Programs (Clean Courtyards), Zero-Tolerance Garbage Zones, Cleanliness Task Force, Advance Locality Management Groups (ALMs), Local Area Citizen Groups (LACG), Recyclers Cooperatives, Slum Adoption Schemes, Litter Cops, and Clean-Up Marshals. Across all these programs, the logic of recycling waste, which was earlier absent in the "official" municipal system but present in the urban waste world, was introduced under a new slogan: "Reduce-Reuse-Recycle." And its aim was to achieve a "Zero-Garbage City."

Identities and Rights

The WPOs have been working on issues related to waste pickers in Mumbai for more than three decades.[10] Their initial work was around specific issues: the appalling working conditions of lower-caste waste pickers, particularly women, and the absence of any social security or provisions to waste pickers by the state. Many of their programs were thus targeted towards providing resources and assistance to waste pickers, such as providing health services, conducting microcredit programs, training the waste pickers, and organizing self-help groups. But post-decentralization, these efforts have been channelized towards demanding rights, resources, and securities for waste pickers from the state, since they can't avail them due to the "informal" nature of their work. These demands included formal recognition of waste pickers through registration and ID cards, with the caveat that only registered waste pickers could pick recyclables; a proposal to organize municipally funded training sessions for waste pickers; free provision of transportation facilities and kiosks for storage and segregation by the municipality; and an agreement that waste will not be sold in the market by waste pickers but that the MCGM will make it mandatory for manufacturers to buy it from the WPOs' waste pickers. These demands were made on the basis that waste pickers' work makes important contributions to city services and provides environmental benefits. Despite these active efforts, the 2000 MSW rules had no mention of the WPOs or the waste pickers. However, the 2006 Supreme Court report did recognize their contribution to urban waste management but also claimed that they were "not being optimally used" by the municipalities. Furthermore, the report went on to make recommendations for the rules and regulations regarding registering waste pickers, organizing them, putting them into the right networks of NGOs, and providing requisite channels of training, infrastructure provision, and organizational support so as to harness their capacities (2006). This brought the WPOs to the forefront in the "official" realm of waste management.

Accounting to Zero

Another player that gained prominence in the field of urban waste post-decentralization was the upper-middle-class residents. They took on different organizational forms through multiple municipal initiatives. One of these forms was the Advanced Locality Managment groups (ALMs). The ALM program was initiated in 1996 to complement the municipal services with the participation of citizen-based groups. The goal of this partnership was to achieve a "Zero-Garbage City" by paying attention to the demands made by ALMs in regular meetings with ward councilors. The process of forming an ALM was simple: "gathering at least three civic-minded citizens and holding a meeting of concerned residents of the area" (Times of India, July 20th 2006). Furthermore, the new rules and regulations for solid waste management encouraged ward councilors to organize a larger number of ALMs against promises of budgetary incentives for their constituencies. In addition to the ALMs, residents in upper-middle-class neighborhoods also organized themselves into Citizens' Cleanliness Teams (CCTs)[11] and Citizens' Task Forces (CTFs). These teams and task forces provide regular reports, monitor cleanliness, and participate in organizing mop-up drives in their areas. The CCTs also suggest spots for litter bins, recommend areas for cleanup, devise beautification plans, and install nuisance detectors called Clean-Up Marshals in their neighborhoods.[12] The latter spot violations, such as open defecation, illegal dumping of garbage and debris, and nonsegregation of garbage by citizens or waste workers.

These rules, regulations, and new organizations have affected the field of urban waste in specific ways. At the household level, ALMs, CTFs, CTS, and others are closely involved in monitoring the collection, segregation, and disposal of waste at the source itself to take control of waste in their neighborhoods. They also follow particular practices and procedures, such as writing

Figure 4.2 Character and Fate

daily reports in specified formats, sending written complaints, videotaping and photographing littering activities, and monitoring the daily operations of waste pickers, garbage truck workers, private sweepers, *muccadams*, and municipal officials. Over the years, a number of ALMs have hired architects, academic research groups, and planners to draw up redevelopment plans for their neighborhoods. These plans involve formalizing markets, beautification of public parks, redesigning sidewalks and boundary walls, and delineating hawking zones in their neighborhoods—in short, reordering public spaces where waste gets dumped de facto.

To exercise further control over neighborhoods and to make them "Zero-Garbage Zones," some ALMs have demanded, in letters and petitions, the removal of municipal bins from their neighborhoods, which they deem are a source of nuisance due to the presence of waste, waste pickers, dogs, and cattle (Karmayog.com, accessed 2013). The MCGM has paid heed to these demands by eliminating municipal bins from these neighborhoods and replacing them with *ghanta gadis* (garbage trucks with a bell). When the bell is rung, the private sweeper or the security guard is to hand waste directly to the workers at the housing society gates. Lastly, with increased complaints about waste spilling into the city space and the lack of space in landfills, the municipality has replaced open garbage trucks or dumpers with compactors. The compactors compress waste in its main compartment and squeeze out the excess liquid into the residue tank below. This compression, however, also produces an immense amount of heat inside the compactor, which gets released when waste is dumped at the landfills and unearthed. Another reason for employing compactors is to avoid the leakage of smell and sight of waste while traveling through the city. But this neutralization of waste's affects is only for outsiders, not for those who do the work of collecting and depositing waste in these compactors. Most waste workers, as their wives who live in Toba Tek Nagar told me during interviews, consume a lot of alcohol to anesthetize themselves. The alcohol helps disconnect their body from their senses: their noses are anesthetized while their eyes and hands continue to work as alienated parts.

Contract

Most "official" waste work carried out at the landfill involves a series of contracts and subcontracts. The municipal office at the Deonar landfill is housed in a small brick shed. Three municipal officers, who are in charge of supervising the private consortium sit here. A few steps away from this municipal office is an enclosed office space made of shipping containers. It's the office of the private consortium. During my visit to the landfill, three well-built, muscular men were posted outside its gate. They are referred to as *bouncers* and are in charge of providing security for the landfill as well as the consortium officers. These *bouncers* are hired from a security agency on contract by Sheikh. And Sheikh holds a contract from the municipality for securitizing the landfill. Most *bouncers* work two shifts, which include providing security at five-star hotels and pubs, at high-profile events, and for high-profile personnel. Those who work at hotels and pubs also work as male sex workers (Interviews 2013).

Opposite this container office is Sheikh's office, a small shed built entirely of galvanized iron sheets. I was there that day to get shown around the landfill. As he walked towards me, I figured that the municipal officials had called him to escort me into the landfill. My visit was an added liability on his otherwise stressful day. He rudely asked me to wait for the engineer from the private company, wishing I wasn't there, but couldn't get rid of me, since I had a letter from the chief municipal engineer. As I later came to know from the bouncers, he was the brother-in-law of a municipal councilor, which had played a huge part in his acquiring the security contract. The kinsman of another municipal councilor, they further added, was awarded a contract to provide garbage trucks to the municipality.

After a few minutes, the private engineer showed up and invited me to sit in his office. It was a hot day, and I decided to forgo my chance to observe the happenings outside the landfill and to wait in the engineer's air-conditioned office instead. The walls of his container office were covered with charts, boards, and maps. As I waited, various men kept entering the office to figure out their time, their duty, and their location. The engineer would look up his register to figure out where waste needed to be moved and organized, and would then instruct these men accordingly. Some of them worked on forklifts, others on bulldozers. The job of the bulldozers is to push the waste once it's dumped by the garbage trucks, and the work of the forklifts is to pick it up and order it into hills so as to maintain the correct height of these hills as per the rules of the airport authority. The forklifts and bulldozers are hired on contract by the private consortium. The men who work these machines are also hired on contract.

A few years ago, I was told, working on the dumping grounds was easier. The bulldozers would work from 9 a.m. to 11 a.m. This would give waste pickers time to pick and sort recyclables from the waste dumped the previous night. The garbage trucks would arrive by 11 in the morning and continue dumping till five in the evening. The bulldozers would start working again only at five in the evening and work till seven. The garbage trucks would then resume dumping waste from seven to 11 in the night. But these days, the work of dumping and organizing waste is now carried out simultaneously by the consortium to reduce labor costs. So, while the trucks dump waste, bulldozers push it, and forklifts organize it in mounds. Amidst these machines and their heavily mechanized movements, waste pickers have to find their way to recyclables, while making sure they do not get crushed under the waste being dumped. Thus, waste picking requires a heightened sense of awareness of the movements of bodies and machines around.

Valves

Similar to four other wards in Mumbai, the municipality had granted SOURCE, a WPO, the authority to collect recyclables from households and municipal bins in the ward. In addition to rights to recyclables, the municipality had also provided trucks for transporting materials, a kiosk to sort and store recyclables, and had mediated between the WPO and different Advance Locality Management Groups (ALMs) to help familiarize residents with the WPO and its registered waste pickers.

"The whole world," Sonaldidi (*didi* refers to elder sister) said to me, "is waste, some man-made and some nature-made. The man-made waste can be recycled and reused, while the nature-made can go back into nature through the soil. The first is called dry-waste and the second wet-waste." Sonal*didi* was the SOURCE officer in charge of the WPO's operations at the kiosk and in the ward. The kiosk was located on a large plot, measuring around 20 by 40 meters, on the city highway. At its entrance was a large open space, where two trucks and a *tempo* were being loaded with huge sacks filled with recyclables to be sent for recycling. The kiosk, an L-shaped structure, was divided into four parts. At the center, right opposite the main entrance, was the WPO office. The office itself was fairly small, just enough to fit three people at a time. In one corner of this small office space was a tall cupboard. Here, different types of recyclables, mostly plastic, were cataloged and labeled according to their pre- (thin strips, grains, soft cotton) and post-recycling (jars, pipettes, toys, shirts, buttons, beads) forms. Their fate seemed sealed in there. The space behind the office was divided into two halves: an enclosed bedroom for Javedbhai (*bhai* refers to brother) and a common room with a cupboard and bedding of the other WPO workers. Adjacent to the WPO office, to its left, was a brick shed. Javedbhai was sitting at its entrance, while two young men in their twenties were making their way through a crowd of used glass and plastic bottles. They first separated the caps from the bottles, throwing the metal caps on one side and plastic ones on the other. Then, as if peeling a vegetable, they made one cut in the plastic wrappers around the bottles to peel them off the bottle, and a second cut to detach the colored rims around the mouths of the bottles. These different parts were then sorted and stored in huge white sacks.

To the right of the WPO office was another shed. Manohar*bhai* was sitting at its entrance, with two men packing heaps of newspapers and cardboard cartons behind him. To the right of Manoharbhai's shed was Rasulmiyan's make-shift shed. He lives at the kiosk and takes care of it at night. That day, he was sorting waste collected from the ward into different recyclables and storing them in large plastic bags. After lingering for a while, I made my way to talk to him. Rasulmiyan (*miyan* refers to a friend or partner) had been working as a waste picker in Mumbai for 40 years. Earlier, he said, waste picking was easier and recyclables were easily available. Then, the only people interested in waste were a few waste pickers and some drug addicts who sold recyclables for their daily dose. Today, however, everyone wants to collect and sell garbage. After inquiring about the technicalities of his sorting process, I asked him who owned the kiosk. He replied there are three *seths* (owners): "the NGOdidi, Manoharbhai, and Javedbhai." The WPO, as I found out later from other waste pickers in the ward, had rented out parts of the kiosk to two *kabadiwalas* for INR 30,000/month (USD 500). Manoharbhai dealt in paper and cartons, and Javedbhai in plastic and glass bottles. The WPO had been sourcing recyclables from its registered waste pickers and selling them to the two of them. However, it made sure that the waste pickers received a higher than the market rate.

The rest of the plot, including the terraces of the kiosk, was covered with soft drink and mineral water bottles. Two workers (both men) were sorting them by color, green, and transparent, and a third worker was using a compressor to flatten them and pack them into square blocks. Sonaldidi later told me that they had been approached by COKE-India to collect, sort, and supply recyclable COKE PET (polyethylene terephthalate) bottles. The deal began with an advance payment, an agreement to collect and supply a fixed amount of PET bottles every month, and free installation of the compressor. The COKE bottles get sent right to the factory and bypass all the channels of recycling through which they had traveled earlier. This saves the company a fair bit of money and provides the WPO and its registered waste pickers a higher-than-market-selling rate. However, the WPO can register only a certain number of waste pickers as the amount of recyclables available in wards isn't enough to involve all waste pickers. The unregistered waste pickers now travel to the city's peripheries for recyclables since the recycling economies there aren't as competitive yet.

After walking around the kiosk for a while, I made my way back into the WPO office to interview Sonaldidi. Over the next hour, she went on to tell me about herself, her work at the WPO, and how she had set up the kiosk all on her own, without any donor support. And yet, she added, the kiosk is more successful than any of the others in the city. Different WPOs compete with each other to acquire operational rights in different municipal wards, while the local WPO officers compete with each other to make their wards most profitable. Her specific role as the SOURCE local head was to spread awareness about recycling among citizens in the ward, ensure segregation at the source, coordinate collection of recyclables by registered WPOs, and mediate between ALMs and the WPO. In addition, Sonaldidi was also in charge of making sure the registered waste pickers had ID cards, proper residential addresses, and savings accounts in banks. Four workers were assisting her at the kiosk: a driver who would go around with a municipal truck collecting recyclables from private sweepers and buying recyclables from registered waste pickers that work at bins and streets. The waste pickers got paid at the end of the week, unless they require advance payment. The other two workers were involved in sorting, compressing, and packing PET bottles. The place of Rasul*miyamiyan* in this schema wasn't clear to me; he seemed like a WPO worker and a waste picker at the same time, and maybe there is no difference between the two anymore.

Just at that moment, a young man walked in with a mobile phone and handed it over to Sonaldidi. She switched her demeanor and began shouting assertively. A waste picker, I figured, was on the other end of the call. Sonaldidi had been inquiring about his whereabouts since the time I had arrived that morning. It seemed that the young waste picker had disappeared with an advance payment from the WPO. To add to that, he had refused to hand over recyclables to the WPO workers on the collection trip that morning. Sonaldidi threatened him to either show up at the kiosk by 5 p.m. that very day or never show up in the area again to collect recyclables. After hanging up she turned to me and said:

We are all thieves. I say this to you honestly. Waste pickers, the municipality, ALMs, NGOs, all of us. We all want to increase our own profits, our productivity, and our values. Earlier, the dealers and recyclers controlled things. We maybe doing the same thing, but we provide a good rate in return.

On Swelling and Containing

Historically, in the Indian context, waste has been integral to restating the hierarchical order of the city under the caste system as well as to the oppression of the lower-castes who were (and are) relegated to that world. The work of cleaning city refuse, night soil, dealing with dead bodies, digging graveyards, and guarding the boundaries of villages was the task of hereditary village servants from the lowest castes—those deemed impure by birth. The British replicated and instituted these casteist orders and roles into its municipal system (Mirza 2018). But if in the caste and the municipal system, the object of waste was tied to the body of the lower-castes so as to demarcate and guard boundaries of purity and impurity, of caste, of work, and of the city, the intense work of collecting, sorting and recycling waste had swollen it and extended these boundaries. A swelling, following Walter Benjamin, is not a boundary or limits but "a zone. Change, passage, flooding lie in the word 'swelling'" (Benjamin 1999c: 494). It refers neither to delimitation or containment nor a linear form of change in a place. Instead, it refers to a crisis in the function of containment such that the container itself distends and overextends beyond itself, beyond its limits, to a point where it becomes unrecognizable (Weber 2008: 233). Thus, swelling is not a boundary that separates and divides but a zone that is caught in tension and a movement of extending itself to become something else. But what is this something else? And what constitutes this intensification within that makes something swell?

Despite the "measures" to weigh, collect, dispose, and contain urban waste and its affects, urban waste has always exceeded its own boundaries of life. These include its "miasmic" discharges, its leachate, its gases, its disgust of smell and sight but also its recyclability. The latter, which has been the focus of this chapter, has catalyzed multiple lives, labors, values, and relationships. Both the "official" and the "unofficial" waste workers work to break things down: private sweepers, municipal sweepers, private workers, municipal workers, waste pickers, dealers, recyclers, and supervisors. This "breaking down of things" involves calculated rhythms and exchanges so that urban waste, despite being in excess and yet limited, can go around. But these calculations are made to make sure that what goes around does not remain but gets recycled. So, exchanges are calculated with the hope that they would provide some form of "leverage" to move things in a way that one's position doesn't remain the same. For instance, individuals are fixed in terms of their positions within the caste system, the "official" waste system, the "unofficial" waste system, and the hierarchical rights it guarantees to them and others. In such a situation, despite being fixed, calculated exchanges provide leverage to move others so that their position changes in relation to them. At the same time, these levers help ensure that recyclables could go around so that others can

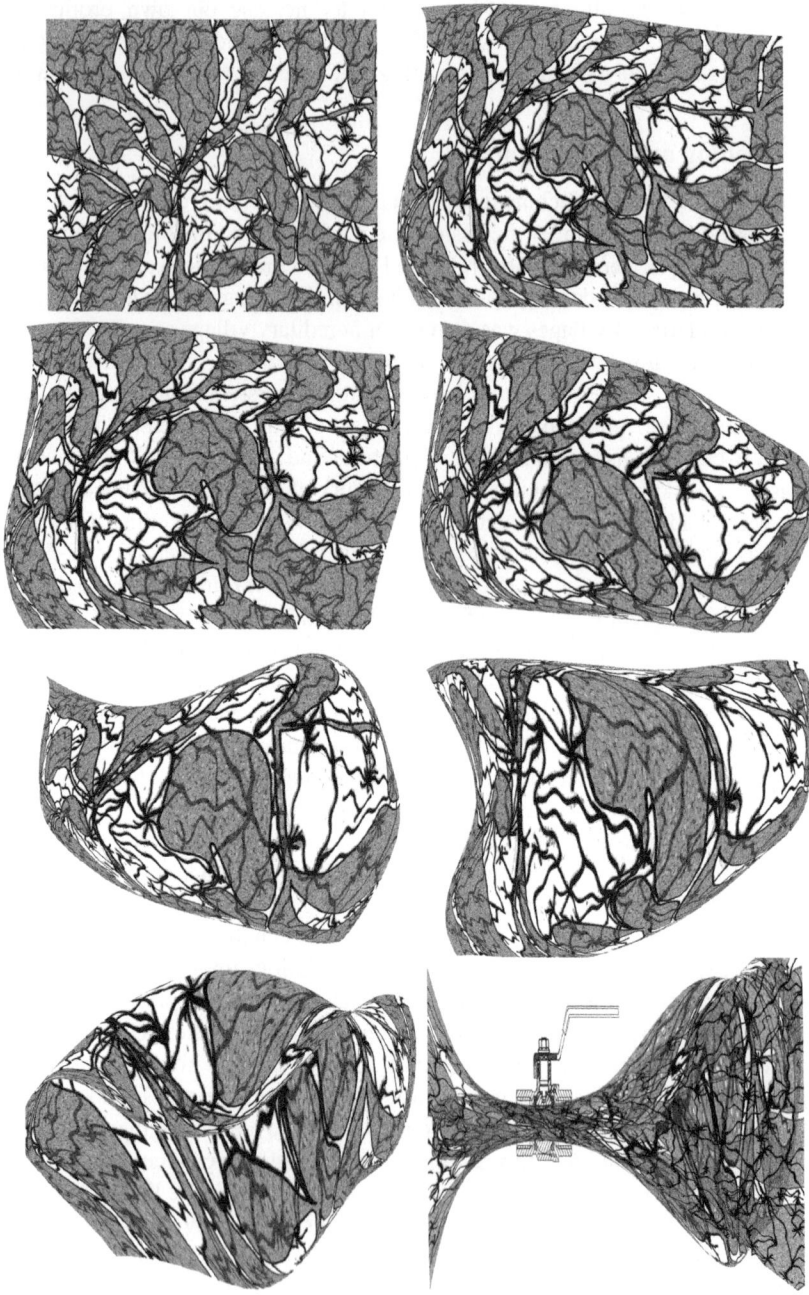

Figure 4.3 Swelling and Containment

get a piece of the action. This involves exchanging customary rights for money, pooling, and branching out to avoid getting bound; attending to and forgoing specific recyclables so that others can participate too; and loosening bodies, waste, time, and space so that they are flexible enough to expand or swell. Here levers do function to raise oneself to a higher position but to expand and distend time, space, and resources at different points in the "official system." In doing so, these points do not remain points, stations, or ends but expand into zones. The affect of these exchanges, levers, and expansions is recyclability—recyclability of not just waste but also the waste world itself. For instance, it isn't that the "official" and the "unofficial" waste worlds exist separately within their limits, but the "official" is broken down and into, so that it distends to the point of its unrecognizability—where things have the appearance of being "official" but aren't. For instance, public spaces, municipal bins, and landfills become spaces for work, resources, and exchanges, while the "official" system swells through "unofficial" dealings. In this swollen system multiple logics of waste, property forms, value systems, and relationships are at play. And it is in this play that waste and the city go live— become operational, while gesturing towards the possibility of rendering older forms an inoperative.

But given the ability of waste to contaminate, discharge, release, and swell, the state has to "take measures" and "measure" waste in order to contain, manage, and govern it. These measures have taken on different forms in Mumbai: contracts, accounting, rights, valves, and decentralization. But in many ways, the form of the urban waste world was already decentralized, since it had worked its way into households, bins, streets, slum localities, and landfills, where different actors worked, exchanged, and transacted. So, what does decentralization do? It is important to note here that the larger goal of decentralization in terms of waste was to achieve a "Zero-Garbage City." Given that, decentralization has multiplied the locations where the affects of waste on the city could be contained and contained in a way that they amount to zero—anesthetized (Osborne and Rose 1999). In this process, citizens, NGOs, and WPOs are enrolled who keep an "account" of the affects, monitor them, and make sure that the entry and exit of entities were controlled but not completely stopped so that it could have the desired effects, which account to zero. Thus, these points and organizations work as "valves," which could account for and keep a count of what passes in and out, without allowing the system to swell (Massumi and Dean 1992). But yes, they also had to do "right" by those who were unaccounted for—the waste pickers and private workers. So, the former had to be given rights, but only if they could be counted or registered. On the other hand, "contracts" do make things legitimate and accountable, but also "contract" times, space, resources, and possibilities of partaking in the waste world. As one municipal official said about her efforts of formalizing recycling industries, "The owners of the industrial clusters just could not agree upon any of our suggestions, since it would mean a radical reorganization of their form both physical and organizational, which cannot work under municipal systems" (Interviews 2013). Thus, flexibility here, despite its risks, uncertainty, and precarity, is not so much a matter of "informality," as it is a matter of not allowing any sovereign control over logics, time, space, exchanges, and meanings, so that they can all be kept in play—an interplay (Gandolfo 2013). This interplay allows for tensions and intensifications that recycle cities into something that is undetermined in the present. Thus, the recyclability of waste gestures towards its ability to swell the city, where multiple logics, values, and practices can be kept in play, which includes wasting values without any returns.

On Laying Waste

In the midst of researching the life of the waste recycling industry in Toba Tek Nagar, I interviewed Rafiq and Nafisa who work as waste pickers. After an hour-long conversation with them, which involved my ten questions about their work, their migration history, the garbage business and how it changed, the landfill, and their waste pickers' organization, I decided to end the interview with "the eleventh question"[13]: "Do you ever find things in the dumping ground that are special or priceless?" Rafiq replied, there are times when some waste pickers find a small piece of jewelry, a particle of gold, or even silver, but nothing substantial enough to change their life. These pieces of precious metal travel to the dumping ground on garbage trucks from Zaveri Bazaar (the Jewelers' Market in South Mumbai). The merchants are known to carefully sift through the shop garbage themselves before allowing sweepers to even touch it; hence it's rare for these fragments to reach the dumping ground. Nafisa added that most waste pickers collect and store these small pieces of metal until there is enough to sell to the nearby jewelers. If the piece of jewelry is made of silver, they just use it. Besides precious metal, waste pickers find a number of objects of everyday use such as dishes, bowls, spoons, forks, or shoes, which they use. But I was looking for something more and hence repeated my question awkwardly as if the question wasn't making sense: "Not things of value that you would sell, but things that you would want to keep for yourself." Rafiq smiled and pointed towards one of the walls on his house.

There on the bright blue wall behind him were framed photos of mosques, religious calendars, and quotes from the Quran. Among these different divine artifacts were a number of other small things, such as clocks, sculptures, and wall-hangings that were nailed to the wall. At the rightmost corner was a bright red fridge with the television above it. Above the television, two shelves nailed to the wall held another set of things. Next to the fridge, on the left side, was a sewing machine that Nafisa used for her second work of tailoring laces onto a cloth. But on the right side were two shelves that were beautifully arranged with plates, glasses, cups, vases, and a series of small artifacts. These were carefully arranged on the wall but in no particular order or hierarchy, simply as things. The shelves were laced with a triangular green *toran* (door hanging) that had yellow prints of sun and moon on them. There were many vases among these artifacts, both small and big. Some were made of glass, others ceramic; some were glossy with baroque designs resembling natural forms of plants, fruits, and flowers; while others were unfinished but decorated with glittering beads, colors, and fake jewels. The bigger vases were being used to hold plastic flowers, which were

Figure 4.4 Wasting Values

also found in the dumping yard. On the television was a nonworking small lamp with a ceramic base decorated with leaf prints. Next to it were a few miniature houses: a small, glossy ceramic villa with a chimney and pine trees around it, and a small apartment building. I smiled and insisted on seeing them. Rafiq emptied the shelves and brought them down to where we were sitting. These things are washed with cold water, then warm water, dried in sun, and then placed onto the shelves. Such careful displays of collected things weren't peculiar to Rafiq and Nafisa's house. I had seen them in many houses in Toba Tek Nagar. Some of them were complemented with dimly lit fish tanks, some with paintings of countryside settings, still others with poster-sized photographs of scenes from nature (water-falls, spring flowers, a European villa with doves, a path through trees, and so on). After Rafiq and Nafisa finished their stories of how they found these things, I asked them curiously if they gift these to his relatives or friends or sell them to the local *kabadiwalas* for money. They plainly refused, as if both they and the things were disinterested in any kind of exchange.

Notes

1 The workers' strikes have been important events around which the city municipality often reorganizes its structure and sets up new acts and policy. Jim Masselos shows how, since the 1880s, the recurring municipal workers strikes particularly in the sanita-tion sector became important events to set up more stringent rules around criminalizing strikes and changing organizational structures of the municipal departments (Masselos 1982: 101–39). The municipal sweepers strikes became more frequent post-World War II in Indian cities due to labor crises (Ahuja 2020).

2 The numbers of municipal bins provided in each ward are based on population densities. However, new municipal bins are installed frequently based on repetitive complaints by residents about a de facto garbage site in their vicinity.

3 The word *ward* itself designates a city administrative division that came up under colonial rule when the city was hit by the Bubonic plague of 1896. Ward, a medical term used in hospitals, was set up as a geographical unit to carry out a large city sanitary improvement scheme based on locations of hospitals, sanitary officers, health officers, and municipal bodies.

4 It's impossible to trace out an exact date for it, but different articles point out the presence of private sweepers even before the colonial conservancy department was set up in Bombay Presidency. The municipal sweepers, although from the same caste, are differentiated from private sweepers (Masselos 1982).

5 The residential waste accounts for 60 percent of the city waste and is more accessible to different actors. Other waste such as debris and biomedical waste get collected and disposed separately. Of the total solid waste generated in Mumbai region only 17 percent can be recycled completely (Srivastava et.al. 2015). In poorer neighborhoods, particularly slum localities, residents do not have the financial capacity to hire a private sweeper and hence dispose waste themselves into the municipal bins.

6 The use of mobile phones has made their visits to neighborhoods less frequent. They drop off their visiting cards with their mobile numbers on it.

7 For a more detailed study of these relationships from a political economy and insti-tutional framework perspective, see Kaveri Gill's work on plastic recycling in Delhi (2009).

8 In his discussion of sweepers and scavengers in colonial Bombay, Jim Masselos observes that under colonial rule the members of Bhangi (a derogatory term), Mehtar,

and Halalkhore. Those who ate meat and dealt with dead bodies and night soil as per the caste hierarchies were employed to do the same jobs by the colonial municipal corporation. The Mahars, on the other hand, were employed as city sweepers. The latter were from the lower-castes but regarded scavenging as work done only by the lowest of castes. In rural and urban contexts of Maharashtra, the job of the scavengers was to collect night soil from dry latrines and carry it to the city drain or into the sea and to dig graves, remove carcasses, etc. (Masselos 1982).

9 A 2017 study reveals that almost 90 percent of *Safai Karamcharis* in the municipality belong to the Scheduled Castes (SCs) and Other Backward Classes. Those belonging to Mahar, Matang, Meghwal, Harijan, Valmiki, and Chambhar castes are higher in number, while members of Kathewadi, Kunbi, Vadar, and Devendrakulathan castes are in smaller numbers (Salve, Bansod, and Kadlak 2017).

10 Some of the WPOs, like NGOs, get formed as a result of internal conflicts within larger NGOs. Members from these larger organizations split and start their own organization. A lineage history of NGOs will probably point towards possible organizational kinship relations among these various groups.

11 CCTs, formed in wards, are to file reports online in a "simple standard format," which then get delivered to the relevant MCGM officials, displayed publicly online, and handed to ALMs. The MCGM allocated a monthly budget of INR 10,000 (USD 2,000) for proper monitoring of garbage sites by CCTs. A fast-track method to get immediate attention was set up through the "Use Pen to Clean Garbage" program. The program was set up under the mayor to send complaint letters regarding matters of waste to the MCGM; action regarding the same was promised within 24 hours. These letters usually include complaints from citizens about cattle nuisance, waste pickers, or unclean municipal bins. A brief review of these letters suggests that they are usually articulated around two issues: first, "waste is a cause of epidemic outbreaks in the city" and second, reminding the MCGM of its legal responsibilities by quoting written documents such as news articles, MSW rules, and/or quotes from mayors.

12 In order to implement the MSW Rules, the MCGM decided to deploy Clean-Up Marshals in different wards. In 2007, MCGM began contracting out the role of Nuisance Detectors to private agencies. They collect fines and share it on a fifty-fifty basis with the MCGM. Their performance was judged on the basis of deliverables like no litter in the area of operation after sweeping, all spots of open urinals have been eliminated, no litter bins are overflowing or been stolen, and so on. Third-party auditors, such as NGOs and ALMs, oversee these private squads. Furthermore, surprise checks are organized in wards at any time, day or night, to encourage compliance.

13 The first ten questions, the Cybermohalla Ensemble tells us, come easily. With them, we create a traffic of experience with the other, form a story in our minds, but the 11th is the "after question" that can lead us into the unknown realm (Cybermohalla Ensemble 2012).

References

Ahuja, Ravi. 2020. "'Produce or Perish'. The Crisis of the Late 1940s and the Place of Labour in Post-Colonial India." *Modern Asian Studies* 54 (4): 1041–112.

Alexander, Catherine, and Joshua Reno, eds. 2012. *Economies of Recycling: The Global Transformation of Materials, Values and Social Relations*. New York, NY: Zed Books Ltd.

Banerjee-Guha, Swapna. 2002. "Shifting Cities: Urban Restructuring in Mumbai." *Economic & Political Weekly* 37 (2): 121–28.

Benjamin, Walter. 1927. *The Arcades Project*. Edited by Rolf Tiedemann. Translated by Kevin McLaughlin and Howard Eiland. Cambridge, MA and London, UK: Belknap Press of Harvard University Press.

———. 1999a. "The Cultural History of Toys." In *Selected Writings, Volume 2: 1927–1934*, edited by Michael W. Jennings, Gary Smith, and Howard Eiland, translated by Rodney Livingstone, 113–16. Cambridge, MA: The Belknap Press of Harvard University Press.

———. 1999b. "Toys and Play." In *Selected Writings, Volume 2: 1927–1934*, edited by Michael W. Jennings, Gary Smith, and Howard Eiland, translated by Rodney Livingstone, 117–21. Cambridge, MA: The Belknap Press of Harvard University Press.

———. 2014. "Berlin Toy Tour I." In *Radio Benjamin*, edited by Lecia Rosenthal, translated by Lisa Harries Schumann and Diana Reese, 37–43. New York, NY: Verso Books.

Bhide, Amita, and Martina Spies. 2013. "Dharavi-Ground Up: A Dwellers-Focused Design Tool for Upgrading Living Space in Dharavi, Mumbai." 184. Wien, Austria: Commission for Development Studies at the Austrian Academy of Sciences.

Blomley, Nicholas K. 2002. "Mud for the Land." *Public Culture* 14 (3): 557–82.

Brown, Bill. 2016. *Other Things*. Chicago, IL: University of Chicago Press.

Chatterjee, Syantani. 2019. "The Labors of Failure: Labor, Toxicity, and Belonging in Mumbai." *International Labor and Working-Class History* 95 (Spring): 49–75.

Cybermohalla Ensemble. 2012. "The Eleventh Question." In *Cybermohalla Hub*, edited by Nikolaus Hirsch and Shveta Sarda. Berlin: Sternberg Press.

Dean, Kenneth, and Brian Massumi. 1992. *First & Last Emperors: The Absolute State and the Body of the Despot*. New York, NY: Autonomedia.

Dossal, Mariam. 1991. *Imperial Designs and Indian Realities: The Planning of Bombay City, 1845–1875*. New York, NY: Oxford University Press.

Douglas, Mary. 1966. *Purity and Danger: An Analysis of Concepts of Pollution and Taboo*. London, UK: Routledge.

Dumont, Louis. 1970. *Homo Hierarchicus: The Caste System and Its Implications*. Chicago, IL: University of Chicago Press.

Fredericks, Rosalind. 2018. *Garbage Citizenship: Vital Infrastructures of Labor in Dakar, Senegal*. Durhman, NC: Duke University Press.

Frow, John. 2002. "Invidious Distinction: Waste, Difference, and Classy Staff." In *Culture and Waste: The Creation and the Destruction of Valué. Ed. Gay*, edited by Gay Hawkins and Stephen Muecke, 25–38. Lanham, MD: Rowman and Littlefield.

Gandolfo, Daniella. 2013. "Formless: A Day at Lima's Office of Formalization." *Cultural Anthropology* 28 (2): 278–98.

Gidwani, Vinay, and Amita Baviskar. 2019. "The Lives of Waste and Pollution." *Economic & Political Weekly* 54 (47): 33–35.

Gidwani, Vinay, and Rajyashree N. Reddy. 2011. "The Afterlives of 'Waste': Notes from India for a Minor History of Capitalist Surplus." *Antipode* 43 (5): 1625–58.

Gill, Kaveri. 2009. *Of Poverty and Plastic: Scavenging and Scrap Trading Entrepreneurs in India's Urban Informal Economy*. Oxford, UK: Oxford University Press.

Hawkins, Gay, and Stephen Muecke, eds. 2002. "Introduction: Cultural Economies of Waste." In *Culture and Waste: The Creation and Destruction of Value*. Lanham, MD: Rowman and Littlefield.

"Karmayog." n.d. https://karmayog.org/. Accessed August 8, 2021.

Kaviraj, Sudipta. 1997. "Filth and the Public Sphere: Concepts and Practices about Space in Calcutta." *Public Culture* 10 (1): 83–113.

Kumar, Nishant, Aparajita Singh, and Barbara HarRiss-White. 2019. "Urban Waste and the Human-Animal Interface in Delhi." *Economic & Political Weekly* 54 (47): 42–47.

Legg, Stephen. 2007. *Spaces of Colonialism: Delhi's Urban Governmentalities*. Victoria, Australia: Blackwell Publishing.

Luthra, Aman. 2019. "Municipalization for Privatization's Sake: Municipal Solid Waste Collection Services in Urban India." *Society and Business Review* 14 (2): 135–54.

———. 2020. "Efficiency in Waste Collection Markets: Changing Relationships between Firms, Informal Workers, and the State in Urban India." *Environment and Planning A: Economy and Space* 52 (7): 1375–94.

Masselos, Jim. 1982. "Jobs and Jobbery: The Sweeper in Bombay under the Raj." *The Indian Economic & Social History Review* 19 (2): 101–39.

McFarlane, Colin. 2008. "Governing the Contaminated City: Infrastructure and Sanitation in Colonial and Post-Colonial Bombay." *International Journal of Urban and Regional Research* 32 (2): 415–35.

Mirza, Shireen. 2018. "Figure of the Halalkhore." *Economic & Political Weekly* 53 (31): 79.

———. 2019. "Becoming Waste." *Economic & Political Weekly* 54 (47): 36–41.

MoEF. 2000. *Municipal Solid Waste (Management and Handling) Rules 2000*. New Delhi: Ministry of Environment and Forests.

Osborne, Thomas, and Nikolas Rose. 1999. "Governing Cities: Notes on the Spatialisation of Virtue." *Environment and Planning D: Society and Space* 17 (6): 737–60.

Pellow, David Naguib. 2002. *Garbage Wars: The Struggle for Environmental Justice in Chicago*. Cambridge, MA: MIT Press.

Prashad, Vijay. 2000. *Untouchable Freedom: A Social History of Dalit Community*. Oxford, UK: Oxford University Press.

Rao, Anupama. 2012. "Stigma and Labour: Remembering Dalit Marxism." *Seminar*, 633 (May): 23–27.

Reno, Joshua Ozias. 2014. "Toward a New Theory of Waste: From 'Matter out of Place' to Signs of Life." *Theory, Culture & Society* 31 (6): 3–27.

Salve, Pradeep S., Dhananjay W. Bansod, and Hemangi Kadlak. 2017. "Safai Karamcharis in a Vicious Cycle." *Economic & Political Weekly* 52 (13): 37–41.

Seabrook, Jeremy, and Imran Ahmed Siddiqui. 2011. *People without History: India's Muslim Ghettos*. New York, NY: Pluto Press.

Srivastava, Vaibhav, Pooja Singh, Rajiv Pratap Singh, and Sultan Ahmed Ismail. 2015. "Urban Solid Waste Management in the Developing World with Emphasis on India: Challenges and Opportunities." *Reviews in Environmental Science and Bio/Technology* 14: 317–37.

Supreme Court of India. 2006. "Solid Waste Management in Class 1 Cities in India." New Delhi: Supreme Court of India. http://www.almitrapatel.com/supreme.htm.

Taussig, Michael. 2009. "Miasma." In *My Cocaine Museum*, 173–88. Chicago, IL: University of Chicago Press.

Vaibhav, Srivastava, S. A. Ismail, Singh Pooja, and R. P. Singh. 2015. "Urban Solid Waste Management in the Developing World with Emphasis on India: Challenges and Opportunities." *Reviews in Environmental Science and Bio/Technology* 14 (2): 317–37.

Weber, Samuel. 2008. *Benjamin's-Abilities*. Cambridge, MA: Harvard University Press.

5 Conclusion

The Inoperative Operations of Urban Play

How Do We Inhabit Cities?

I lived in Mumbai for the first 26 years of my life, moving across three middle-income high-rise apartments that were located always close to the same railway station. Each of these apartments grew in size, starting from a one-room kitchen to a two-bedroom hall kitchen, while the number of people living in them reduced from five to three. Since the time I could venture outside the apartment complex on my own, the city was a place to move away from what was familiar, but also familial. So, interacting with strangers, wandering around anonymously, hanging out in teashops and cigarette shops, drinking in bars, working nights in colleges, or whiling time away on bikes were a way to get away from a space that often felt like it closed in on me. But what I remember distinctly are two events, both violent, which have shaped my larger inquiry into cities and this book.

First, the 1992–1993 Hindu–Muslim riots, when I was 11. The communal riots brought about a new script and code for how we were to inhabit cities. It brought about new impositions on how one could, and should, relate with others inhabiting cities. It also brought xenophobia into the home, which has only increased since then. But the city itself was also an imposition. It forced us to rely on these others, who we weren't meant to relate to, since the only way we could get around inhabiting the city was through others. The second event, rather a series of events, isn't from Mumbai but other cities, but could have happened in Mumbai too. In 2008, I found myself interning at an international organization working on housing finance for the urban poor in Addis Ababa, Ethiopia. My lure for used goods and boredom from office work led me one morning to the old market area of Addis Mercato. Here, I was stolen, in the middle of the street, in broad daylight, by three guys who pretended to be drunk and could see stars in the day. The others on the street watched it as a performance. A year later, in another city, I was robbed again, but this time, discreetly. A pickpocket had run away with my phone and wallet in the middle of the street, while I was busy looking around. And before I could realize what had happened, strangers had pursued the pickpocket on foot into the alleyways and brought back a few of the stolen goods.

Cities are both a lure and an imposition. And urban residents turn up here in unexpected ways for others, who they don't necessarily know or can claim to

DOI: 10.4324/9781003051848-7

know. This book, although charged with theory and fieldwork about others, is guided by a question that is also self-directed: How do we inhabit cities with others? This question concerns both: what is and what is possible. Rather than arriving at a definitive conclusion on questions concerning slum localities, I want to use these concluding paragraphs to depart from where I began and propose a few ways to think about the question, "how do we inhabit cities?."

Programming Cities

Over the past few decades, most cities have experienced a series of missions that overname them in order to draw global attention and to configure some sense of self-significance in the global scheme of things: the "India Story," the "World-Class City," the Knowledge City, the Green City, the Creative City, and more recently, the "Smart City." Here, the city is constructed by a cast of actors (policy makers, corporate groups, NGOs, foreign consultants, academics, and civil society groups) not just as a problem space that needs to be "fixed" (Simone 2012) but also as an instrument for achieving a speculative, entrepreneurial, and sustainable form of urbanism. These missions for the remaking of cities have involved specific kinds of spatial practices: modeling, inter-referencing, measuring, classifying, and ranking cities (Roy and Ong eds. 2011). And in doing so, cities and urban local bodies are made to enter into comparative and competitive relationships with each other. These missions also introduce new financial instruments, forms of urban governance, legal mechanisms, and jurisdictional boundaries, so that urban local bodies become decentralized, entrepreneurial, and self-sustaining as per global norms (Eslava 2015). This, however, requires building capacities of urban local bodies to account and audit all possible urban flows so as to build their city's credibility in international financial markets. Furthermore, the old forms of "addressing" urban problems through architecture and planning are being rescripted using new networks of Information and Communication Technologies and Spatial Data Infrastructures (Sundaram 2009). This process is driven by corporations, civil society organizations, and central government, who strive to make urban movements, both in the present and in the future, traceable, computable, and programmable, using real-time data and stacks of computational layers (Bratton 2015). To do so, as Jordan Crandall tells us, bodies are dividualized into data points, urban movements are broken down based on attributes, and then analyzed and extrapolated through computational programs (2010). Programs, he writes, are non-differential relational modes that amplify standardizing potentials with the aim of achieving interoperability and a cooperative agreement among different urban actors and their rhythms (ibid.: 85). The latter helps achieve a sense of stabilization across the disparate urban frequencies. Thus programs, he notes, are bound up in materializing norms and normalizing the city, whereby amplification, arrhythmia, and drifts are detected as the exceptions that destabilize the city. These also become the targets in a computable city (Chamayou 2014). Despite their efforts to get a hold on cities, many of these missions and programs don't work out as intended (Anand et.al 2018). They get lost in internal power struggles, the refusal of urban local bodies to loosen their hold on their cities, and the lack of credibility in programs and missions (Datta 2018). In which case, they are not very different from the algorithms that attempt to get hold of the uncomputable infinity that lies in the gap between 0 and 1 (Parisi 2013). And yet, urban local bodies do sign up for these programs and schemes so that capital and resources continue to flow into their constituencies.

The Incalculable: Between 0 and 1

Slum localities too are made calculable but often as the incalculable—that is, as uninhabitable localities that need to be addressed and fixed through a series of schemes and programs or as targets of opportunity that can be converted into developmental values through redevelopment. Urban residents inhabiting slum localities often find themselves in the middle of these schemes and programs that are not their makings. Similarly, they also find themselves inhabiting economic structures, caste systems, communal conflicts, and territorial jurisdictions that are at work in cities. What urban residents can do in such situations is localized—the kind of caste positions they can occupy, the jobs they can take up, the governmental schemes that they are eligible for, the projects they can initiate, the roles and identities they can adopt, the resources they can draw on, the networks and infrastructures they can connect to, and the people they can relate to, all are delimited.

But despite the reality of these delimitations, and regardless of the locality that one is localized to, residents inhabit cities by engaging in different forms of playacts with others in different mediums. The ethnographic stories presented in this book attend to, and draw attention to, some of these playacts: imparting stories, rehearsing roles, performing deceptions, repeating everyday spatiotemporal rhythms, and recycling matter and forms. Furthermore, different abilities that are latent get activated in these playacts. These include impartibility of stories, repeatability of everyday rhythms, citability of gestures, recognizability of self and others, and recyclability of urban forms. In inhabiting through these practices urban residents in slum localities extend and expand the limited space and resources that are on offer to them. They make urban movements possible for the poorer urban residents. For instance, to impart stories is not to communicate or deliberate but to part with and to share parts of oneself, with others, through stories. Often, these stories are shared while idling and waiting in all kinds of spaces. And what is imparted in stories are details about oneself and others. These stories aren't meant to perform a particular kind of work or to be used in specific ways. Neither are they judged based on any qualifications nor do they add up towards truth or totality. Instead, they have a thickness or an excessiveness of details, some of which others might use, waste, or retell in their own ways—that is, they can take them elsewhere. Thus stories are taken elsewhere by others, retold in other ways, and extended beyond what they were. This use of story by others doesn't subtract anything from the story but extends it into a resourceful space for many others so that they too can depart, despite being fixed within structures, localities, and identities.

Figure 5.1 Grid Dance

These departures involve becoming something else as well as transforming one's locality into an elsewhere.

These abilities, to reiterate, are not properties of specific subjects or technological objects but are virtually present in the play between subjects and objects, and bodies and technologies. In that sense, they are not unlike the computational programs that make urban movements calculable, measurable, and computable. And yet, they are different; they are not instrumentalized to program cities towards any specific ends. Instead, they are experimented with, repeatedly, in different mediums (language, bodies, gestures, documents, films, and objects) in the process of inhabiting cities. These experiments involve rehearsing and improvising different playacts (performances, storytelling, recycling, exchanging, citing, deceiving, wasting, collecting), despite the lack of time and space. But unlike in algorithmic experiments, where the goal is to translate rhythms into a sequence that can be used to program cities, the goal of repetitive experiments in play is the emergence of the singular (Weber 2008: 108). In other words, in calculated repetitions, residents read situations and calculate what might be possible but haven't been tried yet—the incalculable infinity that lies between 0 and 1 (Klaeger 2012; Parisi 2013). For instance, waste pickers spread out exchanges with different amounts across different actors to gain leverage and avoid being in debt. Similarly, stories are told with different thicknesses and opacities to different kinds of people; rhythms of work and movement are tried out with different frequencies along different routes at different times; performances are rehearsed using different citations and gestures; new roles, faces, and identities are tried on in playacting; and same films are watched over and over to connect with different worlds. In doing so, residents account possibilities for themselves but not with the intention of foreclosing them for others, at least, not completely. These acts, and the virtual abilities that are part of them, gesture towards a different sense of "how we inhabit cities." And in that different sense, they appear to be a gathering of singular lives that inhabit cities only to depart towards an elsewhere. Thus, despite being spatially bounded, the city is always moving elsewhere.

Cities Swell: In Mediums, We Converge to Depart

Cities, as recent scholarship shows, are a configuration of mediums that connect and disconnect geographies across different scales (Graham and Marvin 2002). These mediums are material and immaterial forms, which mediate matter, capital, discourses, experiences, aspirations, and bodies, and in doing so, they shape different forms of urban collectivities (Larkin 2013). Given these capacities, they are embedded within economies of power, desires, meanings, violence, and capital, as well as realize them. For instance, "Smart Cities" are imagined as a configuration of urban infrastructures and computational technologies that will collect data, transmit it, analyze it, and use it to reprogram cities, recurrently. But these technological mediums, as many have argued, are neither seamless nor complete, nor immortal. They corrode, leak, fail, crumble, and break down and hence require repairs, maintenance, backups, add-ons, and substitutions. They can be hacked, pirated, bugged, and short-circuited to forge new forms of urban relationships and collectivities (Appel et.al 2018).

Urban life, this book argues, takes on distinctive forms *in* different mediums. These forms are an enactment of its inhabitants who engage with others and themselves *in* different mediums. For instance, urban experiences are brought together and imparted to others repeatedly in stories. Residents perform religion by praying with others every day in religious spaces. Information is collected, transmitted, and proven in governmental documents and cards. Films and memories are experienced over and over again in sound images that are screened and received in video theaters. Roles, identities, and gestures are rehearsed and improvised in bodily performances. Collection, segregation, and recycling occurs in waste with different rhythms in different spaces. How we inhabit cities, to a large extent, depends on the abilities of the mediums in which we engage with each other, speak to each other, and act on each other. However, these mediums are not merely mediating instruments that aim to produce interoperability between disparate urban elements. This would construe them as means to an end. Nor are mediums an end in itself, which would render the making of cities into one big mega-infrastructure system as the end in itself. Contradistinctively, urban residents often engage with others in different mediums to become other, which also involves them becoming a medium (Simone 2004). In other words, we come together in cities as different versions of ourselves only to depart from who we are—to become someone or something else.

What is this becoming-other in mediums? For instance, in the process of implementing a slum sanitation program (Chapter 3) in a slum locality, pipes are laid in which water and sewage is carried; information is written into documents and id cards; urban actors and organizations come together in participatory platforms; norms, values, and discourses are produced in models; and stories, gestures, and excreta are circulated in bodies. Thus, the implementation of a slum sanitation program brings different mediums together, and the content of these mediums are other mediums. Urban residents, as I have been suggesting, playact in mediums, whereby models and gestures are made citable—that is, in performing them they are taken elsewhere. As a result, none of the toilets built under the Slum Sanitation Program are alike; each is a singular iteration of the model, whereby the model gets extended to the point that it becomes unrecognizable. In this process, the subjects of the toilet too depart from who they were. They take on new roles and identities while deceiving the ones assigned to them. The instances of youth films, the waste management system, and the shared stories, too gesture towards this becoming-other in mediums. These abilities are latent in cities and lay beside those of calculability, measurability, and programmability. However, while the goal of the latter is to achieve specific goals of a program, the former tend to depart from them. These departures are an interruption of both the program and the script, as well as their transformation into something else.

What does all this tell us about cities, writ large? The city, as Kittler points out, is a medium, the content of which is other mediums (1996). Urban residents inhabit cities by engaging with and acting on others in different mediums. In these inhabitations, disparate urban elements come together, and in this coming together they also depart in unexpected ways. It is this process, wherein singular lives come together and depart in mediums without an overarching framework or predetermined goal, that bears the name urban. It is no coincidence that Henri Lefebvre describes the urban as an implosion and explosion (2003[1970]). Furthermore, these urban convergences and divergences in cities create tensions and intensifications that swell the city, expand it, and extend it, beyond itself. A swelling city, despite its pathological connotations, signals towards change, movement, and passage of that which is contained beyond its limits towards an elsewhere. A swelling city is not a boundary that separates and divides but a zone of experimental becoming (Weber 2008).

A Whatever City

(The) gift of seeing resemblances is nothing other than a rudiment of the power compulsion in former times to become and behave like something else ... Children's games are everywhere interlaced with mimetic modes of behavior, and their range is not limited at all to what one human being imitates from another. A child not only plays at being a grocer or a teacher, but also at being a windmill or a train. (Benjamin 1979[1933])

This book began with the notion of excess as the urban surplus that is expended to make cities work and generate more surplus. And I was primarily interested in the potentiality of inoperative forms and relationships that escape their reabsorption by the dialectic of historical progress. The conceptual notions of play, abilities, and medium opened up a passage to ethnographically explore some of the potentialities of inhabitations. These playacts, as I have argued, interrupt and depart from the urban programs and missions; they render them inoperative. Inoperativity, as Giorgio Agamben tells us in his spin on Georges Bataille, is not the cessation of all work but an activity that renders works and productions inoperative, and in doing so, opens them to new possible uses (2014: 69). The inoperative has no goal. Its aim is not to realize any particular end or self, and is a virtual form of potentiality that is inexhaustible and incomplete.

So rather than trying to rewrite the script or achieve an end, what if we embrace the city as whatever-it-is without subtracting or dividing its divisible layers? What if we embrace the city for whatever-it-is, which includes its irreparable relationships that cannot be recovered or resolved? What if we embrace the city for whatever-it-is, which includes the group coupons that have expired and cannot be redeemed anymore? What if we embrace the city for whatever-it-is so that no matter what it is, it always matters? What if we embrace the city, neither as something to be achieved or actualized nor a destination but as a medium when played in opens up the possibility to become whatever? What if we extend the ability of a child to play at becoming whatever to the city—a whatever city? This is not to dismiss the fact that this ability to become whatever, or this fungibility as Tiffany Lebotho King points out in her work on "Black fungibility," was key

Figure 5.2 Whatever Cities

to the self-actualization of colonialism, capitalism, and Whiteness, which imagined, used, and destroyed bodies, objects, and landscapes as being fungible in its geographical conquest (2019). But at the same time, King notes, fungibility also gestures towards instability in borders, processes, and forms of power relations, as well as towards a state of prefiguration and flux. Fungibility is thus a fertile site for movement, processes, and stories that depart from the entrapments of the "man" or, in this case, "the city" (ibid. 122–24). It marks a space wherein things are not what they appear and are always on the verge to become otherwise.

In this sense, cities, as whatever they are, are always deceptive. They appear to be working as cities as per a given order of things, but they are always on their way to become something other than what they are. They appear to be fixed by the lines and rules of "the city," but are also always on the move to somewhere else. Urban residents in slum localities, those rendered as inoperative, are attentive to the infinite playful abilities in cities to become whatever and are drawn to it despite its impositions. They do find themselves inhabiting cities in the middle of things and restricted by them. But this middle or this medium is also a threshold between what is and a black sky of unknown possibilities. And it is this magical ability of cities that makes them so enchanting, despite all their limitations.

References

Agamben, Giorgio. 2014. "What Is a Destituent Power?" *Environment and Planning D: Society and Space* 32 (1): 65–74.

Anand, Ashwathy, Ajai Sreevatsan, and Persis Taraporevala. 2018. "An Overview of the Smart Cities Mission in India." New Delhi, India: Center for Policy Research and French National Research Insitute-Sustainable Development. https://smartnet.niua.org/sites/default/files/resources/scm_policy_brief_28th_aug.pdf.

Appel, Hannah, Nikhil Anand, and Akhil Gupta. 2018. "Introduction: Temporality, Politics, and the Promise of Infrastructure." In *The Promise of Infrastructure*, 1–38. Durhman, NC: Duke University Press.

Benjamin, Walter. 1979. "Doctrine of the Similar (1933)." Translated by Knut Tarnowski. *New German Critique*, no. 17 (1933): 65–69.

Bratton, Benjamin H. 2015. *The Stack: On Software and Sovereignty*. Cambridge, MA: MIT Press.

Chamayou, Grégoire. 2014. "Patterns of Life: A Very Short History of Schematic Bodies by Grégoire Chamayou." *The Funambulist*, December 4, 2014. https://thefunambulist.net/editorials/the-funambulist-papers-57-schematic-bodies-notes-on-a-patterns-genealogy-by-gregoire-chamayou.

Crandall, Jordan. 2010. "The Geospatialization of Calculative Operations: Tracking, Sensing and Megacities." *Theory, Culture & Society* 27 (6): 68–90.

Datta, Ayona. 2018. "The Digital Turn in Postcolonial Urbanism: Smart Citizenship in the Making of India's 100 Smart Cities." *Transactions of the Institute of British Geographers* 43 (3): 405–19.

Eslava, Luis. 2015. *Local Space, Global Life: The Everyday Operation of International Law and Development*. Cambridge, UK: Cambridge University Press.

Graham, Steve, and Simon Marvin. 2002. *Splintering Urbanism: Networked Infrastructures, Technological Mobilities and the Urban Condition*. London, UK: Routledge.

King, Tiffany Lethabo. 2019. The Black Shoals: *Offshore Formations of Black and Native Studies*. Durham, NC: Duke University Press.

Kittler, Friedrich A. 1996. "The City Is a Medium." Translated by Matthew Griffin. *New Literary History* 27 (4): 717–29.

Klaeger, Gabriel. 2012. "Rush and Relax: The Rhythms and Speeds of Touting Perishable Products on a Ghanaian Roadside." *Mobilities* 7 (4): 537–54.

Larkin, Brian. 2013. "The Politics and Poetics of Infrastructure." *Annual Review of Anthropology* 42: 327–43.

Lefebvre, Henri. 2003. *The Urban Revolution*. Translated by Robert Bononno. Minneapolis, MN: University of Minnesota Press.

Parisi, Luciana. 2013. *Contagious Architecture: Computation, Aesthetics, and Space*. Cambridge, MA: MIT Press.

Roy, Ananya, and Aihwa Ong, eds. 2011. *Worlding Cities: Asian Experiments and the Art of Being Global*. Vol. 42. Lanham, MD: Blackwell-Wiley.

Simone, AbdouMaliq. 2004. "People as Infrastructure: Intersecting Fragments in Johannesburg." *Public Culture* 16 (3): 407–29.

———. 2012. "Ghostly Cracks and Urban Deceptions: Jakarta." In *In the Life of Cities: Parallel Narratives of the Urban*, edited by Mohsen Mostafavi, 121–33. Cambridge and Baden: Harvard Graduate School of Design and Lars Müller Publishers.

Sundaram, Ravi. 2009. *Pirate Modernity: Delhi's Media Urbanism*. London, UK: Routledge.

Weber, Samuel. 2008. *Benjamin's-Abilities*. Cambridge, MA: Harvard University Press.

Index